ZAGATSURVEY®

2001/2002

SEATTLE/ PORTLAND RESTAURANTS

Editors: Troy Segal and Laura Mitchell

Local Editors: Cynthia Nims and Angela Allen

Local Coordinators: Kristine Britton and Kathryn Kurtz

Published and distributed by
ZAGAT SURVEY, LLC
4 Columbus Circle
New York, New York 10019
Tel: 212 977 6000
E-mail: seattleportland@zagat.com
Web site: www.zagat.com

Acknowledgments

In Seattle, Cynthia Nims would like to thank her family and friends for their support during the many head-down-fingers-to-keyboard hours that went into the guide, particularly the troupe of e-mail foodie pals who helped spur things with inspiration and humor. Cynthia would also like to thank her hubby extraordinaire, Bob Burns, for his constant love and encouragement, as well as Kristine Britton, who was a joy to work with, so overwhelmingly conscientious about the nitty-gritty details that it made the job easier.

Kristine Britton would like to thank Bridget Charters for organizing mailing parties and collecting last-minute restaurant data; Matt Castle and Carmella Telling for their calm and "can do" support in survey distribution; and special thanks to Alec Britton for his data organizing brainstorms and computer technical support.

In Portland, Angela Allen and Kathryn Kurtz would like to thank Gary Kurtz and Charlie Stanford for their dedicated filing and detail work; their loyal friends for getting the survey out and about; and Beeka Kurtz and Willie Stanford for unflagging support.

This guide would not have been possible without the exacting work of our staff: Deirdre Bourdet, Phil Cardone, Reni Chin, Anne Cole, Erica Curtis, Liz Daleske, Jessica Fields, Jeff Freier, Shelley Gallagher, Curt Gathje, Jessica Gonzalez, Sarah Kagan, Diane Karlin, Natalie Lebert, Mike Liao, Dave Makulec, Jefferson Martin, Lorraine Mead, Andrew O'Neill, Doug Ornstein, Rob Poole, Brooke Rein, Jason Roth, Robert Seixas, Zamira Skalkottas, LaShana Smith, Charlie Suisman and Kyle Zolner.

Contents

What's New. 5

About This Survey 6

Key to Ratings/Symbols 7

	SE	PO
Most Popular	8	142
TOP RATINGS		
By Food, Cuisine, Features, Location .	10	144
By Decor, Interior, Outdoor,		
Romantic, View	14	148
By Service	15	149
Best Buys.	16	150
RESTAURANT DIRECTORY		
Names, Addresses, Phone Numbers,		
Ratings and Reviews.	18	152
INDEXES		
Cuisines	108	200
Locations	115	204
Special Features	122	207
Breakfast.	122	–
Brunch	122	207
Buffet	122	207
Business Dining.	123	207
Caters	123	207
Cigar Friendly.	124	208
Delivers/Takeout	124	208
Dessert/Ice Cream	125	209
Dining Alone	125	209
Entertainment	126	209
Fireplace.	126	210
Game in Season	127	210
Historic Interest	127	210
Hotel Dining	127	210
"In" Places	128	210
Late Late – After 12:30.	128	211
Meet for a Drink	128	211
Noteworthy Newcomers.	129	211
Offbeat	129	211
Outdoor Dining	130	212
Oyster Bar	131	–
Parking/Valet	131	212
Parties & Private Rooms.	132	213
People-Watching	134	214
Power Scene	134	215
Pub/Bar/Microbrewery	134	215
Quiet Conversation	134	215
Romantic	135	215
Senior Appeal	135	215

Singles Scene	135	216
Sleepers	136	216
Teenagers & Other Youthful Spirits	136	216
Teflons	137	217
Theme Restaurant	137	217
Visitors on Expense Account	137	217
Wine/Beer Only	138	217
Winning Wine List	139	218
Worth a Trip	139	218
Young Children	140	218
Wine Chart	220	

What's New

Although the Seattle area is abuzz with dot-coms becoming not-coms (plus news of Boeing's HQ flying the coop), economic doldrums don't seem to be casting much of a shadow over the Emerald City's food scene. Folks are still responding to the dinner bell en masse, though some might be paying more attention to the bill than they did last year.

With the Downtown crush getting ever more congested, Seattleites are happy to go neighborhood-hopping in search of the next great meal. Such new players as Blue Onion Bistro in the University District, Market Street in Ballard, Stumbling Goat in Greenwood and Supreme in Madrona indicate that all the town's a stage for good eating now – especially the creative spins on comfort food offered by these Americans.

Steak is still taking Seattle by storm. Fleming's Prime Steakhouse & Wine Bar is a notable Downtown newcomer, while DC's Steakhouse of Sammamish comes to us courtesy of the folks behind that beloved veteran the Metropolitan Grill. Moderately priced JaK's Grill has opened an offshoot in West Seattle, proving that beef eating needn't break the bank.

While celebrating the newcomers, we must bid farewell to a few old friends. After 27 years, chef-owner Philippe Gayte hung up his toque at Kirkland's Bistro Provençal. (Raga has snatched up its prime space.) Wallingford won't seem the same without its Honey Bear Bakery, though the cafe's two bookstore outposts remain intact. And the surprise shutdown of Stars Bar & Dining saddened the entire town.

In Portland, the Pearl District continues to glow as the "it" neighborhood. Its most spectacular newcomer is Bruce Carey's Bluehour, which debuted after the chef-owner closed his trendsetting Zefiro. Another addition to this onetime warehouse district is Giorgio's, an intimate Italian.

That Eastside antique mecca, Sellwood-Westmoreland, is also in full bloom with a mixed bouquet of culinary styles. The haute-Greek Eleni's Estiatorio and Springwater Grill, a Northwesterner in Fiddleheads' former site, are both attracting admirers.

With development, renovation and art galleries sprucing up North and Northeast Portland, scenesters are swarming into Counter Culture, a haven for adventurous vegans, and Taqueria La Sirenita. Jazz and wine buffs, however, mourn the closing of the Downtown classic Atwater's.

As for the good shaking the Pacific Northwest got last Ash Wednesday, our restaurants rode out the seismic wave pretty well. And with the cost per average meal $24.99 in Seattle and $22.99 in Portland, dining out is still a good deal in these parts. The Rockies may tumble, Gibraltar may crumble, but our strong food scenes seem here to stay.

Seattle, WA   Cynthia Nims
Portland, OR   Angela Allen
May 10, 2001

About This Survey

Here are the results of our *2001/2002 Seattle/Portland Restaurant Survey*, covering over 960 restaurants in the Seattle and Portland areas.

By regularly surveying large numbers of local restaurant-goers, we hope to have achieved a uniquely current and reliable guide. More than 1,900 people participated. Since the participants dined out an average of 2.9 times per week, this *Survey* is based on about 289,000 meals per year.

We want to thank each of our participants. They are a widely diverse group in every respect but one – they are food lovers all. This book is really "theirs." Our reviews are designed to synopsize our surveyors' opinions, with exact comments shown in "quotes."

Of the surveyors, 58% are women, 42% are men; the break-down by age is 13% in their 20s, 23% in their 30s, 25% in their 40s, 25% in their 50s and 14% in their 60s or above.

Of course, we are also grateful to our editors, Cynthia Nims, food editor at *Seattle Magazine*, and Angela Allen, a Portland-based national award-winning food writer, fashion columnist and opera reviewer for *The Columbian*, Vancouver, Washington's, daily newspaper; and our coordinators, Kristine Britton, a caterer and culinary consultant in Seattle, and Kathryn Kurtz, a restaurant reviewer for *The Columbian* in Vancouver, Washington, and a food writer for Northwest and overseas publications. A world traveler, she takes small culinary groups to Asia.

To help guide our readers to Seattle and Portland's best meals and best buys, we have prepared a number of lists. See Seattle's Most Popular restaurants (page 8–9), Top Ratings (pages 10–15) and Best Buys (page 16) and Portland's Most Popular restaurants (page 142–143), Top Ratings (pages 144–149) and Best Buys (page 150). To assist the user in finding just the right restaurant for any occasion, we have also provided handy indexes.

As companions to this guide, we also publish *America's Best Meal Deals* and *America's Top Restaurants*. To check out these or any of our other *Zagat Surveys* to more than 40 major markets, including London, Paris and Tokyo, see our Web site, zagat.com, where you can also vote or shop.

Your comments, suggestions and even criticisms of this *Survey* are also solicited. There is always room for improvement with your help. Contact us at seattleportland@zagat.com.

New York, New York
May 10, 2001

Nina and Tim Zagat

Key to Ratings/Symbols

Name, Address & Phone Number

Zagat Ratings

Hours & Credit Cards

			F	D	S	C
			▽ 23	9	13	$15

Tim & Nina's ◐ 🅂 ⇎

4 Columbus Circle (8th Ave.), 212-977-6000

◪ Open 24/7, this "crowded", "overpopular" joint started the "Swedish-Mexican craze" (i.e. herring or lox on tiny tacos with mole or chimichurri sauce); though it looks like a "garage" and T & N "never heard of credit cards or reservations" – yours in particular – "dirt cheap" tabs for "*muy bien* eats" draw demented "debit-account" diners to this "deep dive."

Review, with surveyors' comments in quotes

Restaurants with the highest overall ratings, greatest popularity and importance are printed in CAPITAL LETTERS.

Before each review a symbol indicates whether responses were uniform ■ or mixed ◪.

Symbols: ◐ serves after 11 PM, Monday–Thursday
🅂 open on Sunday

Credit Cards: ⇎ no credit cards accepted

Ratings: Food, Decor and Service are rated on a scale of **0** to **30**. The Cost (C) column reflects our surveyors' estimate of the price of a meal including one drink.

F	Food	D	Decor	S	Service	C	Cost
23		9		13		$15	

0–9	poor to fair	**20–25**	very good to excellent
10–15	fair to good	**26–30**	extraordinary to perfection
16–19	good to very good	▽	low response/less reliable

A place listed without ratings is either an important **newcomer** or a popular **write-in**. For such places, the estimated cost is indicated by the following symbols.

I	$15 and below	**E**	$31 to $50
M	$16 to $30	**VE**	$51 or more

Seattle's Most Popular

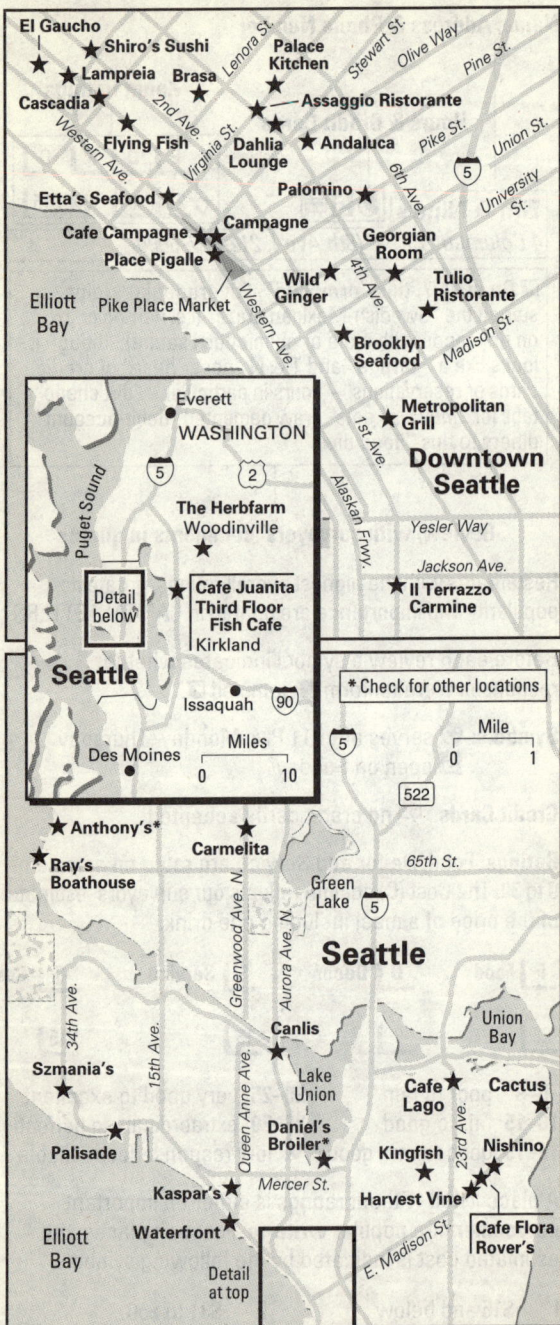

El Gaucho ★

★ Shiro's Sushi

★ Lampreia

Brasa ★

★ Palace Kitchen

Cascadia ★

★ Assaggio Ristorante

★ Flying Fish

Dahlia Lounge

★ Andaluca

Etta's Seafood ★

Palomino ★

Cafe Campagne ★

★ Campagne

Georgian Room ★

Place Pigalle ★

Wild Ginger ★

Tulio Ristorante ★

Elliott Bay

Pike Place Market

Brooklyn Seafood ★

Metropolitan Grill ★

WASHINGTON

Everett ●

Downtown Seattle

Puget Sound

The Herbfarm
Woodinville

Yesler Way

Jackson Ave.

Cafe Juanita
Third Floor
Fish Cafe
Kirkland

Il Terrazzo Carmine ★

Detail below

Seattle

Issaquah ●

* Check for other locations

Des Moines ●

Miles
0   10

Mile
0   1

★ Anthony's*

Carmelita ★

★ Ray's Boathouse

Green Lake

Seattle

Union Bay

Szmania's ★

Canlis ★

Lake Union

Cafe Lago ★

Cactus ★

Daniel's Broiler* ★

Nishino ★

Palisade ★

Kingfish ★

Harvest Vine ★

Kaspar's ★

Mercer St.

Waterfront ★

Cafe Flora
Rover's ★

Elliott Bay

Detail at top

Seattle's Most Popular

Each of our reviewers has been asked to name his or her five favorite restaurants. The 40 spots most frequently named, in order of their popularity, are:

1. Wild Ginger
2. Dahlia Lounge
3. Rover's
4. Metropolitan Grill
5. Canlis
6. Campagne
7. Flying Fish
8. Brasa
9. Palisade
10. Cafe Campagne
11. Daniel's Broiler
12. Herbfarm, The
13. Etta's Seafood
14. El Gaucho
15. Il Terrazzo Carmine
16. Ray's Boathouse
17. Palace Kitchen
18. Georgian Room
19. Cascadia
20. Kingfish
21. Tulio Ristorante
22. Szmania's
23. Kaspar's
24. Lampreia*
25. Anthony's
26. Cafe Flora
27. Cactus
28. Assaggio Ristorante
29. Brooklyn Seafood
30. Cafe Juanita
31. Palomino
32. Harvest Vine
33. Cafe Lago
34. Place Pigalle*
35. Third Floor Fish Cafe*
36. Andaluca
37. Shiro's Sushi*
38. Carmelita
39. Waterfront
40. Nishino

It's obvious that many of the restaurants on the above list are among the most expensive, but if popularity were calibrated to price, we suspect that a number of other restaurants would join the above ranks. Thus, for frugal gourmets, we have listed 80 Best Buys on page 16.

---

* Tied with the restaurant listed directly above it.

Top Ratings

Top lists exclude restaurants with low voting.

Top Food Ranking

29	Rover's		Flying Fish
28	Herbfarm, The		JaK's Grill
	Espresso Vivace		Nell's
27	Salumi	25	Macrina Bakery
	Georgian Room		Cafe Juanita
	Mistral		Monsoon
	Campagne		Chez Shea
	Cafe Campagne		Sanmi Sushi
	Harvest Vine		Pecos Pit BBQ
	Dahlia Lounge		Toyoda Sushi
26	Canlis		Kingfish
	Wild Ginger		Place Pigalle
	Szmania's		Paseo
	Le Gourmand		Hunt Club
	Nishino		Etta's Seafood
	Shoalwater*		Ark Restaurant
	Fullers		Eva
	Shiro's Sushi		Union Bay Cafe
	Il Terrazzo Carmine		Cascadia
	Metropolitan Grill		Waterfront

Top Food by Cuisine

American (New)
- 26 Nell's
- 25 Eva
- Union Bay Cafe
- Restaurant Zoë
- Lampreia

American (Regional)
- 23 Roy's Seattle
- Cactus
- 21 Sante Fe Cafe
- 20 Delcambre's
- 19 5 Spot

American (Traditional)
- 23 Maltby Cafe
- Dish, The
- 21 Original Pancake Hse.
- 19 5 Spot
- Paragon

Deli/Sandwich Shop
- 22 Three Girls Bakery
- 21 Bakeman's
- 20 Sisters European
- 19 Bagel Oasis
- 18 Roxy's Deli

Dessert
- 25 Macrina Bakery
- 21 Dilettante Chocolates
- 20 Famous Pacific
- B&O Espresso
- Caffe Ladro

Eclectic/International
- 25 Eva
- 24 Palace Kitchen
- 23 Yarrow Bay Grill
- Marco's Supperclub
- 22 Jimmy's Table

French
- 29 Rover's
- 27 Campagne
- 26 Le Gourmand
- 24 Maximilien
- 20 Brasserie Margaux

French (Bistro)
- 27 Cafe Campagne
- 24 Cassis
- 23 Le Pichet
- Boat Street Cafe
- 22 Avenue One

---

* Tied with the restaurant listed directly above it.

Hamburgers
23 Red Mill Burgers
22 Two Bells Tavern
18 Dick's Drive-In
17 Kidd Valley
16 Red Door Alehouse

Italian
26 Il Terrazzo Carmine
25 Cafe Juanita
24 Cafe Lago
    Salvatore Ristorante
    Tulio Ristorante

Japanese
26 Nishino
    Shiro's Sushi
25 Sanmi Sushi
    Toyoda Sushi
24 Izumi

Mediterranean
24 Brasa
    Adriatica
    Phoenecia at Alki
22 Andaluca
    Mona's Bistro

Mexican/Tex-Mex
23 El Puerco Lloron
22 Gordito's
21 Rosita's Mexican
20 El Camino
    Galerias

Northwest (Contemporary)
28 Herbfarm, The
27 Dahlia Lounge
25 Chez Shea
    Cascadia
24 Inn at Langley

Northwest (Traditional)
26 Canlis
    Shoalwater
    Fullers
25 Hunt Club
    Ark Restaurant

Pan-Asian
26 Wild Ginger
23 Shallots
    Roy's Seattle
22 Chinoise Café
21 Dragonfish

Pizza
22 Pegasus Pizza
21 Delfino's
    Pagliacci Pizza
20 Pazzo's
    Piecora's

Seafood (Contemporary)
26 Flying Fish
25 Etta's Seafood
    Waterfront
24 Third Floor Fish Cafe
23 Ponti Seafood Grill

Seafood (Traditional)
24 Dash Point Lobster
23 Oyster Bar/Chuckanut
    Shucker
    Ray's Boathouse
    Brooklyn Seafood

Southern/Soul
25 Kingfish
24 Ezell's Famous Chicken
22 Sazerac
    Catfish Corner
21 Alligator Soul

Spanish/Latin American
27 Harvest Vine
23 Tango
    Fandango
22 Bandoleone
20 Dulces Latin Bistro

Steakhouse
26 Metropolitan Grill
    JaK's Grill
24 Ruth's Chris
    Daniel's Broiler
    Fleming's Prime

Thai
24 Bai Tong
    Typhoon!
22 Bahn Thai
21 Fremont Noodle Hse.
20 Racha Noodles

Vegetarian
23 Carmelita
22 Cafe Flora
20 Green Cat Cafe
18 Still Life in Fremont
    Bamboo Garden

Top Food

Top Food by Special Feature

Breakfast*
27 Cafe Campagne
25 Macrina Bakery
23 Maltby Cafe
   Dish, The
21 Original Pancake Hse.

Brunch
25 Etta's Seafood
23 Roy's Seattle
   Ponti Seafood Grill
   Yarrow Bay Grill
   Boat Street Cafe

Hotel Dining
27 Georgian Room
   Four Seasons Olympic
26 Fullers
   Sheraton Seattle
25 Hunt Club
   Sorrento Hotel
24 Inn at Langley
   Inn at Langley
23 Painted Table
   Alexis Hotel

Lunch Spot
27 Salumi
25 Macrina Bakery
   Pecos Pit BBQ
24 La Panzanella
23 El Puerco Lloron

Newcomers/Rated
27 Mistral
25 Restaurant Zoë
24 Fleming's Prime
23 Le Pichet
   Fandango

Newcomers/Unrated
   Barking Frog
   Blue Onion Bistro
   Café Ambrosia
   Stumbling Goat
   Supreme

Offbeat
25 Paseo
21 Alligator Soul
   Dragonfish Asian
19 Ohana
   Luau Polynesian

People-Watching
25 Restaurant Zoë
24 El Gaucho
   Palace Kitchen
23 Tango
   Fandango

Pub/Tavern
22 Two Bells Tavern
20 Hilltop Ale House
   74th St. Ale House
19 Maple Leaf Grill
   Paragon

Worth a Trip
26 Shoalwater
   Seaview
25 Ark Restaurant
   Nahcotta
24 Inn at Langley
   Langley, Whidbey Island
23 Oyster Bar/Chuckanut
   Bow
   Salish Lodge
   Snoqualmie

Top Food by Location

Bellevue
25 Tosoni's
24 Daniel's Broiler
   Shanghai Garden/Cafe
23 I Love Sushi
   Sea Garden

Belltown
27 Mistral
26 Shiro's Sushi
   Flying Fish
25 Macrina Bakery
   Cascadia

Capitol Hill
28 Espresso Vivace
25 Monsoon
   Kingfish
24 Cassis
   La Panzanella

Downtown
27 Georgian Room
   Dahlia Lounge
26 Wild Ginger
   Fullers
   Metropolitan Grill

---

* Other than hotels.

Kirkland
25 Cafe Juanita
24 Shamiana
Izumi
Third Floor Fish Cafe
23 Yarrow Bay Grill

Pike Place Market
27 Campagne
Cafe Campagne
25 Chez Shea
Place Pigalle
Etta's Seafood

Pioneer Square/SODO
27 Salumi
26 Il Terrazzo Carmine
25 Pecos Pit BBQ
23 Torrefazione Italia
21 Bakeman's

Queen Anne/Seattle Center
24 Kaspar's
23 Banjara Restaurant
Pasta & Co.
22 Bahn Thai
Uptown Espresso

Top Decor Ranking

28 Georgian Room
27 Canlis
26 Palisade
    Salish Lodge
    Waterfront
25 Dahlia Lounge
    Cascadia
    Rover's
    Hunt Club
    Herbfarm, The
    Brasa
    Inn at Langley
    Chez Shea
    Fullers
24 Campagne
    Shoalwater
    Calcutta Grill
    Il Terrazzo Carmine
    Spirit of Washington
    Wild Ginger

Dash Point Lobster
Maximilien
SkyCity at the Needle
23 Cafe Campagne
Restaurant Zoë
Fleming's Prime
El Gaucho
Andaluca
Painted Table
Ray's Boathouse
Oyster Bar/Chuckanut
Place Pigalle
Third Floor Fish Cafe
La Rustica
Serafina*
Nikko Restaurant
Eques Restaurant
Torrefazione Italia*
Yarrow Bay Grill
Ponti Seafood

Dramatic Interior

Brasa
Canlis
Cascadia
Dahlia Lounge

El Gaucho
Georgian Room
Herbfarm, The
Painted Table

Outdoor

Anthony's Pier 66
Calcutta Grill
Christina's
Hiram's at the Locks
Madison Park Cafe

Pink Door
Ray's Cafe
Salty's
Waterfront
Waypoints

Romantic

Adriatica
Avenue One
Boat Street Cafe
Campagne
Chez Shea
Hunt Club

Il Bistro
La Fontana Siciliana
Le Gourmand
Madison Park Cafe
Rover's
Serafina

View

Cliff House
Copacabana Cafe
Cutters Bayhouse
Elliott's Oyster House
Palisade
Prego

Ray's Boathouse
Salty's
SkyCity at the Needle
Spirit of Washington
Waterfront
Yarrow Bay Grill

---

* Tied with the restaurant listed directly above it.

Top Service Ranking

28 Rover's
    Georgian Room
27 Herbfarm, The
    Canlis
26 Le Gourmand
25 Campagne
    Restaurant Zoë
    Fullers
    Dahlia Lounge
24 Mistral
    Szmania's
    Metropolitan Grill
    Nell's
    Chez Shea
    El Gaucho
    Hunt Club
    Il Terrazzo Carmine
    Cafe Juanita
    Inn at Langley
23 Dash Point Lobster

Cafe Campagne
Waterfront
Palisade
Il Bacio
Fleming's Prime
Adriatica
Cascadia
Eva
Matt's in the Market
Shoalwater*
Salish Lodge
Assaggio Ristorante
Ruth's Chris
Union Bay Cafe
Kaspar's
Lampreia
La Rustica
Nishino*
22 Daniel's Broiler
Izumi

---

* Tied with the restaurant listed directly above it.

Best Buys

Top Bangs for the Buck

This list is derived by dividing the cost of a meal into its combined ratings.

1. Espresso Vivace
2. Torrefazione Italia
3. Dick's Drive-In
4. Uptown Espresso
5. Caffe Ladro
6. Bakeman's
7. Pecos Pit BBQ
8. Frankfurter, The
9. Bagel Oasis
10. Burrito Loco
11. Three Girls Bakery
12. Gordito's
13. Dish, The
14. Sisters European
15. El Puerco Lloron
16. Red Mill Burgers
17. B&O Espresso
18. Kidd Valley
19. Famous Pacific
20. Ezell's Famous Chicken
21. Original Pancake Hse.
22. La Panzanella
23. Honey Bear Bakery
24. Taco Del Mar
25. Salumi
26. Paseo
27. Macrina Bakery & Cafe
28. Still Life in Fremont
29. Louisa's Cafe
30. Two Bells Tavern
31. My Favourite Piroshky
32. Green Cat Cafe
33. Mae's Cafe
34. Maltby Cafe
35. Pasta & Co.
36. Sit & Spin
37. Roxy's Deli
38. Luna Park Cafe
39. Dilettante Chocolates
40. Briazz

Additional Good Values

Moderately priced restaurants that give you your money's worth.

Agua Verde Cafe
Armadillo Barbecue
Bai Tong
Buca di Beppo
Bungalow Wine Bar
Café Soleil
Catfish Corner
Delcambre's
Delfino's
Dixie's BBQ
Emmett Watson's
Fremont Noodle Hse.
Grapes
Greenlake Bar & Grill
Hale's Ales
Hilltop Ale House
Hi-Spot Cafe
Jack's Fish Spot
Kingfish
Krittika Noodles

Machiavelli
Malay Satay Hut
Mama's Mexican Kitchen
Mandalay Café
Matt's Famous
Mediterranean Kitchen
Noodle Ranch
Olympia Pizza
Pagliacci Pizza
Pazzo's
Pegasus Pizza
Piecora's
Racha Noodles
Shanghai Garden
Shultzy's
611 Supreme
Taqueria Guaymas
Triangle Lounge
World Class Chili
Zaina

Seattle Restaurant Directory

Seattle

	F	D	S	C
Adriatica [S]	24	22	23	$40

1107 Dexter Ave. N. (north of Mercer St.), 206-285-5000

■ Surveyors say this "ultra-romantic", converted "old house" is a "precious hidden gem" where the long climb "up, up, up" (think of it as numerous "steps = more room for dessert") leads to "memorable", "consistently excellent" Mediterranean meals; while "high-rises have ruined" a once-glorious vista, regulars hint that there's still a "good view of Lake Union from the [top-floor] bar", so "try to stay upstairs for dinner."

	F	D	S	C
Afrikando [S]	19	13	19	$18

2904 First Ave. (Broad St.), 206-374-9714

◪ "Something different" is afoot at this Belltowner – namely, "good West African food" that's "just like mama makes, if mama is from Senegal"; advocates applaud the "large portions" of nicely "flavored and spiced" fare ("the mustard-and-onion sauce is great") served by a "friendly and helpful staff"; critics, however, complain that they often "don't have everything on the menu"; P.S. "no alcohol" served.

	F	D	S	C
Agua Verde Cafe & Paddle Club	–	–	–	I

1303 NE Boat St. (Brooklyn Ave.), 206-545-8570

Such a "nice place to hang out" say surveyors of this vibrantly colored, "casual" eatery in the University District, where those in on the "well-kept secret" go for "terrific smoked salmon" and "spicy catfish" tacos – to name just two examples of the "clever Mexican" cuisine that's offered with a "killer view of the Montlake Cut" and its bustling boats below; N.B. like to do more than watch? kayak rentals are available in season downstairs.

	F	D	S	C
Al Boccalino [S]	19	19	19	$34

1 Yesler Way (Alaskan Way), 206-622-7688

◪ This "intimate Italian" in historic Pioneer Square "feels like a secret hideaway" decorated with lots of "brick and wood"; although a few foes find the trattoria "not as good as in its prime", the "quality food" keeps regulars coming back for more.

	F	D	S	C
Alligator Soul	21	14	19	$25

2013½ Hewitt Ave. (Broadway), Everett, 425-259-6311

■ "Not a bad choice on the menu" say soul mates of this "exemplary" Southerner where the "hot and savory" "Cajun food" ("yummy corn salad") and "fun staff" are "worth the trip from Seattle" to Everett; "live music on weekends adds to the festive atmosphere" in a "funky setting."

Andaluca S   22 | 23 | 22 | $37
Mayflower Park Hotel, 407 Olive Way (bet. 4th & 5th Aves.),
206-382-6999
■ A "colorful" and "stylish decor", combined with a
"creative menu", makes this "welcoming" Downtowner a
good "antidote to Seattle rain"; fans "love the crab tower"
and the "gourmet tapas", not to mention the "terrific
cocktails", "excellent sherries" and "standout" desserts;
in short, "if you like Mediterranean food, this is the place
for you" – whether you "eat big-time or just nibble"; P.S.
"great valet parking" is a plus.

Andy's Diner   13 | 14 | 17 | $20
2963 Fourth Ave. S. (bet. Hanford Ave. & Lander St.), 206-624-4097
☑ "1950 is alive and breathing" in this recently re-opened
SODO American where "seating in old railroad cars"
provides a bit of "novelty" in a "nostalgic" (some say
"dated") setting; new owners have spiffed the place up a
bit but retained the no-frills, "working-man's menu", which
sophisticates sniff is "standard stuff."

Angelina's Trattoria S   13 | 13 | 16 | $19
2311 California Ave. SW (Admiral Way), 206-932-7311
☑ This "cozy neighborhood" "Italian joint" in West Seattle
draws a "local" clientele; while eating here "feels like
coming home" to the devoted, less neighborly types yawn
"ho-hum"; N.B. it serves only wine and beer.

Angel's Thai Cuisine S   16 | 11 | 15 | $16
235 Broadway E. (Thomas St.), 206-328-0515
■ The Capitol Hill crowd flocks to this mirrored Siamese
for "surprisingly good Thai food" served in a "quiet
atmosphere"; though perhaps "not the best, [it's] quick
and convenient" and "great for takeout."

ANTHONY'S AT   19 | 19 | 19 | $30
POINT DEFIANCE S
5910 N. Waterfront Dr. (Vashon Ferry Dock), Tacoma,
253-752-9700
ANTHONY'S BEACH CAFE/HOMEPORT S
Edmonds Marina, 456 Admiral Way (Dayton St.), Edmonds,
425-771-4400
ANTHONY'S HOMEPORT S
6135 Seaview Ave. NW (near Shilshoe Marina), 206-783-0780
Everett Marina Village, 1726 W. Marine View Dr. (bet. 16th &
19th Sts.), Everett, 425-252-3333
135 Lake St. S. (Moss Bay Marina), Kirkland, 425-822-0225
704 Columbia St. NW (Market St.), next to
Olympia Farmer's Mkt.), Olympia, 360-357-9700
ANTHONY'S OYSTER BAR & GRILL/HOMEPORT S
Des Moines Marina, 421 S. 227th St. (Marine View Dr.),
Des Moines, 206-824-1947

(continued)

(continued)

ANTHONY'S WOODFIRE GRILL S
*Everett Marina Village, 1722 W. Marine View Dr. (bet. 16th &
19th Sts.), Everett, 425-258-4000*

▧ "No matter which one you go to", there's "always a great
view" from these "comfortable" waterside fish houses; add
in "consistently good seafood" – the "Sunday crab feed
can't be beat" – and this chain becomes "a safe bet for
entertaining out-of-town guests"; but "it's hard to keep the
act fresh for in-towners", who crab about "unimaginative",
"middle-of-the-road meals."

Anthony's Pier 66 S   21 | 21 | 20 | $32 |
Pier 66, 2201 Alaskan Way (Bell St.), 206-448-6688

■ "Beautiful views" from a "terrific location" reel 'em into
this Waterfront seafooder where the "cioppino is superb"
and the "crab cakes exceptional"; being a "must for out-
of-town visitors" ("a hit with New York guests" in particular),
it garners the occasional "touristy" label – though even
foes admit it's "better than the usual joints" on the pier.

Aoki Japanese Grill & Sushi Bar   22 | 14 | 18 | $22 |
621 Broadway E. (Roy St.), 206-324-3633

■ The "stark decor" doesn't keep away fans of the
"wonderful sushi" at this Capitol Hill Japanese; it's a
"reliable neighborhood spot" where the "quick service"
and a "kid-friendly" attitude make for an A-ok experience.

Ark Restaurant & Bakery, The S   25 | 20 | 22 | $35 |
*Nahcotta Dock, 273 Sandridge Rd. (Hwy. 103), Nahcotta,
360-665-4133*

■ "Still good after all these years" declare devotees, who
"drive two-plus hours" to this NW-American to dine on
chef/co-owners Jimella Lucas and Nanci Main's "great
oysters" and "creative seafood" ("I dream of the Scotch
salmon regularly"), "promptly served" with an "excellent
view" over Willapa Bay; all admit it's "a long way to go", but
the reward is "amazing food in the middle of nowhere."

Armadillo Barbecue S   17 | 9 | 12 | $14 |
13109 NE 175th St. (131st Ave.), Woodinville, 425-481-1417

■ "Roll up your sleeves for the messy little bit of hog
heaven" that makes this "funky BBQ spot" a "must-stop in
Woodinville"; if you can "get past the surly manner of the
staff", you're in for an evening of "down-home grit and wit."

Arnies S   17 | 16 | 18 | $29 |
*The Landing, 300 Admiral Way (Dayton Ave.), Edmonds,
425-771-5688*
714 Second St. (Mukilteo Spdwy.), Mukilteo, 425-355-2181

▧ This pair of seafood standbys on the Edmonds and
Mukilteo waterfronts offers "wonderful views", along with
NW fare that's "reliable" – albeit "very predictable" and
(critics carp) "uninspired"; still, the "price is right."

Asian Wok & Grill [S] ▽ 18 | 14 | 17 | $17

3601 Fremont Ave. N. (36th Ave.), 206-675-8508

Broadway Wok & Grill ◐ [S]

614 Broadway E. (Roy St.), 206-568-0505

◪ Fans would wok a mile to this Fremont favorite for the fresh Pan-Asian "food that's always good" and "served quickly" by a "polite" staff, but less-generous reviewers grump the cuisine's "not as exciting as it could be" and bemoan the "dumpy grounds"; N.B. the Capitol Hill location is new and unrated.

ASSAGGIO RISTORANTE 23 | 21 | 23 | $34

2010 Fourth Ave. (Virginia St.), 206-441-1399

■ "No restaurant in Seattle has as much heart" as this "truly Northern Italian" Downtown where "great food" ("those mussels – *bellisimo*!") and "stellar service" make for an "awesome" experience; owner Mauro Golmarvi – his "personality alone is worth the price of the meal" – "runs a tight ship" but still creates a "warm atmosphere" that manages to be "both noisy and romantic."

Asteroid Cafe, The [S] – | – | – | M

1605 N. 45th St. (bet. Densmore & Woodlawn Aves.), 206-547-2514

"Small" and cozy Wallingford Italian whose inviting decor is filled with artwork that changes every couple of months; by day, it's a casual setting for great coffee and a plethora of panini; by night, on comes a menu where the "pasta dishes are good and the entrees are [even] better", all served up in generous portions at "great prices."

Athenian Inn 13 | 15 | 14 | $16

Pike Place Mkt., 1517 Pike Pl. (Pine St.), 206-624-7166

◪ A "Seattle institution" (established 1909) that's "a real joint, in the most positive way"; regulars love to "take in the Pike Place Market flavor" while eating American "plebs' food" (especially the "early breakfast") or choosing from all the microbrews available at the "crusty sea-dog bar"; the less-sentimental snap that since *Sleepless in Seattle* fame, it's become "tourist"-ridden and that the "food used to be good" (happily, the Puget Sound "view still is").

Atlas Foods [S] 16 | 17 | 16 | $23

University Village, 2820 NE University Village (25th Ave. & 45th St.), 206-522-6025

◪ After you've made the rounds at University Village, come on in to this "kid-friendly" American, which has replaced its revolving 'round-the-world menu with "good, solid comfort food", along with "great wine prices", supporters say; critics claim it "lacks personality" ("it's in a mall – enough said") and gets "too darn loud", but most feel it offers "excellent shopping-center refreshment."

Avenue One S 22 | 21 | 21 | $40
1921 First Ave. (bet. Stewart & Virginia Sts.), 206-441-6139
■ "Delicious" French bistro fare and a "relaxing, romantic atmosphere" keep regulars returning to this Pike Place Market one-and-only, where they advise that you "try for a table in the intimate back room" with its "fabulous view of the Sound"; a few feel the place is "kinda pricey", but keep in mind that you're getting "sumptuous dining" with a "lovely European feel"; P.S. don't overlook the "great bar" for cocktails or *digestifs*.

Axis ◑S 18 | 19 | 17 | $33
2214 First Ave. (bet. Bell & Blanchard Sts.), 206-441-9600
◪ The "food is good [but] the bar scene is better" at this "quintessential Belltown spot" where the "young, hip crowd" sips "fun cocktails" (raspberry kamikazes, anyone?) and digs into "very tasty", "great-for-sharing" International fare, like pizzas from the wood-fired oven; it gets "terribly noisy on weekends" and sometimes the "service is poky", but requesting a table away from the "Singles-R-Us atmosphere" can help if eating, not meeting, is your MO.

Ayutthaya S 19 | 12 | 17 | $16
727 E. Pike St. (Howard St.), 206-324-8833
■ "Don't let its looks fool you" – the food's much "better than you'd expect" at this compact Capitol Hiller, whose regulars love to Thai one on with the "great green curry" and "sublime coconut chicken"; it's "genuine" fare that comes "at a cheap price", delivered by a "friendly staff."

Azteca S 13 | 13 | 15 | $16
Shilshole Marina, 6017 Seaview Ave. NW (57th Pl.), 206-789-7373
1823 Eastlake Ave. E. (Yale Pl.), 206-324-4941
Northgate Mall, 543 NE Northgate Way (5th Ave.), 206-362-0066
150 112th Ave. NE (bet. Main & 2nd Sts.), Bellevue, 425-453-9087
31740 23rd Ave. S. (320th St.), Federal Way, 253-839-6693
25633 102nd Pl. SE (Smith St.), Kent, 253-852-0210
12015 124th Ave. NE (bet. 116th & 124th Sts.), Kirkland, 425-820-7979
15704 Mill Creek Blvd. (Bothell-Everett Hwy.), Mill Creek, 425-385-2209
4801 Tacoma Mall Blvd. (bet. S. 48th & 49th Sts.), Tacoma, 253-472-0246
17555 Southcenter Pkwy. (south of Minkler Blvd.), Tukwila, 206-575-0990
◪ Seattle's "handy" chain comes with "lots of locations" and "lots of choices" on the "no-brainer Mexican" menu; allies argue it's "great for kids" and for those craving "cheap eats" that "arrive in a hurry", but critics complain about "bland, generic" offerings and a "decor as formulaic as the food"; oh, and "stop calling me amigo."

Baccano Ristorante & Vinoteca ◐ Ⓢ 14 | 20 | 17 | $30 |
2218 Western Ave. (bet. Bell & Blanchard Sts.),
206-770-9000
◪ This "family-style" Italian at the edge of Belltown has a
"fun decor" – a dining room-cum-piazza complete with
vast columns, faux storefronts and fountains – but surveyors
split on the "festive atmosphere": though "great for big
groups", it strikes more sedate types as "loud" and "simply
embarrassing"; almost all parties agree, however, that
this yearling should pay "more attention to the food"
("mediocre at best").

Bacchus Greek Cuisine Ⓢ   18 | 19 | 16 | $19 |
806 E. Roy St. (Broadway), 206-325-2888
■ "Beautiful murals" and a "delightful room" create a
"romantic" atmosphere (hint: it's "great for a date") at this
Capitol Hill spot, where the "authentic Greek food"
("we'll be back for more flaming cheese") compensates
for "charmingly ditzy" service; P.S. "believe it or not"
they do a pretty good breakfast, too.

Bagel Oasis Ⓢ   19 | 7 | 11 | $8 |
462 N. 36th St. (bet. Dayton & Francis Aves.),
206-633-2676
2112 NE 65th St. (bet. Ravenna & 21st Aves.),
206-526-0525
◪ "Though [they're] not the NYC paragon", the "best bagels
in Seattle" get turned out by this Fremont and Ravenna deli
duo, which uses the classic "boiled, then baked" method
to produce "chewy", "hot-out-of-the-oven" specimens;
non-noshers gripe about the "ornery staff" (it's "amazing
how complicated a simple order can become") and the
"need [for] ambiance", but for most, the only question is
"why get bagels anywhere else?"

Bahn Thai Ⓢ   22 | 15 | 18 | $19 |
409 Roy St. (5th Ave. N.), 206-283-0444
■ Located in lower Queen Anne, this "tasty" Thai offers
"big portions" of "delicious" fare that's especially "nice for"
novices, since the "cooking can be adjusted to American
tastes"; best of all, "fast service" ensures you'll be "in and
out in time for the Sonics game" or whatever else has you
heading to the Seattle Center.

Bai Tong Ⓢ   24 | 12 | 18 | $17 |
15859 Pacific Hwy. S. (160th St.), 206-431-0893
■ "Ignore the location" – it's "worth a detour" to SeaTac
"near the airport" to the "best Thai around", whose
"extraordinary food" "never fails to amaze"; so who cares
if the decor "needs a total makeover" – the fact that it
draws devotees among Siamese "airline personnel"
suggests this is "the real thing", not to mention "the place
to try a dish other than pad Thai."

Bakeman's ⊖   21 | 6 | 15 | $8
122 Cherry St. (2nd Ave.), 206-622-3375

■ "It's the day after Thanksgiving every day" at this Pioneer
Square deli where you "gotta love the turkey-with-cranberry
on wheat with attitude"; "learn to order fast and enjoy"
because they're all about getting people ("lots of lawyers"
and other Downtown business folks) through the line and on
their way; the "subterranean location" and "depressing
dining area" leave some opting for "takeout", but either
way it's "still the best lunch deal around."

Bamboo Garden   18 | 11 | 17 | $16
Vegetarian Cuisine S
364 Roy St. (bet. 3rd & 4th Aves.), 206-282-6616

◩ "Amazing what they can do with tofu" chime converts
to this "well-priced" kosher Chinese-Vegetarian in lower
Queen Anne; but while the "creative use of soy" products
("best fake sweet 'n' sour chicken anywhere") pleases
some, nonbelievers bemoan flavors that are "a little bland"
and wonder "why impersonate the taste of meat?"

B&O Espresso S   20 | 18 | 14 | $12
Broadway Mkt., 401 Broadway E. (Republican St.), 206-328-3290
204 Belmont Ave. E. (Olive Way), 206-322-5028 ◑
Cherry Street Coffee House
2121 First Ave. (bet. Blanchard & Lenora Sts.), 206-441-7176
103 Cherry St. (1st Ave.), 206-621-9372 ⊖

■ The pastries take pride of place at this American coffee
shop quartet where you can satisfy that sweet tooth with
"mammoth slices" of some of the "best desserts in town"
(including "heart-palpitating chocolate" tarts) accompanied
by "tasty variations of favorite espresso drinks"; while all
four "encourage lingering", the original Belmont "institution"
stays open late, making it a "fun place after theater."

Bandoleone S   22 | 19 | 19 | $28
2241 Eastlake Ave. E. (Lynn St.), 206-329-7559

■ Ease on over to this "cozy" Eastlake eatery, which offers
the "tantalizing flavors" of an "inspired Latino cuisine" (start
off with some "killer tapas" and "great sangria"); local art
graces the walls to embellish the "intimate atmosphere",
creating a "very comfortable neighborhood feel"; there's
also a "great [albeit small] bar for meeting friends and
sipping" Iberian Peninsula wines – just be aware it can
get "smoky", particularly on Monday cigar nights.

Banjara Restaurant S   23 | 17 | 20 | $18
2 Boston St. (Queen Anne Ave. N.), 206-282-7752

■ "Homey preparations" are on hand at this "jewel" "buried
in Queen Anne"; regulars swear by the "super tandoori
oven" that turns out "delicious" "Indian favorites", often
with a "delightfully different spicy twist"; given the "great
food and great prices", small wonder that "when you crave"
a taste of the Raj, "nothing else will do."

Barking Frog S
– – – E

Willows Lodge, 14580 NE 145th St. (Redmond-Woodinville Rd.), Woodinville, 425-424-2999

The casual, welcoming dining room of the posh new Willows Lodge (also home to the relocated Herbfarm) recently opened in the midst of Woodinville's wine country, very near the Chateau Ste. Michelle and Columbia wineries; chef Stephane Desgaches (ex Brasserie Margaux) brings his sophisticated French technique to NW foods, with results like seafood *pot-au-feu* and a "top-notch duck cassoulet"; the vino, naturally, is 99 percent Washington state.

Bay Cafe S
21 16 20 $25

9 Old Post Rd. (opp. post office), Lopez Island, 360-468-3700

◪ This relaxed San Juan Islands cafe serves a seafood-infused menu in a "beautiful atmosphere" looking out over the bay and beyond; fans find the New American fare and "hearty [weekend] breakfasts" "wonderful" (especially "on the deck"), but naysayers bay that since the advent of new owners, the experience is "not as unique" and a little "too dependant on the server's mood."

Bella Rosa Bistro S
▽ 21 17 18 $30

3410 NE 55th St. (35th Ave.), 206-527-3400

■ Life is indeed rosy at this "romantic, cozy spot" in the University District where regulars keep returning for "wonderful Italian dishes", Moroccan specialties (couscous, tagines) that reflect the chef-owners' heritage and "outstanding desserts"; small wonder that many a surveyor says "eating here makes me hot" (oh, so *that's* why "it's a great place on a crisp night").

Bell Street Diner S
17 16 16 $20

Pier 66, 2201 Alaskan Way (Bell St.), 206-448-6688

◪ On the Seattle Waterfront this downstairs and downscale sibling of Anthony's Pier 66 rings a bell with many reviewers for its "very reasonably priced menu" of NW seafood favorites (especially the "rich fish tacos"), served on a "nice dining deck" whose "great view" over Elliott Bay is an added plus; critics, however, carp that the "menu could use some sprucing up" and while the "staff is always upbeat", "service can be slow."

Belltown Billiards ◐S
11 13 13 $19

90 Blanchard St. (1st Ave.), 206-448-6779

◪ "It's not really a place to eat", but for a "fun spot to hang out with friends" and nibble "decent snacks to fuel pool" (thin-crust "pizzas are a good choice", given the kitchen's Italian focus), this "casual joint" in Belltown makes the shot; it may be "a little overpriced for what you get", but consider that "great people-watching" is thrown in for free.

Belltown Pub & Cafe S   18 | 18 | 18 | $18
2322 First Ave. (bet. Battery & Bell Sts.), 206-728-4311
◩ That it provides the "best Guinness pour in the city" is
reason enough for some to come to this pub "in the heart
of Belltown", where a "fun atmosphere" and "nice casual
ambiance" make it a "great place to just hang"; though a
few feel the NW "food doesn't satisfy", others find the
burgers and salads perfectly "good."

Bick's Broadview Grill S   20 | 16 | 19 | $21
10555 Greenwood Ave. N. (107th St.), 206-367-8481
■ "After a long day it's nice" to go and unwind at this
Greenwood "find", where the "hot-sauce-laden" tables
hint at the vibrant flavors of the "exciting New American
food" to come; equally attention-getting are the wine prices
($9 over wholesale); throw in "great ambiance and energy"
and it's clear why "every 'hood should have a place like this."

Big Time:
The Uncommon Pizzeria S   18 | 15 | 15 | $15
7824 Leary Way NE (Cleveland St.), Redmond, 425-885-6425
■ "Tasty pizzas and calzones" are the name of the game
at this Redmond pie parlor; count on some interesting flavor
combos sprinkled over the "excellent crust" – like the
Cascade Loop, which includes dried cranberries and apples
on a garlicky base, or the barbecued chicken ("a must");
wash 'em down with one of the "best microbrews in town."

Billy McHale's S   12 | 13 | 14 | $18
*Factoria Sq. Mall, 4065 128th Ave. SE (Coal Creek Pkwy.),
Bellevue, 425-746-1138*
4301 Guide Meridian (Kellogg Rd.), Bellingham, 360-647-7763
*1800 S. 320th St. (bet. I-5 & Pacific Hwy.), Federal Way,
253-839-4200*
18430 33rd Ave. W. (184th St. SW), Lynnwood, 425-775-8500
15210 Redmond Way (Willows Rd.), Redmond, 425-881-0316
241 SW Seventh St. (Rainier Ave.), Renton, 425-271-7427
10115 S. Tacoma Way (Hwy. 512), Tacoma, 253-582-6330
◩ Okay, so this chain of American-barbecue joints is "a bit
tacky" and the "cheap" fare "one step up from fast food",
but "the kids love it", especially the "crazy decor" with
"trinkets on the walls" that makes for plenty of "fun"(and,
not surprising, plenty of "noise"); among the adults, some
go for the "onion loaf" and some for the "great selection
of margaritas", but others just "won't go again."

Bing's Bar & Grill S   – | – | – | M
4200 E. Madison St. (42nd Ave.), 206-323-8623
The "great cheap, hearty eats" offered by this yearling have
injected a little ba-da-bing into Madison Park's dining
options; the all-American menu ranges from "awesome
omelets and awesome eggs Benedict" at weekend
breakfast to their 'bodacious burgers', chili, ribs and
signature prime rib sandwich served daily.

Bis on Main [S] 22 20 22 $32

10213 Main St. (102nd Ave. NE), Bellevue, 425-455-2033

■ "Bellevue finally has a great restaurant" exclaim locals who relish the "tasty, imaginative menu" at this young New American–Continental; adding glitter to the "undiscovered jewel" are its "sinful desserts" and "good wines", proffered by a "personable and professional staff"; it all confirms the reviewers' refrain: this is "the place to eat" on the Eastside.

Bistro Pleasant Beach [S] ▽ 23 22 22 $30

241 Winslow Way W. (bet. Finch Pl. & Wood Ave. SW), Bainbridge Island, 206-842-4347

■ There's "a pleasant surprise tucked away" at this Bainbridge Island "favorite" where "hard-working" chef/co-owner Hussein Ramadan is "a master, especially with fresh seafood" and other local ingredients that he embellishes "with a Mediterranean flair"; the result is an "interesting combination of taste, texture and color."

Bizzarro Italian Cafe [S] 18 22 19 $24

1307 N. 46th St. (Stone Way), 206-545-3520

■ "A very strange and wonderful" place, this "quirky Wallingford Italian" "combines a surrealistic [setting] with quality cuisine"; the "zany, madcap decor", complete with "chairs on the ceiling", can keep you entertained on those busy nights when "service can be lax" and the "food spotty."

Black Pearl 19 11 16 $17

7347 35th Ave. NE (75th St.), 206-526-5115 [S]

14602 15th Ave. NE (146th St.), Shoreline, 206-365-8989

■ Denizens of Wedgewood and, more recently, Shoreline can count on this pair of pearls – each a "household staple" for "solid Chinese" food that's "cheap" and "always fresh" ("be sure to get the homemade noodles"); the "diner/coffee shop atmosphere" makes them lose some luster, however.

Blue Onion Bistro [S] – – – M

5801 Roosevelt Way NE (58th St.), 206-729-0579

While this University District 1930s filling station-turned-bistro has the funky, retro decor you might expect, it serves up vittles you might not: chef/co-owner Scott Simpson prepares fun American comfort food, with specialties like balsamic marinated portobellos, pizza with house-smoked salmon, and puff pastry–topped smoked-chicken pot pie.

BluWater Bistro ◐ [S] 16 18 14 $23

Yale St. Landing, 1001 Fairview Ave. N. (bet. Eastlake & Mercer Aves.), 206-447-0769

■ For "one of the best congregations of beautiful people", head to this popular deck-endowed eatery overlooking Lake Union; it's "a fun place to meet" for "great appetizers", blue-tinted margaritas and a "decent menu" of American fare with a strong steakhouse bent; P.S. since the kitchen serves until 1 AM, night owls find it a hoot.

Boat Street Cafe [S] ⊄ 23 | 18 | 20 | $25

909 NE Boat St. (Pacific Ave.), 206-632-4602

■ "Chef-owner Renee Erickson makes the evening tops" at this "simple yet elegant" "old boathouse"-turned-French bistro that offers "a bit of class on the edge of the University District"; amidst the "unhurried ambiance", "dine with the UW profs" on "consistently fantastic food" that makes "unique use of NW" ingredients; weekend breakfast is also a big draw, "so get there early to get in line."

Brad's Swingside Cafe [S] 22 | 17 | 21 | $25

4212 Fremont Ave. N. (bet. 42nd & 43rd Sts.), 206-633-4057

■ There's "always a line out the door" of this "funky", "adorable hideaway" in Fremont; chef-owner Brad Inserra injects plenty of personality into the menu, with an Eclectic lineup that includes Cajun and North African influences alongside the "unique twists on classic Italian dishes" (including an "exquisite pasta" that swings); N.B. there's now a garden courtyard complete with fountain.

BRASA [S] 24 | 25 | 22 | $42

2107 Third Ave. (bet. Blanchard & Lenora Sts.), 206-728-4220

■ Chef/co-owner "Tamara Murphy does it right" at this "gorgeous" Belltowner where the "inventive menu" takes you on an eclectic tour of "Mediterranean-with-a-twist" fare; "equally impressive" is the "smashingly sharp, modern look" of the "spacious yet intimate" dining room; the "service can range from perfection to perfunctory, depending on who you get and who you know", but all in all, this is one "very civilized" and "classy" place; P.S. the "ultimate bar menu" is perfect for a post-midnight snack.

Brasserie Margaux [S] 20 | 20 | 18 | $36

Warwick Hotel, 401 Lenora St. (4th Ave.), 206-777-1990

◪ A stylishly revamped interior, crowned by a muraled ceiling, has made this yearling a presence on the Downtown dining scene; while some shrug it's "not quite living up to the remodeling", others "don't understand why it's not busier", given the "tasty food" (classic French with NW influences) and variety of varietals ("brava for [having] splits on the wine list"); undisputed is its handy location "across from the Cinerama", perfect for a pre- or post-movie bite.

Briazz 14 | 11 | 12 | $10

1400 Fifth Ave. (Union St.), 206-343-3099 [S]

The Bon Marché, 300 Pine St., main fl. (3rd Ave.), 206-447-7599 [S]

The Bon Marché, 300 Pine St., 6th fl. (3rd Ave.), 206-341-9009

1000 Second Ave. (bet. Seneca & Spring Sts.), 206-224-3100

Metropolitan Towers W., 1100 Olive Way (Boren Ave.), 206-587-2557

(continued)
Briazz
Westin Bldg., 2001 Sixth Ave. (Virginia St.), 206-256-4595
601 Union St. (6th Ave.), 206-381-5730
Newport Corporate Ctr., 3625 132nd Ave. SE (Newport Way), Bellevue, 425-373-3177
One Bellevue Ctr., 411 108th Ave. NE (4th St.), Bellevue, 425-635-0353
15900 SE Eastgate Way (35th Pl.), Bellevue, 425-401-9301
◪ "Great salads and sandwiches on-the-go for lunch" are the trademark of this chain of delis that also serve breakfast; but while they offer a "quick", "convenient" and "healthy" option that "beats fast food", critics call the "plastic-wrapped" quality "hit-or-miss" and wallet-watchers warn they're "overpriced."

Bridges on Eastlake [S] 14 | 14 | 14 | $20
2947 Eastlake Ave. E. (Allison St.), 206-320-0785
◪ Everyone agrees that the "outside deck" of this NW place offers a "fantastic" Eastlake setting to enjoy "drinks and appetizers" or "brunch with a view" of the aquatic action on Lake Union; but bridge-burners say the scenery trumps the "marginal" cuisine.

Broadway Grill, The ◐ [S] 14 | 13 | 15 | $18
314 Broadway E. (bet. Harrison & Thomas Sts.), 206-328-7000
◪ "People-watching" is the primary pastime of patrons at this Capitol Hill "hangout" "where all the action is"; expect an "easygoing atmosphere" with "the sassiest servers in town" and a "fun happy hour"; the all-American "food is unreliable" ("overhyped and underflavored" carp critics) but "not bad for late eats" for Broadway babies with the midnight munchies.

BROOKLYN SEAFOOD, STEAK & OYSTER HOUSE [S] 23 | 20 | 21 | $35
1212 Second Ave. (University St.), 206-224-7000
■ This "comfy" Downtown "landmark" across the street from Benaroya Hall "is still the place to go on symphony nights" or for "birthday dinners", "business lunches" and "fantastic happy hours"; regulars recommend you "sit at the counter and watch the chefs do their thing" with "first-class seafood and meats" and beer-and-oyster samplers; a few dodgers decry the "get-in-and-get-out" pace.

Brusseau's [S] ▽ 19 | 14 | 16 | $17
117 Fifth Ave. S. (Dayton St.), Edmonds, 425-774-4166
◪ For years this "small-town cafe"/bakery has been serving Edmonds loyalists who amble for fresh pastries in the morning and homestyle soup 'n' sandwiches at lunch; a few feel the goods are now just "mediocre", but there's unanimity that the patio makes a charming shopping respite or waiting room for the Kingston ferry.

Buca di Beppo 🔲   15 | 21 | 18 | $22

701 Ninth Ave. N. (Roy St.), 206-244-2288
4301 Alderwood Mall Blvd. (44th Ave.), Lynnwood,
425-744-7272

■ "Yeah, they're campy" admit followers of these "over-the-top" chain outposts in Lynnwood and Queen Anne, but they're also "a blast for groups" hungry for kitsch and "family-style" Italian fare served in such "overwhelming" portions you could "work on the leftovers" for weeks; epicures gripe "this isn't dining", but most agree you'll have "fun, fun, fun till your daddy takes the vino away."

Bungalow Wine Bar & Café   21 | 21 | 21 | $23

2412 N. 45th St. (bet. Eastern & Sunnyside Aves.),
206-632-0254

■ Oenophiles searching for a "relaxing" "oasis" "that nobody knows about" head for this "cozy old house on a busy street" in Wallingford, where they're "passionate" about wine, offering "a tremendous selection by the glass"; in between sips, you can sample a "luscious cheese plate", "decent tapas" and "tasty" Eclectic offerings from a small, dinner-only menu.

Buongusto Ristorante 🔲   19 | 17 | 19 | $27

2232 Queen Anne Ave. N. (McGraw St.), 206-284-9040

☑ Regulars relish this "reliable and pleasant" converted house at the top of Queen Anne as a "lovely place to linger over a dinner" of "solid Italian food" such as the signature osso buco; skeptics, however, sniff that the "no-frills" fare is "consistently inconsistent."

Burk's Cafe   20 | 16 | 18 | $22

5411 Ballard Ave. NW (22nd St.), 206-782-0091

■ Ballard's "genuine taste of N'Awlins" earns its Big Easy stripes with "tasty gumbo", "good 'jamba'" and other "spicy", "fantastic Cajun-Creole" fixin's; you can grill the "friendly staff" about the new alder-wood pit barbecue that's beefed up the menu, squelching critics who claim it "never changes"; P.S. be sure to save room for the "best pecan pie in the world" (well, in Seattle anyway).

Burrito Loco 🔲   22 | 12 | 18 | $11

9211 Holman Rd. NW (13th Ave.), 206-783-0719
University Village, 4508 NE University Village (25th Ave. &
45th St.), 206-729-2240

■ Flying low on the radar screen but high on praise, this "authentic", "dirt-cheap" Mexican (definitely "not Tex-Mex") is "a delightful surprise" with "burritos to die for" and what might be the "best chile rellenos ever"; Locophiles just "wish they had a better location" than busy Crown Hill (a wish soon to be granted, with a University Village sibling due to be born at press time).

Bush Garden 🅂   19 | 17 | 17 | $26 |
614 Maynard Ave. S. (bet. Lane & Weller Sts.), 206-682-6830
◪ A different Bush dynasty that's "been around forever"
attracts diners to this ID institution for the "good sushi and
bento" and other Japanese favorites; sure, it's "cheesy",
but that doesn't keep away the karaoke crowds whose
nightly sing-alongs make for a grand old party.

Byzantion, The 🅂   16 | 15 | 13 | $20 |
601 Broadway E. (Mercer St.), 206-325-7580
◼ You can count on "good quality Greek" (including a
"fabulous *avgolemono*") with an "authentic, homemade"
touch at this Capitol Hill taverna, whose "inexpensive"
entrees are so "massive" you might need a "shovel and bib";
this is no Trojan horse – you'll "get what you expect."

CACTUS 🅂   23 | 20 | 19 | $25 |
4220 E. Madison St. (43rd Ave.), 206-324-4140
◼ This succulent Southwestern–Tex-Mex in posh Madison
Park has "mouthwatering", "fabulous food" that runs the
gamut from "great tapas" and margaritas to the "best flan";
since it's an "'in'-crowd hang", "get there early" or "be
prepared to wait" – though you can always "borrow a
pager" and "take a leisurely stroll around the neighborhood."

Café Ambrosia 🅂   – | – | – | E |
2501 Fairview Ave. E. (Roanoke St.), 206-325-7111
What a transformation: housed in a former Azteca, this "new
Vegan on the shore of east Lake Union" offers "organic
fine dining" where *nachos grande* once reigned; some
find the elegant, white-tablecloth decor "a little sparse",
but the focus is clearly on the "delicious" and healthful
food that even omnivores can find ambrosial.

Cafe Bengodi 🅂   ▽ 19 | 17 | 15 | $20 |
700 First Ave. (Cherry St.), 206-381-0705
◪ Located just around the corner from sibling Luigi's Grotto
(formerly La Buca), this Pioneer Square hole-in-the-wall
prepares many of its Italian specialties tableside; though not
well-known to surveyors, it's already garnered both fans
("nice menu variety", "flavorful" food) and foes ("bland").

CAFE CAMPAGNE 🅂   27 | 23 | 23 | $31 |
Pike Place Mkt., 1600 Post Alley (Pine St.), 206-728-2233
◼ Smitten transients "want to move in", while gambling
gourmets "play the lottery to be able to eat every day" at
this "oooh"- and "aaah"-worthy "French bistro in the heart
of Pike Place Market", which offers "wonderful" cassoulet,
the "best pâté" and other "comfort food *à la française*";
it's also ideal for brunch, for "relaxing with a glass of Rhône
wine" "on a blustery afternoon" and as an alternative when
you can't get into Campagne, its upstairs sibling.

CAFE FLORA S
22 | 21 | 21 | $24

2901 E. Madison St. (bet. Lake Washington Blvd. & MLK Jr. Way), 206-325-9100

■ Even confirmed carnivores "see the light" at this Madison Park Vegetarian featuring "fabulous", "inventive" dishes (like the "excellent portobello Wellington") from a menu that offers "something for everyone"; the "charming staff" and "serene", "non-granola-ish" "greenhouse setting" alone may be enough to "convince you to go 'veg.'"

Café Huê S
▽ **17 | 11 | 19 | $19**

312 Second Ave. S. (bet. Jackson & Main Sts.), 206-625-9833

■ Those who've spotted this "undiscovered gem" in Pioneer Square declare it delivers "terrific", "creative" Vietnamese fare, even though perfectionists grumble its large dining room won't win awards for decor; still, less fastidious habit-huês just plain "love this place."

CAFE JUANITA S
25 | 20 | 24 | $39

9702 NE 120th Pl. (97th St.), Kirkland, 425-823-1505

■ "Hurrah for new chef-owner" Holly Smith, who has taken this hard-to-find "local institution to a new level" – one that's "worth searching for" if you're seeking "innovative" Northern Italian cooking, an "outstanding wine cellar" and "always excellent service", all in a "quaint", "creekside" setting in Kirkland; no wonder cosmopolites croon it's one of the "most sophisticated" venues around.

Cafe Lago S
24 | 18 | 21 | $28

2305 24th Ave. E. (bet. Lynn & McGraw Sts.), 206-329-8005

■ Ardent fans "dream of the gnocchi" and "live for the lasagna" served at this recently "remodeled" and enlarged Montlake Italian, a "must-go" for "amazing antipasto", "perfect pizza" straight out of a wood-fired oven and other items from the "small menu"; a few fussbudgets fret the place is "not as cozy since the expansion."

Cafe Langley S
21 | 17 | 20 | $33

113 First St. (McLeod Alley), Langley, Whidbey Island, 360-221-3090

■ A "wonderful" kitchen awaits at this Med hidden "in the hinterlands" of Downtown Langley on Whidbey Island; owned by the Garibyan brothers, it offers plenty of incentive (including a signature rack of lamb with cherry demi-glace) to take the "lovely ferry ride" to a "pleasant" respite.

Cafe Nola S
19 | 16 | 16 | $20

101 Winslow Way E. (Madison Ave.), Bainbridge Island, 206-842-3822

☑ Expect "quaint, hearty fare" (and a particularly "good brunch") at this Bainbridge Island Eclectic near the ferry; alas, the tide has been ebbing since the place "changed hands": surveyors register "disappointment" that there's "no bakery" any longer and say the new "concept doesn't work."

Café Septieme S | 15 | 16 | 13 | $19 |
214 Broadway Ave. E. (bet. John & Thomas Sts.), 206-860-8858
■ Stellar "people-watching" is a given at this hopping Capitol Hill cafe, thanks to a prime Broadway address that attracts a "colorful crowd" seeking amusement "after a show"; its "tempting dessert table" is more memorable than the just-ok Continental menu and "pretentious" servers.

Café Soleil S | ▽ 20 | 14 | 16 | $16 |
1400 34th Ave. NW (Union St.), 206-325-1126
■ This split-personality corner cafe in Madrona shines with "excellent" all-American breakfasts in the morning (when there's "never a wait") and "interesting" Ethiopian eats after dark; its large windows are cheering even on a gray day, making it a "comfortable" "neighborhood delight."

Cafe Starbucks S | 12 | 13 | 14 | $13 |
4000 E. Madison St. (McGilvra Blvd.), 206-329-3736
Pacific Pl., 600 Pine St. (6th Ave.), 206-652-4683
▨ "From the Starbucks machine" come these dual cafes in Madison Park and Downtown; reviewers roast the "bland", edibles and slow-drip service but admit they're "handy hangouts" – as long as you "stick to coffee" and pastries.

Cafe Veloce S | ▽ 15 | 15 | 13 | $19 |
12514 120th Ave. NE (Totem Lake Blvd., opp. Totem Lake Mall), Kirkland, 425-814-2972
■ Easy riders and "motorcycle history buffs" collide at this well-trafficked Kirkland Italian near Totem Lake Mall that fills 'em up with "wonderful pasta" packing "lots of garlic"; the Vespa-esque decor is a gas, but service can be a drag, veering from "really friendly" to screechingly "slow."

Caffe Ladro S | 20 | 18 | 19 | $10 |
600 Queen Anne Ave. N. (Roy St.), 206-282-1549
2205 Queen Anne Ave. N. (Boston St.), 206-282-5313
7011 California Ave. SW (south of Fauntleroy Way), 206-938-8021
Tower at 801, 801 Pine St. (8th Ave.), 206-405-1950
452 N. 36th St. (Francis Ave.), 206-675-0854
■ "In a town of great coffee", this "trendy" chain of 'thieves' (as the name translates) steals hearts with "beat-the-chill" lattes and "sinful" desserts including "wonderful home-baked pies"; beating the rap of many other java joints, their *baristas* are "quick" and "cheerful all day long."

Caffè Minnie's ◖S | 12 | 8 | 9 | $14 |
101 Denny Way (1st Ave.), 206-448-6263
611 Broadway E. (bet. Mercer & Roy Sts.), 206-860-1360
▨ Midnight-oil burners muster minnie-mal zeal for these "smoky, loud" American diners in Queen Anne and Capitol Hill that generate "greasy spoon" "grub" 24/7; the bleary-eyed blast the "lousy atmosphere", and even those adorned with the "requisite piercings and tattoos" say the "hipper-than-thou staff" "barely notices your existence."

Calabria Ristorante Italiano [S] 21 | 17 | 20 | $30

132 Lake St. S. (Central Way), Kirkland, 425-822-7350

◩ Fans of "simple", "reasonably priced" fare head to this Southern Italian in Downtown Kirkland for its "delicious seafood" and a "favorite penne Gorgonzola"; some say they "lost their character" following last year's expansion, but loyalists cite the winning combination of "perfect" live music and first-rate cocktails – particularly when co-owner Rhonda Bafaro takes an occasional turn behind the bar.

Calcutta Grill [S] 19 | 24 | 19 | $33

Golf Club at Newcastle, 15500 Six Penny Ln. (155th Ave. SE), Newcastle, 425-793-4646

◩ This Newcastle Golf Course Northwestern on a high perch in Bellevue boasts a "dark, British Empire look" and "top-of-the-world" views; a chef change may account for its birdie-to-bogey food comments ("great" vs. "disappointing") and equally hard-to-handicap service ("outstanding" vs. "snobbish"), but overall, most find it "up to par."

CAMPAGNE ◐ [S] 27 | 24 | 25 | $49

Pike Place Mkt., 86 Pine St. (1st Ave.), 206-728-2800

■ Owner Peter Lewis' "classic Country French" "all-star" at Pike Place Market is "still one of the best in the city" by virtue of "exquisite food that's treated as respectfully as the customers", an "excellent wine list" and a "sexy yet refined" atmosphere; romance-seeking regulars "pop into the bar without a reservation", while penny-pinchers recommend the "bargain" early-evening prix fixe – but whatever route you take to the *campagne*, "a great evening is assured."

CANLIS RESTAURANT 26 | 27 | 27 | $55

2576 Aurora Ave. N. (Halladay St., south of Aurora Bridge), 206-283-3313

■ Passing its golden anniversary, this Seattle "landmark" with a "beautiful setting" overlooking Lake Union seems to get "more and more modern while staying completely timeless"; credit chef Greg Atkinson's "updated" menu of "NW treats" ("top-notch steaks", "out-of-this-world seafood"), complemented by a "superb" wine list of over 1,000 selections and "impeccable" service, especially the "impressive" valet parking; granted, this "classic" is "expensive", so "it should be perfect and usually is."

Capitol Club [S] 18 | 21 | 17 | $27

414 E. Pine St. (bet. Bellevue & Summit Aves.), 206-325-2149

■ "Exotic discoveries" await at this "bohemian hideaway" on Capitol Hill where the cool Casbah decor (sleek banquettes, "great cushions and lighting") casts a spell over the "sexy", "black-clad, dot-commer" crowd that grazes on the "fabulous" Mediterranean menu of chef Michael Ruiz (ex Marco's Supperclub); late arrivals slip upstairs for a snack of hummus and baba ghanoush topped off with "a nightcap in the very happening bar."

Carmelita S 23 20 20 $29
7314 Greenwood Ave. N. (bet. 73rd & 74th Sts.), 206-706-7703
■ "Even a carnivore can dine well" at this Greenwood Vegetarian where the "inventive", "decadent" dishes and "amazing combinations" ensure no "veggie suffering" (even though chef Johnathan Sundstrom has moved on, leaving his toque to protégé Daniel Braun); you can also expect "friendly" service in art-filled, "homey" surroundings.

CASCADIA 25 25 23 $65
2328 First Ave. (bet. Battery & Bell Sts.), 206-448-8884
■ Pushing NW cuisine to ever greater heights (he only uses ingredients from the Cascade Mountain Range region), chef Kerry Sear turns out "ambitious", "cutting-edge" dishes at this Belltown "original" that's further enhanced by "stunning decor" (including a "beautiful waterfall"); a few groan at the "temple-of-gastronomy attitude", but ultimately this "gift to Seattle" leaves most patrons feeling "incredibly pampered" from beginning to "pleasant adieu."

Cassis S 24 20 22 $37
2359 10th Ave. E. (Miller St.), 206-329-0580
■ Inspiring floods of purple (or should we say cassis-colored?) praise, this "incredible" French bistro at the "low-key end of Capitol Hill" makes regulars feel "like the most-wanted guests" thanks to a "warm atmosphere", "one of the friendliest staffs in Seattle" and "fabulous food"; even better, it manages to be both a "great neighborhood" find and the "next best thing to Paris."

Catfish Corner ♥ 22 10 16 $16
2726 E. Cherry St. (MLK Jr. Way), 206-323-4330
■ "Deep-fried food" fanatics are "in heaven" at this "authentic" Central District Soul Fooder that dishes out "killer greens", "melt-in-your-mouth hush puppies" and some of the "best fried catfish ever", all "excellent values"; "transplanted Southerners" say it's "like visiting family."

Chandler's Crabhouse S 20 20 19 $34
901 Fairview Ave. N. (Valley St.), 206-223-2722
■ The "whiskey crab soup will change your life" at this Lake Union seafooder that also showcases a "good variety" of "dependable" crustacean creations; granted, it's "a little pricey" and "touristy", but "more often than not, they get it right" – and there's a "nice marina setting" with a "spectacular view" as a bonus.

Chanterelle Specialty Foods S ▽ 17 15 11 $16
316 Main St. (bet. 3rd & 4th Aves.), Edmonds, 425-774-0650
☑ Downtown Edmonds American cafe that lures locals who keep it simple and "go for soup, sandwiches and dessert" or take out the house specialty, chilled tomato bisque; otherwise, many yawn "tired", noting it "falls apart when more ambitious entrees are produced."

Charlie's on Broadway ◐ [S] 14 | 13 | 13 | $22
217 Broadway E. (bet. John & Thomas Sts.), 206-323-2535
◪ "Interesting characters" (both those "servicing your table" and those passing by) make for provocative "people-watching" at this Capitol Hill all-American that turns out "reliable" pub grub but is probably most memorable because it's "open late"; if the dark decor isn't to your taste, there's always "patio seating during the summer."

Chevys Fresh Mex [S] 17 | 16 | 15 | $16
19920 44th Ave. W. (200th St.), Lynnwood, 425-776-2000
3702 S. Fife St. (38th St.), Tacoma, 253-472-5800
■ Bring the gang to these "always happening" Mexicans in Lynnwood and Tacoma for "tasty tortillas" made on-premises and "excellent salsa" blended hourly; though snobs sniff they're strictly "mass market" and the "cheesy decor has got to go", at least they're "affordable."

CHEZ SHEA [S] 25 | 25 | 24 | $42
Pike Place Mkt., 94 Pike St. (1st Ave.), 206-467-9990
■ If you're in the market (Pike Place Market, that is) for a "romantic, delightful oasis", seek out this "quaint" NW eatery where "attentive" yet "discreet servers" deliver "inventive" offerings from a prix fixe menu; you "can't beat the view" of Puget Sound, nor the "candlelit" "elegance" of "one of the best, least-known restaurants in town."

Chile Pepper 17 | 11 | 15 | $16
1427 N. 45th St. (bet. Stone Way & Wallingford Ave.), 206-545-1790
◪ This Wallingford favorite offers "good Mexican food with an authentic touch", with some of the "best enchiladas" outside of Texas, along with an "ancho chile relleno that's worth the trip"; peppery patrons protest it's "average and unexciting", except for the decor, which is "depressing."

China Gate ◐ [S] 19 | 11 | 14 | $18
516 Seventh Ave. S. (King St.), 206-624-1730
■ For dim sum that's "a cut above" the competition, roll by this ID Chinese "early on the weekends" to snag your share of "seafood choices and fresh vegetables" (the "Peking duck on demand is a winner" too); the "lively" "family atmosphere" is just the ticket "for a large group."

Chinoise Café [S] 22 | 17 | 18 | $23
610 Fifth Ave. S. (Weller St.), 206-254-0413
12 Boston St. (Queen Anne Ave. N.), 206-284-6671
Chinoise on Madison
2801 E. Madison St. (28th Ave.), 206-323-0171
■ "Tasty", "eclectic Pan-Asian fare" and a "big" selection of "awesome sushi" make this neighborhood trio a "once or twice-a-week" treat for many; they "can get crowded" and the "slow service" could use some pep, but "reasonable prices" and a "cozy atmosphere" keep regulars regular.

Chinook's at Salmon Bay § 19 | 18 | 18 | $23
Fishermen's Terminal, 1900 W. Nickerson St. (west of Ballard Bridge), 206-283-4665
■ Locals take "out-of-town guests" to this "no-fuss" Fishermen's Terminal place for its expansive "view of the marina" and "broad selection of fresh seafood"; its "high-energy atmosphere" attracts "lots of families", so more retiring types "go late to beat the noise and crowds."

Christina's § ∇ 26 | 23 | 25 | $40
Porter Bldg., 310 Main St., 2nd fl. (Horseshoe Hwy.), Eastsound, Orcas Island, 360-376-4904
■ Chef-owner Christina Orchid continues to blossom at this Orcas Island "destination" that's "truly worth the trip", since she "knows her NW cuisine" but can also "turn great local classics into sophisticated dishes" (there's a "super wine list" too); look for candlelit, copper-topped tables in a dining room that's "cozy in winter" and a "great deck" overlooking East Sound that's a pleasure in summer.

Chutney's § 19 | 15 | 16 | $22
519 First Ave. N. (bet. Mercer & Republican Sts.), 206-284-6799
☑ Whether you're in the neighborhood for basketball or ballet, this "fabulous find close to the Seattle Center" in lower Queen Anne dishes up "very tasty", "simple Indian food that anyone will like" (particularly since they offer "all levels of spice"); nevertheless, a few detractors beg to differ, finding this tandoori house "disappointingly tame."

Chutney's Bistro § ∇ 20 | 16 | 18 | $18
Wallingford Ctr., 1815 N. 45th St. (Wallingford Ave.), 206-634-1000
■ "I'll be back" pledge basmati buffs who relish the "delicious, healthy Indian food" (including a "tandoori chicken that melts in your mouth") served at this Wallingford Center cousin of the original Chutney's; some also swoon over the "always awesome service."

Chutneys Cuisine of India 19 | 14 | 16 | $20
938 110th Ave. NE (8th St.), Bellevue, 425-467-0867
■ "We're happy they're now in Bellevue" Eastsiders enthuse about this latest addition to the Chutneys clan (each of which is individually owned); this newcomer features a "warm ambiance" with an open kitchen where you can watch chefs feeding the big tandoor oven as they put finishing touches on the signature curried mussels or mango cheesecake – "choose the right item and you're in heaven."

Chutneys Grille on the Hill § 19 | 15 | 16 | $21
605 15th Ave. E. (Mercer St.), 206-726-1000
■ This "friendly and low-key" Indian (one of the few on Capitol Hill) earns admirers for "excellent lamb dishes" and "mmm . . . that tikka masala!"; although it's a "nice, leisurely family and date place", some "good fast" takeout is available too.

Ciao Bella S 20 | 16 | 20 | $27
5133 25th Ave. NE (54th St.), 206-524-6989
Ciao Bella Too S
7115 Roosevelt Way NE (72nd St.), 206-527-4778
■ What a "well-kept secret" this "nice University District spot" (along with its year-old Roosevelt sibling) is; the unpretentious food is "always very good", and you can count on heaping plates of "great pasta" served by a "pleasant staff"; it's one "authentic Italian", down to "the singing waiters" who harmonize if the mood strikes.

Circa Neighborhood Grill & 18 | 14 | 16 | $18
Ale House S
2605 California Ave. SW (Admiral Way), 206-923-1102
■ "West Seattle would be lost without" this "homey" haven circa the busy Admiral district, a "favorite neighborhood spot for a burger and a beer" – though enthusiasts insist the Eclectic-American menu goes beyond "your average pub" grub to offer "high-level comfort food", including seasonal NW specialties.

CJ's Eatery S 15 | 11 | 17 | $15
2619 First Ave. (Cedar St.), 206-728-1648
☑ At a "laid-back" end of boisterous Belltown, a place some consider "Seattle's top spot for eggs" and other breakfast fare "runs like a well-oiled machine" (with "faster-than-the-blink-of-an-eye" service) until 4 PM; but skeptics sneer that "quality has slipped" of late, and while it'll do "if you're in the area, this is not a destination spot."

Claim Jumper S 15 | 15 | 16 | $21
Redmond Town Ctr., 7210 164th Ave. NE (Hwy. 520), Redmond, 425-885-1273
5901 S. 180th Ave. (Southcenter Pkwy.), Tukwila, 206-575-3918
☑ "Be prepared to wait" to stake a claim at these American-BBQ chain links in Redmond and Tukwila, where some say they've struck gold with the "monster portions" of "hearty down-home fare" and "to-die-for desserts"; more peeved prospectors protest that the "menu's an epic of mishmashed styles", the "decor is bad Old West" and the "hilariously sized" helpings "are obscene": "if you're all about quantity, not quality, this is designed for you."

Cliff House Restaurant S 22 | 22 | 21 | $37
6300 Marine View Dr. NE (Slayden Rd.), Tacoma, 253-927-0400
■ At this "longtime standard" with a cliff-top perch, reviewers rave about the "breathtaking" "view over the Tacoma waterfront" as they dine on "wonderful food" with an International emphasis; while the main menu has modern touches (e.g. pork loin with lentils and hazelnut chutney), tradition dominates for dessert, with classics such as "great cherries jubilee" flambéed tableside capping off an "elegant dining" experience; P.S. for those not up to the "expense-account pricing", there's Guido's Downstairs.

Coastal Kitchen [S] 20 | 16 | 17 | $23

429 15th Ave. E. (Republican St.), 206-322-1145

■ "Casual and energetic", this Eclectic eatery is a "local favorite" with the Capitol Hill crowd that "expects a wait on the weekends" before eating "fantastic corn pancakes" or the egg-a-licious "rumbles"; despite sometimes "spotty service", at night it's "fun" for its "rotating menu" that highlights a different coastal region each quarter ("the only frustration: I can't get what I loved last time"); P.S. no, "the voices you hear in the bathroom are not the occupants of the next stall" – they're "language tapes playing."

Coho Café [S] 20 | 20 | 19 | $24

Bella Bottega, 8976 161st Ave. NE (Woodinville-Redmond Rd.), Redmond, 425-885-2646

■ Some swear by this outpost in the bustling Bella Botega shopping center, whose seafood-heavy menu offers a "very tasty" "example of NW cuisine"; while it's "great before a movie" at the nearby cinema, be prepared for a wait at peak mealtimes, when critics carp the place gets "too noisy"; N.B. an Issaquah spawn is due to arrive in May.

Copacabana Cafe [S] 18 | 14 | 12 | $19

Pike Place Mkt., 1520½ Pike Pl. (Pine St.), 206-622-6359

◪ If you're looking for a "nice change of pace" in Pike Place Market dining, just look up to the "wonderful terrace" boasted by this Bolivian; connoisseurs happily cope with the cabana's specialties ("viva paella!" and "*tres leches* cake – can't have just one piece") while they "watch the ferries" ply across the Sound and gaze on a "fab view of the Olympic Mountains."

Costas Greek Restaurant [S] 17 | 13 | 16 | $18

4559 University Way NE (bet. 45th & 47th Sts.), 206-633-2751

■ The "clientele is 90 percent students" at this "University District dive" where you can tuck into "decent Greek food" (including "nice lemon soup" and "really good moussaka"); the scruffy decor's a drawback, but it's hard to beat the "large portions" served at college-budget prices.

Costas Opa [S] 18 | 16 | 17 | $20

3400 Fremont Ave. N. (34th St.), 206-633-4141

◪ This big Greek's "funky atmosphere" matches its bustling Fremont corner locale, across the street from the quirky Waiting for the Interurban statue; while devotees are drawn in by the "smell" of "great souvlaki" and other "tasty", "solid fare", others wish there was a more "authentic cuisine and decor"; the "service, though eccentric, is very friendly."

Coyote Creek Pizza [S] 18 | 13 | 14 | $17

Crossroads Shopping Ctr., 15600 NE Eighth St. (156th Ave.), Bellevue, 425-746-7460

(continued)

(continued)
Coyote Creek Pizza
228 Central Way (2nd St.), Kirkland, 425-822-2226
■ "Thin, crispy-crunch" pies rule at this pair of pizzerias with Western-themed settings in Bellevue and Kirkland; there are "lots of toppings to choose from", in cutely named "adventurous combos" such as Popeye's Pleasure (sautéed spinach and Gorgonzola) and The Road Runner (ham and artichoke hearts); it's all "tasty, if somewhat pricey", though the service and decor could use "some improvement."

Crab Cracker S
18 14 15 $28
452 Central Way (Lake St.), Kirkland, 425-827-8700
☑ Kirklanders appreciate the "convenient location" of this "fun seafood eatery" Downtown; but while converts love to get crackin' on their share of crab legs ("leave your white gloves at the door") and "good clams and mussels", the crabby-minded complain of a "rather dull menu" and the "nondescript" seafood-shack decor.

Crêpe de Paris
19 17 18 $29
Rainier Sq., 1333 Fifth Ave. (Union St.), 206-623-4111
■ For the lunchtime working and shopping crowd, this Downtown French crêperie offers an "ooh-la-la, interesting play on" pancakes (the "delicious dessert" varieties are especially recommended); however, critics hang the crêpe for the "forgettable" bistro menu served when the place morphs into a cabaret at night (at least the "shows are worth the price").

Crocodile Cafe S
13 14 14 $16
2200 Second Ave. (bet. Bell & Blanchard Sts.), 206-448-2114
☑ A "home away from home" for scenesters, this "funky" Belltowner is known mostly as a music venue with a "hip atmosphere" that's "great for a microbrew and a loud Seattle band"; reviews are mixed, though, for its Eclectic-American fare, ranging from raves for "surprisingly good and even inventive" dishes (e.g. the "best veggie Reuben in town") to rants about "worse-than-institutional food."

Cucina! Cucina! ● S
15 15 15 $21
Chandler's Cove, 901 Fairview Ave. N. (Mercer St.), 206-447-2782
Bellevue Pl., 800 Bellevue Way NE (8th St.), Bellevue, 425-637-1177
2031 S. 316th St. (west of Pacific Hwy.), Federal Way, 253-941-4800
Pickering Pl., 1510 11th Ave. NW (56th St.), Issaquah, 425-391-3800
Carillon Pt., 2220 Carillon Pt. (Lakeview Dr.), Kirkland, 425-822-4000
Redmond Town Ctr., 16499 74th St. NE (Hwy. 520), Redmond, 425-558-2200

(continued)

(continued)
Cucina! Cucina!
4201 S. Steele St. (opp. Tacoma Mall), Tacoma, 253-475-6000
Southcenter Mall, 17770 Southcenter Pkwy. (S. 180th St.), Tukwila, 206-575-0520
◪ "A consistent, cheerful crowd-pleaser" characterizes the feeling about this "pasta! pasta!" chain that's "fun for the kids" ("they get to play with the pizza dough"); fans find the "something-for-everyone" menu "consistently good" (with a "don't-miss" chopped salad), but the supercilious sniff that the experience here boils down to "overpriced", "boring Americanized Italian" cuisine in a "noisy setting."

Cutters Bayhouse [S] 20 21 20 $32
2001 Western Ave. (Lenora St.), 206-448-4884
◪ From its prime perch near Pike Place Market, this seafooder's sweeping views of Elliott Bay make it "a great place for tourists and locals too" to "sit by the window and eat the oysters" or "delicious, creative entrees"; dissenters cuttingly declare they're "disappointed, [given] the prices and the expectations driven by the decor."

Cyclops [S] 16 18 14 $20
2421 First Ave. (Wall St.), 206-441-1677
◪ "Quirky and fun" quip the hipsters about this "cool, trendy" spot "in the heart of Belltown", a "happening place for a lively drink" and an "Eclectic, energetic" menu that's "good when it's good", but can be "inconsistent"; the finicky also turn a fish eye on the servers' "snarly attitude."

DAHLIA LOUNGE [S] 27 25 25 $40
2001 Fourth Ave. (Virginia St.), 206-682-4142
■ The verdict is in: this "perennial Downtown favorite" is "as good as ever" in "great new digs" that are "much more roomy [yet] still intimate" and embellished with "fantastic red walls"; you can count on "wonderful use of seasonal NW foods" in "superbly presented" Eclectic dishes "with just the right amount of creativity" ("save room for the coconut cream pie"); owner "Tom Douglas is a Seattle treasure" and his lounge "a sublime experience."

DANIEL'S BROILER [S] 24 22 22 $43
809 Fairview Ave. N. (Valley St.), 206-621-8262
Leschi Marina, 200 Lake Washington Blvd. (Alder St.), 206-329-4191
Bellevue Pl., 10500 NE Eighth St. (Bellevue Way), Bellevue, 425-462-4662
■ Get ready for "an education in beef" at this "very classy" trio where you'll get "excellent steak and great drinks with commendable service"; all three have "fabulous views" (Bellevue's is from a 21st-floor perch, the others are Lake Union- and Washington-side); sure, it's "spendy" (some even opine "overpriced"), but it's "the place to go to celebrate", and after all, "you've got to treat yourself now and then."

Dash Point Lobster Shop 🅂   24 | 24 | 23 | $39
6912 Soundview Dr. NE (Markham Ave., off E. Side Dr. NE), Tacoma, 253-927-1513

Lobster Shop South 🅂
4013 Ruston Way (McCarver St.), Tacoma, 253-759-2165
■ Tacomans and tourists alike relish these "tucked-away" twins that, humble name aside, have offered "fine dining at its best" for 20 years, thanks to the combination of "creative, delicious seafood" (headed by the specialty Australian rock lobster tails), "great ambiance" and "fantastic views", especially from the "wonderful water-level window seats"; the "good Sunday brunch" is a huge draw, and it's definitely worth a dash to the early-bird dinners.

DC's Steakhouse 🅂   – | – | – | E
22850 NE 8th St. (228th Ave.), Sammamish, 425-898-1231
Since their island-themed Coconut Beach Grill sank, the Consolidated Restaurants group (Metropolitan Grill, Union Square Grill) has returned to its steakhouse roots in this Sammamish Plateau space; the large beef house offers all the standards (22-ounce T-bone, prime rib), plus pasta and chicken options for other tastes.

Delcambre's Ragin Cajun   20 | 10 | 19 | $14
Pike Place Mkt., 1523 First Ave. (bet. Pike & Pine Sts), 206-624-2598
■ "What this place lacks in decor is made up for by the food", which is "real Cajun" (e.g. "hot, spicy, delish!"), showing well what chef-owner Danny Delcambre learned from mentor Paul Prudhomme; the bustling Pike Place Market location makes it particularly "funky and fun" for a well- priced "slice of N'Awlins" at lunchtime.

Delfino's Chicago Style Pizza 🅂   21 | 10 | 13 | $14
University Village, 2675 NE University Village (25th Ave. & 45th St.), 206-522-3466
■ The transplanted natives have spoken, and they declare the "best Chicago-style pizza outside of Chicago" is served at this University Villager, where specialties like the "great stuffed spinach" deep-dish pie – cooked in an authentic Windy City oven – truly "satisfy the cravings" for home; the only problem for this storefront spot: it "needs expanding" 'cuz it's just "too little!"

Deluxe Bar & Grill ◗🅂   15 | 14 | 16 | $17
625 Broadway E. (Roy St.), 206-324-9697
◪ They've "recently revamped the decor and menu" at this hallowed all-American haunt on Broadway, and the "change is welcome", as a jump in scores indicates; though traditionalists grumble that they "miss the homey feel" and eats of the old place, fans find they can still count on "seriously good sloppy burgers" and "great bartenders", making this a reliably "cool place to hang" and enjoy the fine art of "people-watching", Capitol Hill style.

Desert Fire [S] 15 | 17 | 16 | $23

Pacific Pl., 600 Pine St. (6th Ave.), 206-405-3400
Redmond Town Ctr., 7211 166th Ave. NE (Bear Creek Pkwy.), Redmond, 425-895-1500

◪ This "fun" pair of Southwestern theme-o-rama spots offers a "good option while shopping" in Redmond and Downtown malls; but while the "reasonably priced" fare's "smoky flavors" catch fire with fans, skeptics say the desert-style "decor upstages food" "that's really of chain quality."

Dick's Drive-In ◐[S]≠ 18 | 10 | 16 | $7

12325 30th Ave. NE (Lake City Way), 206-363-7777
500 Queen Anne Ave. N. (Republican St.), 206-285-5155
9208 Holman Rd. NW (12th Ave.), 206-783-5233
111 NE 45th St. (bet. 1st & 2nd Aves.), 206-632-5125
115 Broadway E. (bet. Denny Way & John St.), 206-323-1300

◪ For many mavens, this quintet of "classic" '50s-style drive-ins isn't just "a Seattle institution" – "it's a way of life" for "gotta-have-it hamburgers", "real ice cream shakes" and "still-the-best fries"; skeptics sniff there's "nothing special" here "other than a little nostalgia value", but for those seeking a "guilty pleasure", the combination of "cheap, filling" fare and "fast, fast, fast" service means you get "absolutely the most bang for your burger buck" – not to mention a place that's "open when most bars close."

Dilettante Chocolates ◐[S] 21 | 14 | 11 | $13

416 Broadway E. (bet. Harrison & Republican Sts.), 206-329-6463

■ The "chocolate rum cake melts hearts" at this Capitol Hill fave that's no dilettante when it comes to "wonderful ice cream treats" and other "magical" desserts that can be polished off in "cozy" surroundings; beyond the sweet stuff, there's "so-so food" delivered by "waiters who operate at slow speed only" – but "how can anyone be unsatisfied amid all that" confectionery?; N.B. there's a Pike Place Market outpost that's strictly retail.

Dimitriou's Jazz Alley [S] 13 | 18 | 16 | $36

2033 Sixth Ave. (Lenora St.), 206-441-9729

■ "Very classy supper club" Downtown, where jazz hounds "come for the music, not for the dinner"; although the eclectic NW "food is certainly acceptable", it's the "awesome shows" that take center stage here.

Dish, The [S]≠ 23 | 17 | 21 | $13

4358 Leary Way NW (8th Ave.), 206-782-9985

■ Devotees dish happily about the "great breakfast" ("eggs all day – hooray!") that awaits at this diner-style Fremont American where a "staff that's a hoot" and a colorful "funky decor" provide for a "fun", if "crowded", atmosphere; on weekends there can be a "long wait, but they provide coffee" while you cool your heels outside; P.S. a lunch menu is available late-morning until the 2 PM closing.

Dixie's BBQ ⌀ — | — | — | I |
11522 Northup Way (116th Ave. NE), Bellevue, 425-828-2460
"Have you met The Man?"; if your answer's yes, then you've
been inducted into a sacred 'cue club that doesn't mind
queuing up to this Bellevue spot for "some of the best
BBQ around", in spite of "zero atmosphere" (hey, not that
long ago folks came here for brake jobs, not brisket); by
the way, 'The Man' refers to the super-hot sauce, not the
character who runs the place; P. S. for dessert, "try the
lemon cake" for a light, fresh finish to the feast.

Dragonfish Asian Cafe ◐S 21 | 21 | 19 | $25 |
Paramount Hotel, 722 Pine St. (8th Ave.), 206-467-7777
▣ "Happy hour is fun and original" at this mod Downtowner
where "cool mixed drinks" are served in the lively bar lined
with vivid pachinko machines (alas, not operational); while
some pan the Pan-Asian fare as "overpriced" and "bland",
others applaud the "quirky menu" full of "tasty bites"
("order a bunch of small plates and share"); at least,
given its proximity to the Paramount, it's a "good option
pre-theater" or after (kitchen closes at 1 AM).

Duke's Chowder House S 17 | 15 | 17 | $23 |
*7805 Green Lake Dr. N. (north shore of Green Lake),
206-522-4908*
901 Fairview Ave. N. (south shore of Lake Union), 206-382-9963
23 Lake Bellevue Dr. (NE 8th St.), Bellevue, 425-455-5775
▣ From the classic clam to "hip" Bombay shrimp and
lobster Pernod versions, the "chowders get a cheer" from
fans of these "convenient" and "consistent" seafooders;
beyond the stylish stews, however, gastronomes gripe
that the "overpriced" offerings are pretty "pedestrian"
("no surprises") and the "decor needs to be refreshed."

Dulces Latin Bistro S 20 | 20 | 19 | $35 |
1430 34th Ave. (bet. E. Pike & Union Sts.), 206-322-5453
▣ Serving an eclectic Med menu (ranging from red-pepper-
and-chorizo ravioli to boeuf bourguignon), this "secluded"
bistro is "a surprise tucked away in Madrona – but what
sort of surprise varies: the sweet-tongued rave about "the
sensual food" and "smoldering atmosphere", while the
hard-hearted find the "presentations listless"; you can
debate the matter in the adjacent cigar room, where
regulars often retire for a post-dinner puff.

Earth & Ocean ◐S — | 19 | 16 | $40 |
W Hotel, 1112 Fourth Ave. (Seneca St.), 206-264-6060
▣ Post-*Survey*, chef Johnathan Sundstrom (ex Carmelita)
took over at this New American in the almost "too hip" W
Hotel, and fans say "it's time [he gets] proper recognition";
those who were "tired of the small-plate idea", take
heart – the new regime offers "hearty" dishes that make
"great use of NW ingredients"; a happy holdover are the
"fabulous desserts" from pastry priestess Sue McCown.

Eating Factory, The [S] 12 | 11 | 10 | $18

Gelati Pl., 10630 NE Eighth St. (bet. 106th & 108th Aves.), Bellevue, 425-688-8202

◪ You can "stuff yourself until it hurts" at this Bellevue buffet with its "all-you-can-eat sushi – what a concept!"; while bargain-hunters believe the "food is ok for the price", dissenters dub this the "McDonald's of Japanese cuisine", where the "mass-produced food" "is as creative as the name", which "should be changed to the Rubber Factory."

Eggs Cetera's Blue Star Cafe & Pub [S] 18 | 14 | 14 | $16

4512 Stone Way N. (bet. 45th & 46th Sts.), 206-548-0345

◪ "A true Sunday-morning spot" (that actually serves breakfast every day) in Wallingford, where you can pick from your choice of 20-plus omelets before picking your way through the newspaper (the sometimes-slow service gives you plenty of time); for the not-quite-early-bird crowd, there's all-American "diner-style food and cheap, good beer" the rest of the day; kudos for being a "no-smoking" place, as well.

El Camino ◐ [S] 20 | 19 | 17 | $23

607 N. 35th St. (Evanston Ave.), 206-632-7303

■ "Great Mexican with a twist" is on the menu at this "hopping Fremont hangout" where you can count on "mouthwatering margaritas", "fabulous appetizers" and the "best specials ever"; "colorful" and "festive", "this is the place" for "fun people-watching" or to "meet friends for a drink", though some occasionally wonder "do the waiters remember they are working?"

EL GAUCHO ◐ [S] 24 | 23 | 24 | $52

2505 First Ave. (bet. Vine & Wall Sts.), 206-728-1337

■ It's "class all the way" at this "sophisticated" Belltown shrine to "superb steaks and superb service", whose worshipers include the "martini, meat and Cuban-cigar crowd" (though "surprisingly, the fish entrees are as good"); what with watching "Caesar salad and bananas Foster prepared tableside" and spotting the "local who's who", this is a real "dinner-as-theater" experience, set in a "dark and dramatic" "supper-club atmosphere" that "takes you back to a time long ago."

El Greco [S] 21 | 15 | 18 | $21

219 Broadway E. (bet. Olive & Thomas Sts.), 206-328-4604

■ "A hidden treat", this "good, casual Mediterranean" serves simple, straightforward preparations, such as the signature crispy penne, that strike ardent admirers as works of art; the most "underrated restaurant in the heart of Broadway" is "fantastic for brunch", too, with "omelets that are to die for."

Elliott's Oyster House [S] | 20 | 19 | 20 | $33
1201 Alaskan Way (bet. Seneca & Spring Sts.), 206-623-4340
◪ "Consistent for many years", this "fish house" is "perfect for out-of-towners", since it boasts a "great Elliott Bayside setting" and it's one of the "best places in town to get" shellfish (particularly at the newly revamped oyster bar); some see it as a "tourist trap", but fans find the dining experience to be "surprisingly good for the Waterfront."

El Niño | 16 | 17 | 16 | $23
113 Virginia St. (bet. 1st & 2nd Aves.), 206-441-5454
◪ "Serious margarita drinkers" dig this "cool" Downtowner for the "great tequila selection" (over 100 varieties), making it a great place to learn what the blue agave is all about; between sips, try nibbling on "pretty tasty" Mexican fare.

El Puerco Lloron [S] | 23 | 15 | 13 | $11
1501 Western Ave. (Pike Pl. Hillclimb), 206-624-0541
■ "You feel like you're in a Mexican cafe" when you hit this rest-stop on the Pike Place Hillclimb, thanks partly to the "wobbly tables" and "folding chairs", but mostly to the "incredibly authentic food", including "amazing *carne asada*" and "pork taquitos with guacamole that can't be beat"; it's a "once-a-week lunch staple" among amigos.

Emmett Watson's Oyster Bar [S] | 19 | 13 | 14 | $15
Pike Place Mkt., 1916 Pike Pl. (bet. Stewart & Virginia Sts.), 206-448-7721
■ "Tucked away in Pike Place Market" is this casual spot (inspired by the veteran *Seattle Times* columnist) where you'll be handed a "menu on a brown paper bag" that lists "excellent fried seafood", "oysters cooked every which way" and "to-die-for salmon soup"; regulars "love, love, love the courtyard" and relish the "reasonable prices."

Eques Restaurant [S] | 18 | 23 | 20 | $39
Hyatt Regency Hotel, 900 Bellevue Way NE (Bellevue Pl.), Bellevue, 425-698-4100
◪ "Elegant surroundings" inside the Hyatt Regency Hotel set the pace for a "good" International mix of dishes, with "excellent service and presentation" ("especially the right-on-the-money wine suggestions"); but radicals remain "underwhelmed", saying it "seems a little stuffy."

ESPRESSO VIVACE ROASTERIA [S] | 28 | 16 | 21 | $7
901 E. Denny Way (Broadway), 206-860-5869
ESPRESSO VIVACE TO GO BAR [S] ⊄
321 Broadway Ave. E. (bet. Harrison & Thomas Sts.), 206-324-8861
■ "Best coffee in town" carols the caffeine crowd that frequents this Capitol Hiller, Seattle's No. 1 Bang for the Buck, where beans are roasted on premises and every espresso drink is crafted with care, down to the aesthetic touch of "decorations in the latte foam"; N.B. don't forget the well-loved To Go Bar a few blocks away on Broadway.

ETTA'S SEAFOOD S | 25 | 20 | 22 | $36 |

2020 Western Ave. (bet. Lenora & Virginia Sts.), 206-443-6000
■ Fish fans say there's almost nothing b-etta than this "longtime favorite" (part of owner "Tom Douglas' dynasty") at the north edge of the Pike Place Market; it's "warm, friendly and informal", with an "eclectic menu" of "superbly fresh seafood" that "gets everything right" (even "the side dishes are a must"); it's a "super weekend-breakfast place" as well, ideal for fueling up before hitting the shops; an "always-pleasant staff" rounds out a supremely "satisfying" experience that even "impresses the in-laws."

Eva S | 25 | 21 | 23 | $34 |

(fka Brie & Bordeaux)
2227 N. 56th St. (Kirkwood Pl.), 206-633-3538
■ Locals have long lavished praise on this Greenwood bistro known for its "wonderful, casual atmosphere", "well-crafted, delicious food" and "knowledgeable staff" ("with no attitude except friendly"); regulars hope that new chef/co-owner Amy McCray (ex Chez Shea) – whose Eclectic–New American cuisine may not be reflected in the above food rating – "will continue the tradition" at this "darling spot"; N.B. at press time, plans were afoot to transform the adjacent cheese and wine shop into a bar.

Ezell's Famous Chicken S⊟ | 24 | 7 | 12 | $10 |

11805 Renton Ave. S. (72nd Ave.), 206-772-1925
501 23rd Ave. (E. Jefferson St.), 206-324-4141
7531 196th St. SW (76th Ave. W), Lynnwood, 425-673-4193
■ "You do not go to Ezell's for the decor – you go for the fried chicken", a "guilty pleasure" that "just doesn't get any better" (if he had known, "Colonel Sanders would never have left Kentucky"); the "rolls and sweet potato pie are also miracles" at this high-frying family of Southerners, but plan on getting it all to go, "unless you eat standing up."

Falling Waters Seafood Restaurant S | ▽ 21 | 23 | 22 | $35 |

2020 Second Ave. (bet. Lenora & Virginia Sts.), 206-374-3707
☑ A rich-toned "comfortable, pleasing decor" framed in wood draws strollers into this new addition to bustling Belltown; inside they'll find some "unique" offerings on the seafood-heavy menu (like the signature Hawaiian monchong); it's a "little stuffy", though, and while it has "potential to be great", so far it falls just short of the mark.

Famous Pacific Dessert Co. | 20 | 11 | 13 | $11 |

127 Mercer St. (Warren Ave. N.), 206-284-8100
☑ The menu's entirely "devoted to desserts" at this Queen Anne eatery near Seattle Center; the sweet-toothed sigh it's "perfect post-theater" for "sinfully delicious" treats and "great coffee" (hey, maybe that location is a little "too convenient"); more sour-minded surveyors, however, are "disappointed" by "cakes that look better than they taste."

Fandango ☽ 🅂   23 | 23 | 21 | $37

2313 First Ave. (bet. Battery & Bell Sts.), 206-441-1188

■ "Chef-owner Christine Keff [of Flying Fish] triumphs again" with this "great newcomer" that brings "authentic Latin to Belltown" in a vividly colored, "electric, hip atmosphere"; start with signature *mojitos* in the bar before slipping into the dining room (with any luck, you'll get one of the "sleek red booths") for a "tasty" trip through the "intriguing" and "refreshing menu" ("try the suckling pig, it melts in your mouth"); some say it's "still working out kinks" service-wise, but already this place is "hot, hot, hot."

Figaro Bistro 🅂   22 | 17 | 21 | $31

11 Roy St. (bet. 1st & Queen Anne Aves.), 206-284-6465

■ This "pleasant oasis in lower Queen Anne" is Seattle Center–goers' favorite "place for an excellent pre-theater meal"; the menu offers "good, traditional French bistro" fare that's "pretty much as you remember it from your first trip to Paris" ("wonderful, rich onion soup" and "fabulous mussels"); though some habitués note that the dining experience can be "inconsistent", the service is dependably "friendly and well informed."

Filiberto's Cucina Italiana   ▽ 19 | 12 | 15 | $24

14401 Des Moines Memorial Dr. (144th St.), 206-248-1944

■ In the shadow of Sea-Tac airport lies this Burien cucina that for 25-plus years has been serving up "genuine Italian home cooking" "at a reasonable price" in a "noisy, friendly" atmosphere; old-timers opine it's "just like the Old Country", complete with regulars who play a little bocce out back.

Firenze Ristorante Italiano 🅂   ▽ 21 | 16 | 21 | $29

Crossroads Mall, 15600 NE Eighth St. (156th Ave.), Bellevue, 425-957-1077

Il Capo 🅂

Third Place Books, 17171 Bothell Way NE (Ballinger Way), Lake Forest Park, 206-364-6001

■ "Romance in a strip mall" may seem like an oxymoron, but owner and "great host Salvatore Lembo" creates an atmosphere that is more "neighborhood-style Italian eatery" than its setting would let on; the menu serves up classics with style, including a wealth of pastas and not-your-average meats (grilled quail, for one); N.B. new bambino Il Capo, which serves an abbreviated menu, is unrated.

5 Spot ☽ 🅂   19 | 18 | 18 | $19

1502 Queen Anne Ave. N. (Galer St.), 206-285-7768

■ "Comfort food done right" has crowds spilling out onto the sidewalk in front of this "witty" Queen Anne American, a "superb twist on a diner", whose menu and decor "take you to a different U.S. city" every few months; while the "awesome breakfast" always hits the spot, a few find the dinner menu all over the map; but hey, if you eat here regularly, think of "the money you'll save on vacations."

Fleming's Prime Steakhouse & Wine Bar [S] 24 | 23 | 23 | $44

1001 Third Ave. (Madison St.), 206-587-5300

■ This "wonderful new steakhouse Downtown" is already proving to be "competition for" Seattle's other beef barons, with its "big portions" of "high-quality" meat and an "enormous selection of wines by the glass" (105, to be exact); "a real treat" too is the light mood provided by the open, window-filled dining area – an effectively airy break from the traditional "good-old-boy" stuffiness.

FLYING FISH ◐ [S] 26 | 22 | 22 | $38

2234 First Ave. (Bell St.), 206-728-8595

◪ "A lot of imagination goes into" the "superb seafood" with an Asian twist that's served by this "bustling and energetic" Belltowner; fans' faves include "out-of-this-world Thai crab cakes" and a platter of salt-and-pepper Dungeness crab that's "great for a crowd" (sharing's highly encouraged here); critics carp that it gets "way too noisy" and that "while the cash register flies, the service crawls", but most feel "this is a catch you should not miss."

Foghorn [S] – | – | – | M

6023 Lake Washington Blvd. (bet. NE 60th & 62nd Sts.), Kirkland, 425-827-0654

Perched on a prime spot overlooking Lake Washington for 28 years, this Kirklander is undergoing a major face-lift; at press time, it's scheduled to reopen with a fully revamped decor, new menus (still mainly seafood, but more emphasis on NW regional ingredients) and a spiffed-up wine list.

Four Seas [S] 18 | 14 | 17 | $21

714 S. King St. (8th Ave.), 206-682-4900

◪ "Excellent dim sum" is what usually brings people down to this ID Chinese, "particularly on weekends", when it can get quite busy despite its vast dining area (400 seats); some folks prefer to "eat in the bar", which gives a little respite from the flurry of activity in the main room.

14 Carrot Cafe [S] 17 | 12 | 14 | $16

2305 Eastlake Ave. E. (Lynn St.), 206-324-1442

◪ Half–health-fooder, half-diner, this '70s standby is "a lovely little treasure of a cafe on Eastlake" to stalwarts, who deem it just the place to go "for a big, traditional breakfast" – so no surprise that it's "always packed on weekends" (thankfully, they offer a "coffee stand outside" while you wait); but critics complain that the service is "a little harried", while the cuisine is both "over-egged" and "undercooked."

Frankfurter, The ⊄ 16 | 7 | 10 | $7

226 S. Orcas St. (3rd Ave.), 206-763-9669

213 Marion St. (bet. 2nd & 3rd Aves.), 206-382-0897

Seattle Ctr., 305 Harrison St. (5th Ave. N.), 206-728-7243 [S]

(continued)

(continued)
Frankfurter, The
11020A Eighth Ave. NE (Northgate Way), 206-367-7569 Ⓢ
Pier 54⅞, 1023 Alaskan Way (Madison St.), 206-622-1748 Ⓢ
Crossroads Mall, 15600 NE Eighth St. (156th Ave.),
Bellevue, 425-746-8607 Ⓢ
■ You'll find a "great variety of hot dogs" at this litter,
"the place to go" when you're "on the go"; while each
chowhound has his favorite – from "the best kielbasa" to
the "tasty low-fat Thai chicken sausage" – they all "love
the [fresh-squeezed] lemonade."

Fremont Classic　　　　　20　13　17　$19
Pizzeria & Trattoria Ⓢ
4307 Fremont Ave. N. (43rd St.), 206-548-9411
■ Its "newly remodeled" space makes this "great
neighborhood Fremont Italian" "bigger and better" at
accommodating the lines of folks willing to wait for
"world-class lasagna", "tiramisu that's made fresh daily"
and, of course, pizza that warms the heart of many a "poor
NY boy"; P.S. the decor rating may not fully reflect the
"long-overdue" expansion.

Fremont Noodle House Ⓢ　　21　16　16　$15
3411 Fremont Ave. N. (bet. 34th & 35th Sts.), 206-547-1550
■ "An awesome deal" awaits at this Fremont Thai where
the "excellent soup cures whatever ails you"; however,
there's "more than just noodles": "good curry", tasty "fried
wontons" and the signature *mieng kahm*, a leaf-wrapped
concoction that's a virtual "taste explosion"; though
"sometimes the wait is too long", the "attractive digs" make
the place "comforting"; N.B. at press time, a move to a yet-
unknown location was in the works.

FULLERS　　　　　　　26　25　25　$49
Sheraton Seattle Hotel & Towers, 1400 Sixth Ave.
(bet. Pike & Union Sts.), 206-447-5544
◪ "Always a great place for business dinners", this
Downtown "class act" offers "excellent NW food" and
regional wines served up "in a formal setting" that
showcases the distinctive art collection peppering the
walls; though "mixed experiences" leave malcontents
muttering it's "no longer the legend" that it used to be,
the full-hearted deem this vet still "one of the city's best."

F.X. McRory's　　　　　18　20　19　$28
419 Occidental Ave. S. (King St.), 206-623-4800
◪ The "testosterone-fueled atmosphere" of this Pioneer
Square "institution" draws the "sports crowd" for "pre-
and post-game" libations from the "great, legendary bar";
spoilsports say "forget the food", but most fans find the
surf-and-turf menu "creditable"; final score: "always
noisy, but it works."

Galerias 🅂 | 20 | 18 | 17 | $23

210 Broadway E. (bet. John & Thomas Sts.), 206-322-5757

■ This "marvelous Mexican" in an unlikely Capitol Hill locale is as famous for its "big-as-your-head margaritas" as it is for its authentic – "not by any means your usual Tex-Mex" – dishes, including the specialty *filete uruapan*, grilled skirt steak with creamy avocado sauce; the "awesome ambiance" boasts some ornate adornments, but there's not a sombrero in sight.

Gaspare's Ristorante Italiano 🅂 | 18 | 13 | 17 | $23

8051 Lake City Way NE (15th Ave.), 206-524-3806

■ "Homey, quiet and romantic" sums up this "solid" Lake City citizen, whose "pasta-lovers' pasta" and "daily seafood specials" "at a decent price" set it apart "from other neighborhood Southern Italian restaurants"; its "comfy" "familial environment" comes naturally – it's run by a husband-and-wife team.

Gelatiamo | – | – | – | I

1400 Third Ave. (Union St.), 206-467-9563

Since opening on a Downtown corner five years ago, this pint-size *gelateria* has gained a following among sweet-toothed surveyors, who can't get enough of the "best gelato outside of Firenze" and "gorgeous homemade Italian pastries" – all made on-premises by owner Maria Coassin; you can also jump-start your day here with a thick shot of espresso before hitting the office.

Geneva ▽ | 25 | 24 | 26 | $44

1106 Eighth Ave. (bet. Seneca & Spring Sts.), 206-624-2222

■ "One of the last bastions of Continental cuisine", this "jewel box" on First Hill offers "brilliant dishes" imbued with a little NW sparkle by Swiss chef-owner Hanspeter Aebersold; gourmands gush it's the "best in intimate dining", augmented by "old-world, professional service" and "elegant" yet "warm decor" – just the ticket "if you can't go to Europe for dinner."

GEORGIAN ROOM, THE 🅂 | 27 | 28 | 28 | $54

Four Seasons Olympic Hotel, 411 University St. (bet. 4th & 5th Aves.), 206-621-7889

■ There's just "no more elegant" place in town than this "posh" Downtowner (voted Seattle's No. 1 for Decor); but this "class act" goes beyond the opulent "carpets and chandeliers" to offer NW "meals fit for a king" and "luxuriant service"; "eventually all of Seattle shows up here", so "don't wait until a special occasion" – just "dress up" and "bring the credit card"; P.S. although well known "for an unforgettable evening", it now serves lunch as well.

Gordito's 🄢   22 | 11 | 17 | $11
213 N. 85th St. (Greenwood Ave.), 206-706-9352
■ "Go hungry, very hungry" to this "authentic Mexican"
in Greenwood that "caters to starving college students
and those interested in great burritos"; the "terrific
owners" serve 'em up "so big, cheap and tasty, you'll feel
like a *gordito*" (which "translates as 'little fat one'") after
finishing; you get "a lot for your money" here ("leftovers
guaranteed"), so "no wonder there's always a line."

Gordon Biersch   16 | 16 | 16 | $21
Brewery Restaurant 🄢
Pacific Pl., 600 Pike St., 4th fl. (Pine St.), 206-405-4205
◪ American "pub food with a large assortment of beers"
sums up this Pacific Place pit stop that's "good while
waiting for a movie" or after hard-core shopping Downtown;
it's "fun for the younger set", but others argue it occupies a
"no-man's-land between brewery and [eatery]."

Grady's Grillhouse ◗🄢   ▽ 15 | 12 | 14 | $15
2307 24th Ave. E. (bet. Lynn & McGraw Sts.), 206-726-5968
■ Sometimes all you need is "a good hamburger joint" that
offers "friendly service" – that's how the regulars rate this
Montlake sports bar where "TVs are going all the time"; a
recent face-lift has lightened up the look of this "hangout",
which may not be reflected in the decor rating above.

Grapes 🄢   ▽ 21 | 15 | 20 | $18
(fka Market Street Wine & Cheese)
5424 Ballard Ave. NW (Market St.), 206-297-1460
■ This "small" (40 seats), understated wine-and-cheese
shop just off Ballard's main drag offers a "nice selection"
of vino available by the two-ounce taste or glass, along
with a light bistro-style New American menu.

Gravity Bar 🄢   17 | 15 | 11 | $15
Broadway Mkt., 415 Broadway E. (bet. Harrison &
Republican Sts.), 206-325-7186
◪ Devotees "go for the juice" at this "sleek and hip" Capitol
Hill health-fooder – not to mention "amazing smoothies" and
"tasty" vegetarian dishes that'll have you "walking out
feeling healthier than ever"; but dissenters grouse about
service that ranges from "slow" to just plain "bad."

Grazie Ristorante Italiano 🄢   18 | 15 | 18 | $25
Factoria Sq. Mall, 3820 124th Ave. SE (I-405 & I-90),
Bellevue, 425-644-1200
23207 Bothell-Everett Hwy. SE (232nd St.), Bothell, 425-402-9600
Grazie Pizza Kitchen 🄢
16943 Southcenter Pkwy. (Strander Blvd.), Tukwila,
206-575-1606
◪ Fans say *grazie* for this triad of "decent" Italians where
the fare is "simple but good"; despite gourmands' gripes that
they're "not compelling", each is "a star in its neighborhood."

Green Cat Cafe S | 20 | 14 | 13 | $12 |
1514 E. Olive Way (Denny Way), 206-726-8756
■ At this "Vegetarian oasis" on Capitol Hill, the "colorful crowd" tucks into "high-quality grub", particularly the "great breakfasts" ("the scrambled tofu rocks!"); less-cool cats find the "extremely casual" scene "a little too healthy" – but how can you say no to a "curried tofu stir-fry that'll cure any hangover"?

Greenlake Bar & Grill S | – | – | – | M |
7200 Green Lake Way E. (NE 72nd St.), 206-729-6179
Early reports are the "food's decent" at this new seafooder where, before or after that volleyball game or blade run around Green Lake, you can tuck into the easy-to-like menu; the grill in question cooks up a variety of fish and shellfish, which comes with your choice of five sauces; the indecisive can content themselves with an "amazing calamari with spicy cilantro mayonnaise" or spinach salad with bacon-and-blue-cheese vinaigrette.

Hale's Ales Brewery & Pub S | 16 | 17 | 16 | $17 |
4301 Leary Way NW (8th Ave.), 206-782-0737
■ The smell of toasted malt greets you as you enter this "relaxed and comfortable" Fremont "hideout", whose "well-thought-out" layout offers both a "spacious dining room" and kick-back area with leather couches and coffee tables; though the "microbrew is the reason for coming" – they pour some of the "freshest tap beer in Seattle" – there's also plenty of "upscale pub grub without pretension."

HARVEST VINE RESTAURANT | 27 | 20 | 22 | $33 |
2701 E. Madison St. (27th Ave.), 206-320-9771
■ "Good things come in small packages" at this "shoe-box–size" Basque in Madison Valley that provides an "unparalleled ethnic experience"; since there are "no reservations", "get there early" to reap a harvest of "authentic" and "exquisite tapas", plus "great Spanish wine" between bites; "sit at the copper-topped bar" so you can watch mustachioed chef/co-owner Joseph Jimenez de Jimenez at work; wife and pastry chef Carolin "is a wonder", so save room for dessert.

Hattie's Hat S | 15 | 13 | 12 | $14 |
5231 Ballard Ave. NW (Vernon Pl.), 206-784-0175
◪ It's "still grim, still smoky and still populated with the more colorful of Ballard's denizens", but the bar's the place to be at this "late-night" icon, where veteran 'tenders serve up a famously zippy Bloody Mary with "great sweet potato fries to snack on"; though some warn "only order it if it comes in a bottle", many find the American "menu better than appearances would indicate"; "sit at the counter" for the full diner experience (including "snippy service").

HERBFARM, THE 🇸 | 28 | – | 27 | $87 |

Willows Lodge, 14590 NE 145th St. (Woodinville-Redmond Rd.),
Woodinville, 206-784-2222

■ Oh, the superlatives that devotees dole out for the "culinary adventure" that results when chef Jerry Traunfeld applies his art to the "creative uses of herbs" ("sublime", "pure alchemy", "inventive NW cuisine at its best"); expect a leisurely multi-course, multi-hour and multi-dollar "gastronomic feast", supplemented by "exquisite service and [table] setting", that's "worth the long wait" for reservations; herbivores "can't wait for their new location" to open in Woodinville (at press time, ETA was early April).

Hillside Manor 🇸 | – | – | – | M |

17121 Bothell Way NE (96th Ave.), Bothell, 425-485-7600

A recent change of ownership has built some changes into this Bothell hillside, including the addition of a front-yard waterfall and redecoration of the 1916 house; those to-the-manor-born find the new American menu, which emphasizes steak and Alaskan king crab, to be "of a higher caliber."

Hilltop Ale House 🇸 | 20 | 16 | 19 | $17 |

2129 Queen Anne Ave. N. (Boston St.), 206-285-3877

■ This "cozy, noisy" Queen Anne spot serves up "tasty" American-Eclectic pub grub ("halibut cakes – yum, yum") that's "perfect with brews" and the "strong" cocktails poured in a "very friendly, neighborhood atmosphere"; it gets "crammed like a closet", but the "cool staff" will make you feel at home – provided yours is a "non-smoking" one.

Hiram's at the Locks 🇸 | 20 | 21 | 20 | $32 |

Hiram M. Chittenden Locks, 5300 34th Ave. NW (south of
Market St.), 206-784-1733

☑ "Welcome back" signal fans to this Ballard American veteran, once again ensconced in its "original" home where you get "a good view of the locks from any table", but particularly the coveted patio seats; nostalgists love to "dine while the fish jump" (in the water below) on a tradition-oriented, seafood-heavy menu, but dissenters "wish the food matched the view", complaining that the "old menu [at] new prices is out of our league."

Hi-Spot Cafe 🇸 | 19 | 16 | 18 | $17 |

1410 34th Ave. (E. Union St.), 206-325-7905

■ Just follow the aroma of "wonderful cinnamon rolls" and "yummy scones" and you'll have little trouble honing in on this Madrona Victorian manse that's home to one of the city's "best breakfast joints"; you can expect a "very long wait" on "weekend mornings" ("too many people!"), but eventually you'll be nourishing yourself on "good ol' cooking like grandma's, in a house that could be hers."

Honey Bear Bakery & Cafe
19 | 13 | 14 | $11

Elliot Bay Book Co., 101 S. Main St. (1st Ave.), 206-682-6664
Third Place Books, 17171 Bothell Way NE (Ballinger Way),
Lake Forest Park, 206-366-3330 S

■ Now down to two locations in Pioneer Square and Lake Forest Park (the bear mascot watches over things at Third Place Books), this iconic bakery/cafe offers "atmosphere for good conversation (or a good read) over coffee", "great baked goods" and "soul-fueling sandwiches" that manage to be "wholesome and decadent at the same time."

Honey Court ⬤S
20 | 10 | 13 | $19

516 Maynard Ave. (Weller St.), 206-292-8828

☑ Late-nighters court this "consistently good" Cantonese-Mandarin "hole-in-the-wall" in the heart of the ID for its "great salt-and-pepper prawns" and other selections from the vast menu; but surveyors have less honeyed words for the visuals and the "impersonal, inattentive service", which has "really gone downhill" since the last *Survey*.

Hong's Garden S
▽ 24 | 13 | 18 | $23

64 Rainier Ave. S. (Airport Way), Renton, 425-228-6332

■ The former owner of the venerable House of Hong serves "dim sum done right" near the Renton Municipal Airport; it's "a great place to take airline refugees when they arrive" – though the "great flavors" make this one of the "best Chinese" in any part of town.

House of Hong S
18 | 13 | 16 | $19

409 Eighth Ave. S. (Jackson St.), 206-622-7997

■ Sip on some "chrysanthemum tea" while taking your pick from the passing carts of "consistently good dim sum" ("everything that one expects") or perusing the massive menu at this Chinese veteran; it's a big and bustling spot, like so many in the ID, with a "very friendly" staff.

Hunan Garden S
17 | 13 | 16 | $18

11814 NE Eighth St. (116th Ave.), Bellevue, 425-451-3595

■ This "good reliable" Bellevue Chinese of the lemon chicken and sweet 'n' sour pork variety offers "very fast" service that makes it "great for a quick lunch during the work week" – a good thing, since the "cheesy atmosphere" is no garden of Eden.

HUNT CLUB S
25 | 25 | 24 | $45

Sorrento Hotel, 900 Madison St. (Terry Ave.), 206-343-6156

■ For a dose of "some of the most elegant, romantic dining in Seattle", smart hunters head to this "landmark" on First Hill where chef Brian Scheehser prepares "great, full-flavored NW food" (he "has a nice way with game" in particular) laced with Med influences that reflect the hotel's Italianate decor; the mahogany-"paneled room" is "quiet" and "comfortable", offering an "old-world ambiance and style" that most find "elegant" but "not ostentatious."

icon Grill S
19 | 23 | 19 | $32

1933 Fifth Ave. (Virginia St.), 206-441-6330

▨ Patrons are polarized about Seattle's newest Downtown icon, which strives "to be both sophisticated and silly"; the "eclectic atmosphere" blends the "granny's attic" look with "glass art everywhere" ("groovy" grin some, while others huff "hate it"); similarly, many marvel at the "great take on American comfort food", while others shrink from the "overpriced" "so-so fare" ("the most expensive mac 'n' cheese you'll ever eat"); many mention the "hilarious staff" (we're still working out if that's a praise or a pan).

Il Bacio S
24 | 20 | 23 | $36

Cleveland St. Sq., 16564 Cleveland St. (164th St.), Redmond, 425-869-8815

■ This Northern Italian in Redmond is another example of a suburban "strip-mall" exterior that belies the "all-around fantastic" experience within; the dining area is split into three "quiet", candlelit rooms (all the better to showcase chef/co-owner Rino Baglio's specialties, like buffalo tenderloin sautéed with Barolo), serviced by a "friendly staff" – so "nice for those special, romantic evenings out."

Il Bistro S
23 | 23 | 21 | $37

Pike Place Mkt., 93A Pike St. (1st Ave.), 206-682-3049

■ Below the hubbub of the Pike Place Market is tucked this "wonderfully sexy hideaway" that's "been a favorite for years", owing to the "fantastic, gorgeous bar" (a "very popular" sipping spot) and the "picturesque" dining room with candlelit, linen-topped tables where you can sup on "delicious" Northern Italian fare, including "the best calamari and Caesar salad"; besides, what's not to love about a place where the perfectly balanced "lighting makes everyone look beautiful"?

Il Fornaio S
19 | 20 | 18 | $29

Pacific Pl., 600 Pine St. (6th Ave.), 206-264-0994

▨ In a "shopper-friendly location", this "mall restaurant with extra class" revives Downtown denizens; the more casual *risotteria* downstairs offers "quick-yet-good fare" (pizzas, etc.), while the *ristorante* upstairs "ventures into different areas of Italian cooking"; fans find it "consistently satisfying", but to detractors, it merely represents "a good argument against corporate" eateries.

Il Gambero
21 | 18 | 19 | $29

2132 First Ave. (Blanchard St.), 206-448-8597

■ Selfish surveyors say "shhh, don't tell anyone" about this cozy Belltowner, where chef-owner Gaspare Trani (who "knows seafood") cooks up Southern Italian "delicious, shrimp-infused, lip-smacking dinners" "with a delicacy that's rare in Seattle"; the intimate brick space is also "very romantic", making it easy to "linger for a few hours" over a bottle of wine from the mother country.

I Love Sushi S 23 14 18 $27
1001 Fairview Ave. N. (Mercer St.), 206-625-9604
11818 NE Eighth St. (bet. 116th & 120th Aves.), Bellevue,
425-454-5706
■ "Hate the name, love the spicy tuna rolls" summarizes
the sentiments of those who brave the "long lines" at this
Bellevue and Lake Union duo of sushi joints that are "short
on ambiance but big on taste"; while the "exquisitely
prepared" rolls rule, the presence of a few cooked dishes
makes it a "great experience even for non–sushi-lovers" –
so "you can't help but become a regular."

IL TERRAZZO CARMINE 26 24 24 $40
411 First Ave. S. (bet. Jackson & King Sts.), 206-467-7797
■ Expect a "continuously superb" experience at this
longtime favorite in Pioneer Square, an "elegant, old-
school Italian" that relies on standards such as the "best
carpaccio" and the signature osso buco Milanese, served
in a setting that's simultaneously "sophisticated" and
"comfortable"; the "ever-watchful eye of owner Carmine
Smeraldo guarantees you" "seamless service", but the
popular "classic" "can be loud."

India Bistro S – – – M
2301 NW Market St. (Ballard Ave.), 206-783-5080
Ballard heaved a big sigh when Scandie's – long the
Scandinavian cafe-of-choice in this Nordic-heritage
neighborhood – closed; but it's taken to heart this "nice
little spot", a "welcome addition" to "the main strip" for its
"superior Indian" "dishes with depth", often accompanied
by "great chutneys" and served by a "very nice staff."

India House S 18 13 16 $20
4737 Roosevelt Way NE (50th St.), 206-632-5072
◪ This 30-year-old, one of Seattle's longest-standing
Indian restaurants, has gotten a bit lost amid the wave of
trendy newcomers springing up around town; the "great
tikka masala and tandoori fish" still seem "fabulous" to
some Moghul mavens, but others could skip this University
District passage to India, citing "lackluster service" and a
"buffet [that's] not as good as before."

Inn at Langley S 24 25 24 $58
400 First St. (bet. Anthes & Park Aves.), Langley,
Whidbey Island, 360-221-3033
■ "When fine dining and weekend escape come together"
it's "the ultimate in romance", and that's what happens at
this Whidbey Island destination, which offers a different
sort of "dinner theater" in an "intimate" inn atmosphere:
the "one-sitting" prix fixe starts off with an "inspiring lecture
by innkeeper-chef Stephen Nogal" ("fun, but a bit precious")
and is followed by a "true NW culinary experience" that
features the best of very local, seasonal foodstuffs; "one
of my top meals of all time" many maintain.

Isabella Ristorante S　　　21 ｜ 21 ｜ 21 ｜ $33
1909 Third Ave. (Stewart St.), 206-441-8281

■ Its unassuming spot on a busy Downtown avenue belies the "warm and romantic" atmosphere behind the door of this Italian; it's "nice, not fancy", so some folks pop in "for a lunch" of "excellent pizza and salads" and at night turn their attention to heartier fare like the signature osso buco and daily seafood specials; "good" as they are, "desserts are even better" and the "service is top-notch."

Ivar's Acres of Clams S　　　17 ｜ 15 ｜ 15 ｜ $19
Pier 54, 1001 Alaskan Way (Madison St.), 206-624-6852

◪ A fixture on the Waterfront for over 60 years, this "Seattle institution" "close to the ferry dock" serves up a seasonal array of "no-nonsense seafood" (including a "great clam chowder" sold as far away as Japan) in a "family-oriented, bare-bones" setting; admirers attest it's the place "to take auntie from Chicago" ("sit outdoors and feed leftovers to the seagulls"), but foes huff the fish house's "heyday" is over and it's now "living on reputation and the glut of tourists."

Ivar's Mukilteo Landing S　　　17 ｜ 17 ｜ 17 ｜ $22
Whidbey Island Ferry Dock, 710 Front St. (Mukilteo Spdwy.), Mukilteo, 425-742-6180

◪ For the Whidbey Island bound, this fish house offers a nice place "to wait for the Mukilteo ferry" or take advantage of the "lightning-quick" "take-out window"; those not in transit enjoy a "nice view of Puget Sound" while perusing the menu that features contemporary NW twists amid the traditional seafood sustenance; clearly, this "is not your father's Ivar's" – but some still sigh that it "never seems to get beyond mediocre."

Ivar's Salmon House S　　　18 ｜ 18 ｜ 16 ｜ $24
401 NE Northlake Way (north shore of Lake Union), 206-632-0767

◪ Wood is the theme at this "old standby", a replica of a cedar longhouse (complete with "Indian artifacts") that boasts a 14-foot alder-wood barbecue pit, the source of the signature "great alder-smoked salmon" and other seafood delights; fans find it's a good place "to take visitors" for a "great view of Lake Union" and a "different" perspective on the "Seattle skyline"; old-timers grumble (what else?) "it's not as good as 30 years ago."

Izumi S　　　24 ｜ 18 ｜ 22 ｜ $25
Totem Lake West Ctr., 12539 116th Ave. NE (124th St.), Kirkland, 425-821-1959

■ "Always crowded and always pleasant", this Kirkland Japanese serves up the "best sushi on the Eastside" (some say it's even "right up there with Shiro's"); belly on up to the sushi bar where a "wide selection" of the "freshest fish" keeps you busy while you banter with the "friendly chefs"; amiable kimono-clad servers and a "comfortable decor" further explain why everyone here is "a happy customer."

Jack's Fish Spot 🆂   ▽ | 19 | 11 | 14 | $11 |
Pike Place Mkt., 1514 Pike Pl. (Post Alley), 206-467-0514
■ Smack in the middle of the Pike Place Market, this
"yummy lunch counter" with "not enough seats" can be
"very crowded and hectic, but worth it" for "great fish 'n'
chips, oysters, chowder" and freshly cooked Dungeness
crab at by-the-pound prices; it's basically an adjunct to a
fishmonger – so don't forget to pick up something for dinner.

JAK'S GRILL 🆂 | 26 | 18 | 22 | $32 |
*4548 California Ave. SW (bet. Alaska & Oregon Sts.),
206-937-7809*
14 Front St. N. (Sunset Way), Issaquah, 425-837-8834
■ "Great steak" at a "low price" might seem an oxymoron,
but this "excellent" West Seattle and Issaquah beef duo
does manage to be one of the "best buys in town" (the
"no-frills" setting helps); "the fact that they don't take
reservations is a pain" and because they're so often
"crowded" they get "noisy", but "service that makes you
feel like family" causes folks to be "weekly regulars."

Jalisco Mexican Restaurant 🆂 | 16 | 13 | 16 | $16 |
12336 31st Ave. NE (Lake City Way), 206-364-3978
8517 14th Ave S. (Cloverdale St.), 206-767-1943
1467 E. Republican St. (15th Ave.), 206-325-9005
122 First Ave. N. (bet. Denny Way & John St.), 206-283-4242
1715 228th St. SE (bet. 15th & 18th Aves.), Bothell, 425-481-3931
115 Park Ln. (Lake Washington Blvd.), Kirkland, 425-822-3355
Taqueria Jalisco 🌑🆂
129 First Ave. N. (bet. Denny Way & John St.), 206-282-1175
■ Since its expansion from its original location (a habitual
stop for Seattle Center–goers), many mope that this chain
"has lost its funky authenticity" ("why karaoke? why?"); but
it's "still worth a try" for "good [if] not great" "Mexican
spreads" and "ass-kicking margaritas"; "fast" service too.

Jimmy's Table | 22 | 18 | 19 | $33 |
2805 E. Madison St. (23rd Ave.), 206-709-8324
☑ "Well-prepared" meals are on the table at this addition to
the Madison Valley's Restaurant Row, where an Eclectic–
New American menu with Southern accents is, to put it
mildly, "interesting" ("where else can you get 10 ingredients
per entree?"); whining it's "way too noisy", dissenters find
it "a disappointment after Plenty", chef/co-owner James
Watkins' old gig, but even they admit there's "potential here."

Jitterbug Cafe 🆂 | 20 | 17 | 19 | $23 |
2114 N. 45th St. (bet. Bagley & Meridian Aves.), 206-547-6313
■ "A fun place to eat", this Wallingford hangout (from the
folks who brought you 5 Spot Cafe) has fans doing the
hand-jive for its "tasty, upscale diner food", which runs
the gamut from "gingerbread waffles that are a must" to
"innovative" Eclectic–New American dinners; it's got "a
lot of charm", even if it's "always packed on weekends."

Judy Fu's Snappy Dragon [S] 22 | 12 | 17 | $19

8917 Roosevelt Way NE (89th St.), 206-528-5575

■ Chef/co-owner Judy Fu is "famous for her noodle dishes, and rightfully so"; "delectable dumplings" and noteworthy soups star among the "tasty and creative food" at this "always-crowded" Maple Leaf Chinese, but Fu fans also insist "don't miss the green onion pancakes" or "tremendous crispy eggplant in tangy hot glaze"; some snap the fare's "heavy."

Julia's of Wallingford [S] 17 | 14 | 15 | $18

4401 Wallingford Ave. N. (44th St.), 206-633-1175

◪ This Wallingford mainstay offers a "laid-back and comfortable atmosphere" that's "still kind of hippie-ish" after all these years; it's "famous for breakfast" with "great bakery goods" (made on-site and available to go) and healthy, veg-heavy Eclectic–New American fare at lunch and dinner, but detractors dis the "long wait for tables and service" and a "quintessentially mediocre" menu that could use "more meat, please."

Kabul Afghan Cuisine [S] 22 | 15 | 18 | $21

2301 N. 45th St. (Corliss Ave.), 206-545-9000

■ It's "worth the hunt" to find this Wallingford "sleeper" and fill up on the Afghani version of comfort food; the "unusual, well-prepared dishes" range from "heavenly appetizers" like the "ecstasy"-evoking *bolani*, potato-scallion turnovers in garlic-yogurt sauce, to the dessert *firni*, a "delicious rosewater pudding"; a sitar player provides ambiance Tuesdays and Thursdays.

Karam's Lebanese Cuisine ▽ 22 | 9 | 18 | $21

340 15th Ave. E. (bet. Harrison & John Sts.), 206-324-2370

◪ When the stinking rose permeates your nose, you're probably near this Lebanese "in a dive of a Capitol Hill location", whose "tasty Middle Eastern food" comes liberally laced with "serious garlic" (perhaps the reason why critics complain it "all tastes the same"); after 8 PM it only serves those with reservations, leading some to quip it's "open as often as you find an honest politician."

KASPAR'S 24 | 22 | 23 | $43

19 W. Harrison St. (1st Ave.), 206-298-0123

■ An "island of civility" isn't exactly what you'd expect so close to the Seattle Center, but the "relaxed ambiance", combined with "elegant food" and a "fabulous wine list", makes this Queen Anne place simply "terrific"; chef-owner Kaspar Donier applies his Swiss training to produce "definitive NW-Continental haute cuisine" that "never disappoints"; N.B. watch out for periodic winemakers' dinners and tastings.

Kells Irish Restaurant & Pub S | 17 | 18 | 17 | $23 |
Pike Place Mkt., 1916 Post Alley (bet. Stewart & Virginia Sts.),
206-728-1916

■ "The closest thing to an Irish pub this side of Dublin", this Pike Place Market spot is the place for pints, "live music seven nights a week" and "crowded, fun, noisy" times; perhaps it's a wee bit "better known for" the booze and bands "than for the food", but would-be Celtics claim the "authentic cooking" (like the signature spud-laden stew) warms the soul "on a cold rainy day."

Kidd Valley S | 17 | 9 | 12 | $9 |
5502 25th Ave. NE (55th St.), 206-522-0890
14303 Aurora Ave. N. (143rd Ave.), 206-364-8493
135 15th Ave. E. (John St.), 206-328-8133
531 Queen Anne Ave. N. (Mercer St.), 206-284-0184
4910 Green Lake Way N. (50th St.), 206-547-0121
Northgate Mall, 418 Northgate Mall (5th Ave NE &
Northgate Way), 206-306-9516
15259 NE Bellevue-Redmond Rd. (north of Northup Way),
Bellevue, 425-643-4165
6434 Bothell Way NE (61st Ave.), Kenmare, 425-485-5514
5901 Lake Washington Blvd. NE (Houghton Park), Kirkland,
425-827-5858
1201 Lake Washington Blvd. (Coulon Park), Renton, 425-277-3324

■ We kidd you not: since the original opened over 25 years ago, this bevy of burger joints has become "a Seattle institution"; "don't think about your waistline" as you munch "mouth-stuffing" patties, "great Walla Walla sweet onion rings (in season)" and 12 flavors of hand-mixed "real shakes" (including banana and peanut butter versions); unfortunately, the "indifferent service" is no laughing matter.

Kikuya S | ▽ 24 | 17 | 21 | $20 |
8105 161st Ave. NE (Redmond-Kirkland Way), Redmond,
425-881-8771

■ "Tucked into a nondescript Redmond strip mall", this amiable Asian offers up "very good Japanese food" that's served in "huge portions" by "the most pleasant staff around"; while it's "great for dinner", the "lunch specials can't be beat", so don't overlook digging into some *donburi* midday or the bento box, one of the "best in the region."

KINGFISH S⊄ | 25 | 22 | 21 | $26 |
602 19th Ave. E. (Mercer St.), 206-320-8757

■ "You go, girls!" cheer fans of the Coaston sisters, who run this "buzzing" "down-home" haunt, which offers "a taste of Southern tradition" at "very reasonable prices"; the "great cookin' with all the fixin's" includes "red beans, rice and cornbread to die for", "huge slices of the cake *du jour* to save room for" and "buttermilk fried chicken worth every minute in line"; admittedly, this can amount to quite a lot of minutes, so "put your name down and go for a drink" or a walk around the mellow Capitol Hill nabe.

Kirkland Roaster & Ale House S 15 14 15 $22
111 Central Way (1st St.), Kirkland, 425-827-4400

◪ "Crowded, noisy" "gathering place" in Kirkland that offers American "comfort food" with many a microbrew on tap; most find the fare "all pretty standard" except for the "very good roasted meats", which admirers argue make for "great lunches" even when the servers are "out to lunch."

Kokeb Restaurant ▽ 21 11 14 $22
926 12th Ave. (bet. Marion & Spring Sts.), 206-322-0485

◪ For nearly 20 years, interest in *injera* (soft, flat native bread) and all that you can pick up with it has sent fans flocking to this Ethiopian near Seattle U; the "large portions" draw those looking for "something different", but some shrug that the cuisine and service "could use more kick."

Krittika Noodles & Thai Cuisine S ▽ 23 20 19 $19
6411 Latona Ave. NE (65th St.), 206-985-1182

◪ This recent addition has hit the ground running with "marvelous Thai food" in a comfortable setting, making Green Lakers "glad to have it" in their neighborhood; "when not busy, it's a great place for a low-key meal", so regulars recommend you "avoid" peak hours, when they are "understaffed" and overwhelmed.

La Fontana Siciliana S ▽ 22 22 23 $30
120 Blanchard St. (bet. 1st & 2nd Aves.), 206-441-1045

▪ 'Midst the hustle-bustle of Belltown, here's a truly tranquil haven where the namesake fountain greets you in the brick courtyard and a "wonderfully cozy atmosphere" awaits within; the "delightful staff" offers "good" "stick-to-your-ribs Southern Italian fare" including a tortellini Gorgonzola that's "orgasm on a platter"; small wonder some call this "the most romantic restaurant in Seattle."

Lake Washington Grillhouse S ▽ 13 19 14 $22
Kenmore Marina, 6161 NE 175th St. (Lake City Way), 425-486-3313

◪ "A beautiful view of the north end of Lake Washington" draws folks to this formula surf 'n' turfer at the Kenmore Marina, as does the proximity to the Burke-Gilman Trail; though there's "friendly service" and a good selection of microbrews, it functions primarily as a convenient pit stop for tired boaters, bikers or bladers.

La Medusa 21 17 20 $26
4857 Rainier Ave. S. (Edmonds St.), 206-723-2192

▪ This "fave in historic Columbia City" earns its self- applied label of "Sicilian soul food" purveyor by serving up "delicious pasta", "must-try thin-crust pizzas" and other "earthy and filling" fare, supplied by the nearby "farmers' market in the summer"; so much "kindness abounds" in the "warm and bustling" atmosphere it'll keep anyone from turning to stone; N.B. the decor score doesn't reflect a recent redo.

LAMPREIA [S] | 25 | 21 | 23 | $58
2400 First Ave. (Battery St.), 206-443-3301
◪ No Emerald City establishment polarizes patrons as much as this Belltowner: the cult-like majority "would sit on an apple box in the alley to eat" chef-owner and "culinary genius" Scott Carsberg's "sublime" Italian-influenced NW–New American fare – though folks don't have to, given the "stylish atmosphere" and "indulgent staff"; to heretics, however, it's a "stuck-up" spot that specializes in "confrontational dining" in the form of "skimpy portions", "robotic waiters" and "austere decor."

La Panzanella ⊅ | 24 | 19 | 16 | $14
1314 E. Union St. (14th Ave.), 206-325-5217
■ Man *can* live on bread alone – provided it's been baked by Ciro Pasciuto, chef/co-owner of this Capitol Hill cafe, aka "Italy's outpost", both for the fare ("delicious panini", the namesake salad and "beautiful pastries") and for its "exceptionally warm atmosphere"; while you're at it, why not get some dough to go – many of the best restaurants in town do.

La Rustica [S] | 24 | 23 | 23 | $27
4100 Beach Dr. SW (Carroll St.), 206-932-3020
■ "The early bird gets the romantic table" at this "small, homey Italian" that's "way off the beaten path" (unless you happen to be a lucky West Seattleite); "all pasta, all the time" characterizes the menu, which is embellished with nightly specials like the signature lamb shanks; all in all, a "delightful, unpretentious experience" at a "great value."

Le Bonaparte [S] | ▽ 19 | 15 | 15 | $39
21630 Seventh Pl. S. (bet. Marine View Dr. & 216th St.), Des Moines, 206-878-4412
■ This midsize Des Moines suburbanite has morphed from Classic to Contemporary French with a renovated "great menu" that hints ever-so-subtly at new chef-owner Masao Nagasawa's Japanese heritage; thrilled neighbors say the once "classiest place in South King County" has made a Napoleonic "comeback" – though perhaps not fast enough to be fully reflected in the above ratings.

LE GOURMAND | 26 | 21 | 26 | $54
425 NW Market St. (6th Ave.), 206-784-3463
■ "A little off the beaten path", this Ballard "oasis of comfortable elegance" offers an "escape from the trendy set" as you enjoy "top-of-the-line French fare"; chef-owner Bruce Naftaly "is a delight" with his "impeccable use of NW ingredients" (some of which may be "grown 20 yards from where you sit", in the adjacent garden); with "exquisite fine food, romantic atmosphere and prompt quiet service, what more can you ask for?"

Le Pichet S | 23 | 22 | 20 | $30 |
Pike Place Mkt., 1933 First Ave. (Virginia St.), 206-256-1499
■ There's now a "little piece of Paris" at the Pike Place Market, offering the "hearty flavors" of "artful" French bistro fare on a selective (some say "limited") menu; it may be "brand-new", but it feels "like it's been there 40 years", with such "authentic details" as the tiled floor, hefty zinc bar, earthenware *pichets* of wine and a bill with phrases *en français*; N.B. it's open only for continental breakfast till noon on Tuesdays and Wednesdays.

Leschi Lakecafe S | 16 | 18 | 16 | $25 |
102 Lakeside Ave. (Alder St.), 206-328-2233
☑ The "beautiful view" of Lake Washington draws crowds to this "stereotypical" "'80s-style bar and grill" on Leschi with "a good deck" and lots of beers; it's "great when boating" but otherwise "just seems ok", with a seafood-infused American "menu that needs a face-lift" (except for the "excellent clam chowder").

Les Tamales ⊟ | ▽ 18 | 18 | 20 | $24 |
3247 California Ave. SW (bet. Hanford & Hinds Sts.), 206-923-3538
■ No, that's not a misprint in the name: this "ambitious", peach-colored West Seattle spot serves "Mexican [fare] with a French flair", including "well-done" specials like shrimp-and-gruyère tostadas, chimichanga con chèvre and Mayan chocolate mousse cake (along with more traditional tamales and bouillabaisse); the "all-Mex margaritas", made with 35 types of tequilas, are "all great" too.

Limelight Cafe S | – | – | – | E |
3656 34th Ave. W. (Emerson St.), 206-282-1282
Stealing the limelight in Magnolia is this "casual yet classy" cafe where the Eclectic menu features "creative classics" such as the signature jambalaya and a spinach-hazelnut cannelloni; the combination of "original" offerings and "omnipresent owners" adds up to a "wonderful", "quiet" refuge that locals love.

Lockspot Cafe S | 14 | 10 | 12 | $13 |
3005 NW 54th St. (south of Market St.), 206-789-4865
☑ This 80-year-old eatery at "the entrance to the Ballard Locks" is famous for "fish 'n' chips served with a bushel of fries" and "killer drinks", though the American menu also includes a "salmon-pesto sandwich good enough to make you cry"; the unconvinced weep it's "only passable", but there's no denying the good "local flavor" here, complete with "spunky servers" and "funky atmosphere."

Lombardi's Cucina S | 19 | 17 | 16 | $23 |
2200 NW Market St. (22nd St.), 206-783-0055
1620 W. Marine View Dr. (18th St.), Everett, 425-252-1886

(continued)

Lombardi's Cucina
695 NW Gilman Blvd. (7th Ave.), Issaquah, 425-391-9097
■ "Go for the garlic" could be the rallying cry of this "reliably good" trio, purveyors of pasta and other "typical-yet-tasty" Italian choices at "affordable" prices; "unpredictable service" can be a drag, but the complimentary "wonderful bread with roasted garlic cloves" is "a definite plus."

Longshoreman's Daughter S　　19 | 15 | 14 | $16
3508 Fremont Pl. N. (bet. Evanston & Fremont Aves.), 206-633-5169
■ There's "nothing fancy", but plenty "positive", about "Fremont's funkiest hangout", which transitions daily from a "crowded", "classic" breakfast spot with some of the "best omelets in town" to a mellow cafe serving "solid staples and adventurous specials" of American grub (sweet potato sandwich, anyone?); sometimes "service is spotty", but that doesn't hurt the overall "good feeling."

Louie's Cuisine of China S　　16 | 14 | 17 | $20
5100 15th Ave. NW (Ballard Bridge), 206-782-8855
◪ This Cantonese "scores big in Ballard" for its "nicely prepared and served food" loyalists say; but snipers slam a "stuck-in-the-'70s decor" and find the "very Americanized Chinese" cuisine quite "bland."

Louisa's Cafe & Bakery S⇄　　18 | 15 | 12 | $12
2379 Eastlake Ave. E. (bet. Louisa & Lynn Sts.), 206-325-0081
■ If you need a spot "to study, talk or just eat" on Eastlake, this "bohemian bakery" satisfies with "fresh" American fare and "good baked goods" (all made in-house); it's the kind of place "where writers can be seen scribbling", undeterred by the "confusing counter service."

Luau Polynesian Lounge S　　19 | 22 | 20 | $24
2253 N. 56th St. (Kirkwood Ave.), 206-633-5828
■ You're near Green Lake, but "you can almost hear the wind and waves of the tropics" as you enter this often-"packed" Polynesian eatery; start with the flaming pupu platter and some "super-fun drinks" (the "Zombies should come with a warning label, not a straw") before digging into the "original and savory" main attractions; it's all "kitsch taken to new extremes", but you'll have a "raucous", rollicking time nonetheless.

Luigi's Grotto S　　∇ 19 | 18 | 17 | $25
(fka La Buca)
102 Cherry St. (1st Ave.), 206-343-9517
■ "Don't be put off by the [nondescript] entrance" to this Pioneer Square Italian; inside is a "charming" and (like the name suggests) "cave-like setting" in which to enjoy "amazing seafood" and a wide variety of pastas; a "perfect haven on a stormy night" patrons proclaim.

Luna Park Cafe [S] | 16 | 18 | 14 | $13

2918 SW Avalon Way (Spokane St.), 206-935-7250

◪ "Fun family" diner in West Seattle, where the "quirky decor" is haute garage-sale (think vintage lunch boxes and old signage); sophisticates quip it's "all show and no go" here, but luna-tics love the "good burgers", "outstanding milk shakes" and other culinary "'50s hits."

Lush Life [S] | 23 | 23 | 21 | $30

2331 Second Ave. (Battery St.), 206-441-9842

■ "Belltown's hidden best" rave romantics about this stylish Italian, where "everything is fabulous", from the "dark and sultry" setting to the "exceptional" eats (clearly, "somebody in the kitchen loves to cook"); it's "fun late at night" and makes for a "very hip date place", though "it can get quite loud" with all those folks leading the lush life.

Machiavelli | 22 | 15 | 20 | $22

1215 Pine St. (Melrose Ave.), 206-621-7941

■ There's a "great vibe" at this "friendly", "small Italian place on the corner" in Capitol Hill, which "still rules after all these years" thanks to its princely portions of "outstanding pasta" (including "the best" homemade ravioli); since the "underpriced menu draws huge crowds", scheme to "get there early" to snag a table (no reservations accepted).

MACRINA BAKERY & CAFE [S] | 25 | 18 | 18 | $16

2408 First Ave. (bet. Battery & Wall Sts.), 206-448-4032

■ Can't choose from among the aptly named "morning glory muffin", the addictive "orange hazelnut pinwheel" or the "best-of-the-best cinnamon monkey bread"?: then just get "one of everything" and you're guaranteed "gustatory bliss", since this "terrific Belltown bakery" purveys pastries "worth getting out of bed for"; later on, a "varied", "rustic" Med- oriented lunch menu is served.

Madame K's Pizza Bistro [S] | 16 | 17 | 16 | $17

5327 Ballard Ave. NW (bet 22nd Ave. & Vernon Pl.), 206-783-9710

◪ Housed in a historic bordello, this Ballard Italian plays on a "bawdy brothel theme", with "saucy staffers" and suggestively named dishes; some surveyors are seduced by the pies (definitely "not your mama's pizza") and the 'Chocolate Chip Orgasm' dessert ("the perfect climax" to any meal), but others get no satisfaction from cuisine they compare to "Army C-rations."

Madison Park Cafe [S] | 21 | 17 | 19 | $28

1807 42nd Ave. E. (Madison St.), 206-324-2626

■ It's like having "a gourmet dinner in your own living room" when you patronize this "cozy bungalow" in Madison Park, where "new chef" Marianne Zdobysz has boosted the food score with her "fresh and tasty French bistro fare", including an "outstanding" lavender-honey rack of lamb; P.S. the garden "courtyard is especially pleasant in the summer."

Mad Pizza S 17 | 9 | 12 | $12
3601 Fremont Ave. N. (36th St.), 206-632-5453
1314 E. Madison St. (13th Ave.), 206-322-7447
4021 E. Madison St. (bet. 41st Ave. & McGilvra Blvd.),
206-329-7037
🗹 "Be adventurous" is the mantra of those mad about the
"most inventive pizza" (like the "Jamaican jerk chicken"
version) tossed by this trio of pie shops; more stick-in-
the-mud surveyors, however, sum the fare up with "two
big Os: overrated and overpriced."

Mae Phim Thai Restaurant ∅ – | – | – | I
94 Columbus St. (bet. 1st & Western Aves.), 206-624-2979
This "hole-in-the-wall Thai" is an "incredible Downtown
lunch spot" with "friendly service" that's "unbelievably
fast" and "fabulous" food that's "cheap" ("oops" sighs
one surveyor, "I shouldn't have told you"); expect a "long
line", since they're always so "busy with take-out service."

Mae's Cafe S 18 | 16 | 15 | $13
6412 Phinney Ave. N. (65th St.), 206-782-1222
■ "Espresso shake and eggs" ("only in Seattle") is on
hand at this "very fun" Phinney Ridge "cow-themed spot",
and indeed, you might "feel like a cow" when you leave,
full of "tons of good American food for not a ton of money";
regulars advise you "arrive early to beat the crowds", since
the "big breakfasts" are "not necessarily worth a big wait."

Maggie Bluff's S 17 | 16 | 17 | $19
Elliott Bay Marina, 2601 W. Marina Pl. (Smith Cove), 206-283-8322
🗹 Casual American in Magnolia that is a favorite for its
"divine" marina-side glimpse of boats and skyline (shared
with upstairs sib Palisade); fans feel the kitchen bluffs its
way through with crave-inducing burgers or a "great ahi
sandwich", but pickier patrons pout that "not even the view"
makes up for "so-so food" and often "inattentive service."

Malay Satay Hut S ▽ 25 | 9 | 19 | $14
Orient Plaza, 212 12th Ave. S. (bet. Boren Ave. & Jackson St.),
206-324-4091
■ An "authentic" Malaysian menu that travels beyond the
signature satay makes this "hole-in-the-wall" one of the
most popular spots in the ID; the "helpful and friendly
servers" guide you through the "great range" of "complex
flavors"; you "can't beat the price", so some "go here often."

Maltby Cafe S 23 | 17 | 19 | $16
8809 Maltby Rd. (bet. Hwys. 9 & 522), Maltby, 425-483-3123
■ "It's always packed, always slow, but when you leave
you're always full" of "real food, made from scratch" at
this "quaint" Eclectic-American "located in an old school";
admittedly, it's a "long way" to this Maltby breakfast/lunch
spot, so "be sure to take home" some of their celebrated
colossal cinnamon rolls to last you until the next field trip.

Mama's Mexican Kitchen S   17 | 16 | 14 | $15
2234 Second Ave. (bet. Bell & Blanchard Sts.),
206-728-6262

◪ "Elvis has *not* left the building"– his spirit lives in a
"kitschy" room at this Mexican veteran, for nearly 30 years a
"classic" for its "eclectic Belltown crowd"; many have a
hunk of burnin' love for the "speedily served" "killer Cadillac
margaritas" and "monster portions" of "cheap and *bueno*"
eats, but some get all shook up over the "overrated" food
and a staff that "has issues."

Mamma Melina S   22 | 19 | 21 | $27
4759 Roosevelt Way NE (50th St.), 206-632-2271
■ Around the corner from the Seven Gables cinema, this
University District spot makes folks "feel like they're part of
the family", thanks to the "charming" hospitality of Mamma
Melina Varchetta, whose son Roberto is the brains behind
the "simple, delicious Italian" cuisine; at no extra charge,
you may be serenaded by Papa V. "singing with your meal"
(yet another talent that runs in this family).

Mandalay Café S   ▽ 23 | 19 | 24 | $21
1411 N. 45th St. (Stone Way Ave.), 206-633-0801
■ Take the road to Wallingford and this charming converted
bungalow, where the "waiters love to artfully describe"
the tempting array of Southeast Asian savories (including
some of the "most delicious curry options") that "cater
to meat eaters and vegetarians alike"; reviewers "only
regret we didn't find it sooner."

Maple Leaf Grill S   19 | 16 | 18 | $22
8929 Roosevelt Way NE (90th St.), 206-523-8449
■ At this "nice low-key place" in Maple Leaf, the notable
"beer list" and "Eclectic menu" (ranging from "huge
sandwiches" to more "imaginative", "spicy" fare) will
please even "a picky eater"; though some still lament the
"move to a new location", devotees deem this "the best
neighborhood bistro – now if we could just keep others
out, maybe we neighbors could get a table."

Marcha Tapas y Copas ◗ S   ▽ 20 | 21 | 19 | $28
1400 First Ave. (Union St.), 206-903-1474
■ "Top-notch tapas" get folks marching to this new
Downtowner that brings "a bit of Barcelona to Seattle",
complete with "occasional salsa dancing", a modern
"exciting" decor, "convivial service" and an interesting
all-"Spanish wine list" (just one type of the copas, or
drinks on hand); other options include "mouthwatering"
octopus and "incredible paella."

Marco's Supperclub [S] 23 | 20 | 21 | $33

2510 First Ave. (bet. Vine & Wall Sts.), 206-441-7801

■ "Romantic but not too chichi", "the vibe could not be better" at this "always hopping" Belltowner that's "still a classic" (eight years makes you an old-timer in this 'hood); the "excellent Eclectic menu" offers "mind-bending" and "high-flavored" fare, from the "not-to-be-skipped fried sage leaves" appetizer to the signature Jamaican jerk chicken.

Market Street ▽ 27 | 24 | 27 | $34

1744 NW Market St. (bet. 17th & 20th Sts.), 206-789-6766

■ Proving that "Belltown has come to Ballard for sure", this upscale newcomer brings a "creative", seasonally changing New American menu, colorfully "great ambiance" and "fabulous service" to a blue-collar 'hood ; folks "can't say enough" about this "great addition", even if it is "hard on the wallet" in a nabe more familiar with lutefisk than lobster.

Mashiko ▽ 26 | 14 | 18 | $28

4725 California Ave. SW (Alaska St.), 206-935-4339

■ "Bring a good appetite and a sense of humor" to this neighborhood Japanese that's definitely not your "standard staid sushi bar" (the chef chooses the music, which ranges from "great" to "terrible"); acoustics aside, West Seattleites welcome the chance to "sit at the bar to watch the pros work" on "melt-in-your-mouth fish" and serious lunchtime bargains of donburi, udon and bento boxes; now if only "chef-owner Hajime Sato [could] clone himself."

Matt's Famous Chili Dogs ▽ 16 | 11 | 14 | $6

6615 E. Marginal Way S. (4th Ave.), 206-768-0418 [no credit cards]

699 110th Ave. NE (8th St.), Bellevue, 425-637-2858

■ "They do dogs justice" at this hot-diggity pair, where the wallet-weary can get their fix of franks with all the fixin's; and if hot dogs aren't your thing, you can always chow down on sandwiches and tamales; N.B. though the beloved Boeing Field original's basically a stand, there's sit-down space at the Bellevue location.

Matt's in the Market 25 | 19 | 23 | $27

Pike Place Mkt., 94 Pike St. (1st Ave.), 206-467-7909

■ Offering "an eagle-eye view of the heart of the Pike Place Market", this "real hole-in-the-wall" is stuffed with some "tasty surprises"– namely, "some of the best seafood in town", "perfect wine suggestions" from owner Matt Janke and "personable service" that all combine to create "an overall wonderful treat"; P.S. for your best chance at one of the 23 seats, regulars recommend you "go early or late" – oh, and "please don't tell the tourists."

Maximilien **S** 24 24 22 $32
Pike Place Mkt., 81A Pike St. (1st Ave.), 206-682-7270
■ This "excellent secret spot in the Pike Place Market" has a prime corner perch that offers a "supreme Puget Sound view", a "wonderful setting" for enjoying such "spectacular" stalwarts of Classic French cuisine as mussels marinière, tournedos Rossini and a distinctive selection of Gallic (and NW) wines; it's also a "romantic" spot for Sunday brunch, with "uncommon pastries" and what some call "the best eggs Benedict ever eaten."

McCormick & Schmick's **S** 21 19 21 $31
1103 First Ave. (Spring St.), 206-623-5500
■ Though part of a national chain, this Downtowner is redolent of a good "old-style fish house"; a "professional staff" moves smoothly through the "clubby", slightly "stuffy" ambiance that "draws WASPs in droves", while the menu offers a "variety of dishes", headed by a daily selection of "always reliable" "fresh seafood" from all over the U.S.; N.B. the legendary happy hours offer good values on the bivalves.

McCormick & Schmick's Harborside **S** 21 22 20 $30
1200 Westlake Ave. N. (southwest end of Lake Union), 206-270-9052
■ "A delightful view" (both from the casual deck and the elegant upstairs room) makes this seafooder a popular stop on the shores of Lake Union; the kitchen offers "tons of choices of fish, fixed any way you like", with regulars raving about the "Monday night lobster special" in particular; don't overlook the "great bar", either.

McCormick's Fish House & Bar **S** 22 21 22 $34
722 Fourth Ave. (bet. Cherry & Columbia Sts.), 206-682-3900
■ "In the tradition of great fish houses", this 22-year-old Downtowner is "still one of the best" (certainly "the best of the McCormicks") with its "clubby yet comfortable" "great old-style decor of wood, brass and tile" and "well-designed menu" of "always delicious" seafood; regulars hint to "avoid the complex dishes" and stick to straightforward fish, and you'll be sure of "a real treat."

Mediterranean Kitchen **S** 21 14 18 $22
366 Roy St. (4th Ave.), 206-285-6713
103 Bellevue Way NE (1st St.), Bellevue, 425-462-9422
Mediterranean Kitchen Express **S**
1417 Broadway (bet. Pike & Pine Sts.), 206-860-3989
■ It's "full garlic ahead" at these Lebanese-Med outposts where some are so devoted to the 'farmer's chicken wings' (marinated, charbroiled and served with a creamy lemon-garlic sauce) that they may never get to the "must-have *shish tawook*" (marinated chicken breast), the "really good lamb" or the "excellent tabbouleh"; the "big portions" mean "plenty of leftovers", making this trio a "good value" to boot.

Meridian Restaurant & Bar S ▽ 15 | 18 | 16 | $37
1900 N. Northlake Way (Meridian Ave., north shore of Lake Union), 206-547-3242
◪ Still remembered as the site of the old Arnie's, this locale has been transformed by that late establishment's manager into a "pricey" American eatery; while its perch above Lake Union's north end makes it a "good place for out-of-towners" (especially if they try the "fabulous" 'Treasures of the Sea', a seafood sampler), more reserved reviewers are "hanging in" to see if the place gets beyond being a "disappointment."

METROPOLITAN GRILL S 26 | 23 | 24 | $45
820 Second Ave. (Marion St.), 206-624-3287
■ "If you need meat, it can't be beat" say supporters of this Downtowner, a "suit-oriented" oldie that's still "the best place for steak in Seattle"; expect "always-done-to-a-turn" "portions the size of Texas" served by the "bright, funny, attentive staff", and an woody "expense-account" ambiance that, when fueled by the "good happy hour", is "busy, energetic, vibrant" – and a tad "too noisy" at times; all in all, though, this is one prime beef baron.

MISTRAL 27 | 20 | 24 | $67
113 Blanchard St. (bet. 1st & 2nd Aves.), 206-770-7799
■ This "intriguing" newcomer has blown into Belltown, establishing itself for "serious, *very* serious, foodies": you pick your prix-fixe price point, choose "fresh ingredients" from the daily-printed list, then "relax and enjoy" chef-owner William Belickis' "wonderful and daring" New French– New American preparations, "impeccably served"; though reviewers register "sticker shock" over the price, they admit that "every course is exquisite" – "maybe too good for Seattle", in fact.

Moghul Palace S ▽ 22 | 15 | 22 | $20
University Bookstore Mall, 10303 NE 10th St. (Bellevue Way), Bellevue, 425-451-1909
■ There is "nothing like the curried mussels" at this eatery, a "favorite Bellevue Indian" among moguls and ordinary folk alike in spite of its less-than-palatial strip-mall setting; also noteworthy are the "very good" curries and tandooris, which sometimes appear on the "fabulous lunch buffet"; "attentive servers" offer the royal treatment at dinner.

Mona's Bistro & Lounge S 22 | 23 | 20 | $28
6421 Latona Ave. NE (65th St.), 206-526-1188
■ "Good art", richly colored walls and subtle lighting create a "dark and moody" atmosphere at this "delightful Green Lake bistro", almost overshadowing the "great" Med menu that could "hold its own with Downtown restaurants"; however, the romance-minded might avoid the twice-weekly jazz nights, as the "live music" makes things "loud."

MONSOON 🟦

25 | 19 | 20 | $30

615 19th Ave. E. (bet. Mercer & Roy Sts.), 206-325-2111

■ Tucked into a section of Capitol Hill, this "delicious Vietnamese" run by the Bahn clan delights with dishes such as "incredibly fragrant soups", 10-spice flank beef and "must-try sea bass" that "combine subtle and spicy flavors" and are joined by "well-chosen wines"; just be prepared – only a monsoon could drown out the "terrible din" when the "spare, bright" room gets packed.

Moonfish 🟦

▽ 19 | 20 | 17 | $34

4738 Lynwood Ctr. Rd. (NE Baker Hill Rd.), Bainbridge Island, 206-780-3473

◪ Located in a turn-of-the-last-century house (previously occupied by Pleasant Beach Grill), this yearling is "still struggling to find its place on Bainbridge Island"; the moonstruck marvel over the "innovative" Eclectic–New American menu that balances land and sea (phyllo-wrapped salmon's the specialty), but the less-impressed feel it "could do better."

Morton's of Chicago 🟦

24 | 20 | 22 | $56

1511 Sixth Ave. (bet. Pike & Pine Sts.), 206-223-0550

■ "Where are Dean Martin and Frankie?" – they'd fit right into the "men's-lounge atmosphere" of this "carnivore's dream" Downtown, where a "well-trained staff" steers you through "mouthwatering" "steak you can cut with a fork" and "fun appetizers"; some beef there's "too much ado with the food cart and vocal menu" (characteristic for this chain) and "expensive" prices (ditto), but the majority rules "go here when you want to feel important."

Musashi's ⊘

22 | 8 | 17 | $16

1400 N. 45th St. (Interlake Ave.), 206-633-0212

■ If you're wondering how folks feel about this Wallingford Japanese, "the line out the door every night tells you it's top-notch"; the "tiny, crowded place" turns out "simply the best cheap sushi in Seattle" ("tremendous value in teriyaki", too), so who cares if the "decor is worn and minimal" – what inquiring minds want to know is "when will they find a bigger space?"

My Favourite Piroshky 🟦

16 | 7 | 13 | $9

124 Broadway E. (bet. Denny Way & John St.), 206-322-2820

Bellevue Sq., 1010 Bellevue Sq. (Bellevue Way), Bellevue, 425-646-9354

■ For "something different" next time you're shopping Bellevue Square or hanging out on Broadway, slip into one of these "authentic" Russian eateries where you'll find sustenance in the "best borscht ever" and a variety of "cheap, filling" namesake turnovers; it's a great option for "takeout when you don't want yet another burger."

My Friends Cafe [S] ▽ 16 | 9 | 12 | $12

310 NE 72nd St. (Green Lake Dr.), 206-523-8929

◪ Green Lakers like the "decent, healthy" fare (primarily of the breakfast-all-day ilk, with soups and sandwiches for the lunch crowd) served at this simple Eclectic-American; however, the "abrupt service" ("don't you dare sit down before ordering!") leaves some so "turned off" that they "never try the food."

Nara Grill [S] ▽ 21 | 17 | 19 | $25

2027 Fifth Ave. (Lenora St.), 206-727-2224

■ "Send someone to this new place immediately!" demand disciples of this sleek Pan-Asian that specializes in tables with a view – from the all-out action of the teppanyaki-style grill stations to the slice-and-dice setting of the sushi bar – amid a streamlined, artifact-filled decor; upstairs offers quieter rooms and an outdoor deck (nearly eye-level with the passing Monorail, alas); N.B. there's a free parking lot alongside, a big plus in this Downtown neighborhood.

NELL'S [S] 26 | 21 | 24 | $45

6804 E. Green Lake Way N. (bet. 2nd & 4th Aves. NE), 206-524-4044

■ Chef-owner "Philip Mihalski is clearly a rising star", and his New American with regional influences serves as a "great successor" to the beloved Saleh al Lago, late of this Green Lake locale; the "new decor" and "excellent service" make for a "friendly atmosphere" in which to enjoy "inventive, faultless food"; whether it's an "old favorite" (beef tenderloin) or a new (black cod), "each dish is a masterpiece", so some say this yearling "will become one of the city's best" (it's already one of this *Survey*'s).

Neo Bistro ◐ ▽ 17 | 17 | 20 | $22

14053 Greenwood Ave. N. (143rd St.), 206-366-0104

◪ For the North Seattle crowd, this friendly bistro offers a chance to enjoy some made-from-scratch Mediterranean fare (with local, seasonal ingredients) without having to drive Downtown; the smitten say "you can't go wrong with" the Italian-influenced specialties and "mandatory desserts", but the jaded find the cuisine "not very exciting"; N.B. there's no-cover live jazz and blues on weekends.

New Orleans Creole [S] 18 | 16 | 16 | $20

114 First Ave. S. (bet. Washington St. & Yesler Way), 206-622-2563

■ "Tastes like you're eating in the real place" proclaim patrons of this Pioneer Square haunt that's plastered with "jazz posters" – a reminder that this Creole is as well known for its "live music" as for its cuisine that includes "yummy gumbo", étouffée and jambalaya; the "staff can be crusty, but you won't notice after a Hurricane or two."

Nickerson Street Saloon S   15 | 14 | 15 | $15
318 Nickerson St. (3rd Ave.), 206-284-8819

■ It's "not much for atmosphere", but this "great gathering spot" at the south end of the Fremont Bridge is a "fun place to eat and drink", with "food that's amazingly varied and good for a saloon"; some folks prefer to "sit outside" with a view of the ship canal, while others "go for the games on TV" inside, but all enjoy the strong selection of brews on tap.

Nikko Restaurant   24 | 23 | 21 | $31
Westin Hotel, 1900 Fifth Ave. (Virginia St.), 206-322-4641

■ This "spectacularly designed" and "authentic Japanese" is reason enough to "stay at the Westin Hotel"; by day, the Downtown crowd relishes the "great all-you-can-eat sushi lunch", though evenings are very much about "fantastic" fine dining, whether you "sit at the sushi bar" or opt for a "beautiful tatami room"; N.B. for an ultimate treat, place an advance order for the formal, multi-course kaiseki dinner.

96 Union S   – | – | – | E
(fka LeoMelina)
Pike Place Mkt., 96 Union St. (1st Ave.), 206-623-3783

At press time, the old LeoMelina is due to morph into this Mediterranean, one that aims to take full advantage of its "great location" adjacent to Pike Place Market by featuring plenty of regional produce in its menu of pastas, grilled meats and seafood; the evolution includes an interior face-lift to change the once-"stuffy" setting into a more perfect union of casual and inviting ambiance.

NISHINO S   26 | 22 | 23 | $39
3130 E. Madison St. (Lake Washington Blvd.), 206-322-5800

■ A careful balance of "inventive Japanese fare, along with the great classics" is maintained by this "elegant, serene" Madison Park hot spot; "there is no better sushi in Seattle", and the rest of the menu is pretty "divine" too, but regulars recommend "splurge on the omakase meal" (which you must reserve in advance) and "let chef-owner Tatsu Nishino feed you whatever he wants", knowing full well that it will be something "exceptional."

Noble Court S   21 | 12 | 15 | $21
1644 140th Ave. NE (Bellevue-Redmond Rd.), Bellevue, 425-641-6011

◪ Folks love to hold court at this vast Bellevue locale that's "nothing to look at" but serves up what many say is the "best dim sum around"; it's "good for big groups", who can lazy-Susan their way through the "diverse" Chinese offerings, though naysayers note that beyond the little bites, the "menu items are mediocre."

Noodle Ranch | 21 | 16 | 16 | $16 |
2228 Second Ave. (bet. Bell & Blanchard Sts.),
206-728-0463

■ The essence of "cheap eats" is offered by this "funky Belltown neighborhood spot" where the Pan-Asian "food is consistently fantastic" and the place is "always crowded and happenin'"; regulars rave about the "amazing spring rolls", "delicious noodle dishes" and "great green curry", all served up in a "cool atmosphere."

Noodle Studio S | 18 | 13 | 16 | $15 |
209 Broadway E. (bet. John & Thomas Sts.),
206-325-6277

■ Moniker aside, this Broadway Thai serves a good variety of salads, soups and rice ("you [just] keep eating more of that red curry beef"); still, the namesake's the thing, and surveyors single out the "good *kao soy*", a northern specialty of egg noodles with yellow curry and coconut milk, for particular praise.

Ocean City S | ▽ 12 | 9 | 12 | $20 |
609 S. Weller St. (6th Ave.), 206-623-2333

◪ Surveyors' esteem ebbs and flows for this huge International District Chinese; though some enjoy the "dim sum" and "hot pot menu items" "at great prices", others say it's just "another ethnic place to eat"; N.B. the adjacent noodle/BBQ shop is a good bet for quick takeout.

Ohana ◐S | 19 | 20 | 17 | $23 |
2207 First Ave. (bet. Bell & Blanchard Sts.), 206-956-9329

■ "Tiki-tacky fun" abounds at this boisterous Belltowner, where the "taste of Hawaii" comes with an all-out "kitschy decor" that includes an "irresistible tiki bar" where the 'tenders pour "great drinks" ("ask for the tropical umbrella crib sheet"); while sipping that sake bomber you can dig into "colorful" "creative Asian" food, which ranges from "out-of-this-world Spam *musubi*" to robata-grilled goodies to "super [mahi mahi] fish and chips."

Olympia Pizza &
Spaghetti House S | 19 | 11 | 16 | $15 |
1500 Queen Anne Ave. N. (Galer St.), 206-285-5550 ◐
4501 Interlake Ave. N. (45th St.), 206-633-3655
516 15th Ave. E. (bet. Mercer & Republican Sts.),
206-329-4500

■ Now all independently owned, this Italian trio keeps 'em coming in for "good old-fashioned pizza", served plenty cheesy and in a "endless variety" of combinations; though the pie is the thing, some also go for the Olympian portions of pasta, proclaiming the "Greek spaghetti [feta, garlic, olive oil] rocks!"

Original Pancake House 🅂   21 ⎮ 11 ⎮ 17 ⎮ $12 ⎮
Park Place Ctr., 130 Park Place Ctr. (Central Way),
Kirkland, 425-827-7575
■ Clearly, not all pancakes are created equal – as indicated
by the "huge lines" outside this Kirkland flapjack joint, full
of folks waiting to dig into "light and heavenly" griddle fare
(especially the signature "warm cake overflowing with
apples and drenched in cinnamon sauce"); a few flap
about the "grungy-looking environment", but it's worth it for
a meal that's not only "the best breakfast on the Eastside",
but "better than breakfast has a right to be."

Oyster Bar on Chuckanut Drive 🅂 23 ⎮ 23 ⎮ 20 ⎮ $33 ⎮
2578 Chuckanut Dr. (Estes Rd.), Bow, 360-766-6185
■ "What a location" declare discoverers of this "hidden
treasure" that affords a "wonderful" view "overlooking
Samish Bay toward the San Juan Islands" to accompany
the "tasty oysters", "great seafood" and other "outstanding"
items on the NW menu (the noteworthy wine list gets a
special nod as well); getting to this "intimate place" in Bow
is a "long drive" for most – but they all agree it's "worth it."

Oyster Creek Inn 🅂   – ⎮ – ⎮ – ⎮ E ⎮
2190 Chuckanut Dr. (Estes Rd.), Bow, 360-766-6179
Renovation delays have kept this "favorite destination"
closed for a spell, but at press time it is scheduled to re-open
in the spring, with more room at the inn; when it does, loyal
followers have faith that this seasonally changing, seafood-
oriented Northwesterner will again be "A-1."

Pagliacci Pizza 🅂   21 ⎮ 10 ⎮ 16 ⎮ $13 ⎮
426 Broadway (Federal Ave.), 206-324-0730
4529 University Way NE (bet. 45th & 47th Sts.), 206-632-0421
550 Queen Anne Ave. N. (Mercer St.), 206-285-1232
■ Acolytes are "agog for the 'AGOG primo'" (roasted
garlic, kalamata olives and goat cheese) – just one of the
"can't-miss" "hand-tossed pizzas" from this mini-chain, a
speed-dial fixture for its "creative seasonal offerings"
and "always-fresh salads"; while the three "eat-in" pie
shops are perfect for a "quick slice", they're best known
for "excellent [delivery] service", leaving some to sigh
"they don't deliver to my neighborhood – bummer!"

Painted Table, The 🅂   23 ⎮ 23 ⎮ 22 ⎮ $44 ⎮
Alexis Hotel, 92 Madison St. (1st Ave.), 206-624-3646
■ "Unique hand-painted dishes" set your place in this
"beautiful", "artsy" dining room Downtown, the perfect
"showcase" for chef "Tim Kelley's gastronomic artistry"; the
'NW Market' menu takes full advantage of nearby Pike Place
Market, using the freshest seasonal foods with "creative
and fabulous" results ("try the tasting menu, you can't go
wrong"); some prefer its "quiet, romantic" ambiance at
night, while others opt for the midday "power lunch"; let's
table the discussion and call this an "absolute knockout."

PALACE KITCHEN ◐ [S] | 24 | 22 | 21 | $36 |
2030 Fifth Ave. (Lenora St.), 206-444-2001
■ Need we say it again?; owner "Tom Douglas is the best", and folks have "nothing but kudos" for his "very hip" "hot spot" Downtown; the "imaginative", made-for-grazing menu serves up Eclectic–New American "food with real flavor", from the "fabulous house-baked bread", through simmered short ribs and applewood-grilled meats, to the cheese plate; add in the "great bar scene" and you've got a "festive atmosphere" that makes for hordes of "happy people"; P.S. it's also "the perfect place for late-night dining."

PALISADE [S] | 23 | 26 | 23 | $42 |
2601 W. Marina Pl. (Garfield St.), 206-285-1000
■ "Wonderful for a special occasion" or "to blow away out-of-town guests", this Magnolia destination dazzles with its "drop-dead dining room" (which features a huge saltwater tide pool) and "stunning" panoramas; "looking at that view, a peanut butter sandwich would taste good" – so you can imagine how "super" the "creative", Polynesian-influenced seafood is; in short, this is "one classy joint", abetted by a "staff that actually seems pleased to be there."

Palomino [S] | 22 | 22 | 21 | $32 |
Pacific First Ctr., 1420 Fifth Ave. (bet. Pike & Union Sts.), 206-623-1300
■ "Fun, happening Pacific First Center place" where the aroma of "garlic and wood smoke in the air" hints at the Italian-influenced New American fare to come, including "great chop-chop salad", "heavenly thin-crust pizza" and "oven-roasted meats"; while the "chic bar" can get quite "noisy" at times, this "sophisticate" regularly satisfies ("ok, so it's a chain – but it's a good chain").

Pandasia [S] | 19 | 11 | 15 | $18 |
1625 W. Dravus St. (16th Ave.), 206-283-9030
◪ Magnolia mavens regularly slip into this "always interesting Asian" for more of those good "homemade noodles", "awesome dry-sautéed string beans" and bargain "lunch combos"; purists pan the "inventive menu that does not work", but it's still a standby for all those within delivery range.

Paragon Restaurant & Bar [S] | 19 | 18 | 18 | $30 |
2125 Queen Anne Ave. N. (bet. Boston & Crockett Sts.), 206-283-4548
■ For such a "fun nightlife place", the cuisine can be surprisingly "decent" at this American atop Queen Anne hill, with the "tasty" skirt steak and spinach salad particularly praiseworthy; it's especially hopping on weekends, when no-cover live music draws a "young crowd", so why not "go for the food and stay for the band."

Paseo ⊘
4225 Fremont Ave. N. (Motor Pl.), 206-545-7440

25 | **11** | **16** | **$13**

■ While "ambiance is not its thing", this tiny Fremont "shack delivers big-time flavors"; the "great half-chicken dinner" and "grilled pork sandwiches" topped with onions are just two examples of "Caribbean scrumptiousness", however takeout might be the best bet until Cuban-born chef-owner Lorenzo Lorenzo heeds the plea to "please expand!"

Pasta & Co. S
University Village, 2640 NE University Village (45th St.), 206-523-8594
2109 Queen Anne Ave. N. (Crockett St.), 206-283-1182
10218 NE Eighth St. (102nd Ave.), Bellevue, 425-453-8760

23 | **14** | **18** | **$15**

■ This "longtime favorite" chain of food shops "continues to shine" as a "great place to grab a take-out lunch or dinner" of "impressive fresh pastas and sauces" and "can't-live-without-it roasted chicken" ("bring it home, heat it up, take all the credit"); most have a handful of seats for on-site consumption of "delights attractively displayed."

Pasta Bella S
5909 15th Ave. NW (bet. 59th & 60th Sts.), 206-789-4933
1530 Queen Anne Ave. N. (Garfield St.), 206-284-9827

21 | **16** | **18** | **$23**

■ "A perfect plate of pasta" and "friendly service" are givens at these *due ristorantes* where "consistently good Italian food" fills the "reasonably priced" bill; both offer "atmosphere", though the Queen Anne site with fireplace has an edge over "newly remodeled" Ballard.

Pasta Ya Gotcha
123 Lake St. S. (Central Way), Kirkland, 425-889-1511

12 | **6** | **10** | **$10**

◪ At this Kirkland stand, loyalists laud the International mix of "good on-the-go pasta" (the "Texas Tijuana Taco Penne is delish"); naysayers, however, are "not impressed": if they getcha to "go once, you never will again."

Pazzo's ◐S
2307 Eastlake Ave. E. (Lynn St.), 206-329-6558

20 | **17** | **17** | **$19**

■ "Great calzones", "wonderful salads and pizzas" and a good selection of microbrews are the mainstays at this "casual" Italian; it's something of a "college hangout" with the added benefit of "college prices", though the "warm, lively atmosphere" attracts all of Eastlake.

PECOS PIT BBQ ⊘
2260 First Ave. S. (bet. Holgate & Lander Sts.), 206-623-0629

25 | **10** | **18** | **$10**

■ This SODO shack has "all the ambiance of a converted gas station, which it is", but it makes up for any decor transgressions with "brontosaurus-size" portions of "soul-satisfying BBQ"; for the ultimate zing, just say "spike mine [with a spicy sausage] and serve it hot" (and they will!); P.S. weekday lunch only ("wish they had longer hours").

Pegasus Pizza [S] 22 | 11 | 17 | $15

2758 Alki Ave. SW (bet. 61st & 62nd Aves.), 206-932-4849
12669 NE 85th St. (126th Ave.), Kirkland, 425-822-7400 ◐
4201 NE Sunset Blvd. (Union Ave.), Renton, 425-271-4510
■ "The best pizza in Seattle, period" has worshipers winging their way to this trio; along with the "great crusty" pies, folks "also love the Greek salad" and the "excellent selection of microbrews" to wash it all down with; P.S. the Alki location has the bonus of a "superb view."

Perché No [S] 21 | 15 | 20 | $30

621½ Queen Anne Ave. N. (bet. Mercer & Roy Sts.), 206-298-0230
◪ A "very convenient location for Seattle Center events" helps boost the popularity of this lower Queen Anne perch; mixed reviews about the "Italian fare" ("delicious" vs. "just ok") suggest it can be "uneven", but "great personal service" makes it a "favorite" "pre-opera" or "post-play."

Pesos Kitchen & Lounge ◐[S] – | – | – | M

605 Queen Anne Ave. N. (Mercer St.), 206-283-9353
"Huge servings" of "quick and delightful Mexican fare" (including a "fantastic *carne asada*") are on the menu at this upbeat lower Queen Anne hangout, though they roll a variety of other dishes into the mix as well; the dynamic decor includes vivid colors and intricate ironwork, and those great margaritas make for a hopping bar scene.

Philadelphia Fevre ▽ 21 | 6 | 8 | $11

2332 E. Madison St. (John St.), 206-323-1000
■ For a taste of the City of Brotherly Love, Seattleites truck out to this no-frills Madison Valley outpost, "the *only* place for cheese steaks" (not to mention TastyKakes for dessert); longtime proprietor and Philly native Renée LeFevre has sold the shop, but the "new owners are really glad to see you."

Phoenecia at Alki [S] 24 | 18 | 21 | $29

2716 Alki Ave. SW (bet. 60th & 61st Aves.), 206-935-6550
■ "Always excellent" is how fans feel about chef-owner Hussein Khazaal's "small" but "friendly" Mediterranean where "intriguingly flavored" meats and seafood anchor the menu; though "expensive", "the many daily specials" are appealing, and the West Seattle location affords a "good view" of Alki Beach (hmm, maybe a walk before dinner?).

Pho Thân Brothers' [S]≠ – | – | – | I

4207 University Way NE (42nd St.), 206-633-1735
7714 Aurora Ave. N. (77th St.), 206-527-5973
516 Broadway E. (Republican St.), 206-568-7218
Nothing beats a "hot bowl of pho on a cold rainy Seattle day", and this "consistent" trio serves up "fresh" helpings of the Vietnamese noodle-soup staple with your choice of chicken or one of 14 beef options; "fast service" will get you on your way, wallet intact; N.B. the cream puffs delivered when you sit down are on the house.

Piecora's NY Pizza S   20   11   13 $14
1401 E. Madison St. (14th Ave.), 206-322-9411
Bridle Trails Mall, 6501 132nd Ave. NE (65th St.), Kirkland,
425-861-7000
■ The aptly named Piecora brothers do it up right at this
Capitol Hill and Kirkland pair of pizzerias where a "colorful
crowd" of longtime locals and "East Coast transplants" alike
can get a great "slice" – adorned with "varied toppings"
on "excellent crust" – of what many call "NY–style pizza
at its best"; they can "sometimes be smoky", however, so
opt for "takeout unless you enjoy cigarette flavoring."

Pike Pub & Brewery S   16   15   15 $18
Pike Place Mkt., 1415 First Ave. (bet. Pike & Union Sts.),
206-622-6044
☑ Lots of beeraphernalia is on display at this Pike Place
Market bar, which is actually built around its brewing
equipment; malt mavens find it a "fun, cool place" to drink
the "great" homemade hops and munch locally flavored
American classics like Dungeness crab chowder and
king salmon, but more sober types shrug it off as "typical
brewpub: the beer is fine, the food is uninspired."

Pink Door, The ●   21   21   19 $29
Pike Place Mkt., 1919 Post Alley (bet. Stewart & Virginia Sts.),
206-443-3241
■ For nearly 20 years, this "Pike Place Market institution"
has been a nonstop draw for its combination of "classic
Italian fare", "very hip" bar and entertainment that runs
from tarot card reading to cabaret; there's always a
delightfully "funky atmosphere", but come summer, tons
of thumbs go up for the "outstanding" "outdoor deck"; for
first-timers, "finding this place is half the fun" (hint: look
for a rose-colored entryway across the alley from Kells).

Place Pigalle Restaurant & Bar   25   23   22 $39
Pike Place Mkt., 81 Pike St. (Pike Pl.), 206-624-1756
■ This "very Euro" and "absolutely charming place" is a
"real treat if you can find it behind the Pike Place Market
pig" statue; your efforts will be rewarded with a view
"overlooking Puget Sound" and an "inspired", "consistently
delicious" Eclectic-NW menu that's complemented by "one
of the city's best, and most fairly priced, wine lists"; no
wonder this intimate bistro has become a "perennial"
"must-get- back-to" for locals and visitors alike.

Planet Hollywood S   7   14   9 $22
1500 Sixth Ave. (bet. Pike & Pine Sts.), 206-287-0001
■ Ah, the place Seattle loves to hate: while the "entertaining
environment" can be "fun" for "kids or people coming to
the big city", the "overpriced" "mundane food" and "lowest-
common-denominator service" mean a plethora of pans for
this Downtowner; reviewers rant the name "'Hollywood'
says it all – all style and no substance."

Pogacha [S] 19 15 17 $20

Bellevue Plaza, 119 106th Ave. (Main St.), Bellevue, 425-455-5670

120 NW Gilman Blvd. (Front St.), Issaquah, 425-392-5550

■ "Quick, reliable and friendly", this Adriatic pair's "perfect after work for a casual meal", especially "for the price"; and not to worry if you don't know Croatian cuisine – you'll quickly become a convert, thanks to the chewy-good pogacha dough that comprises their "great homemade rolls" and "designer pizzas"; also "worth repeat trips" to Bellevue and Issaquah is the signature dobar chicken, affectionately known as "the purple dish" for its port-soaked grapes and sauce.

Pon Proem [S] ▽ 20 10 20 $19

3039 78th Ave. SE (bet. 77th & 78th Sts.), Mercer Island, 206-236-8424

■ For the Mercer Island crowd, this "sweet place" offers "good" and "very consistent Thai food" with an extra pinch of spicy "authenticity"; it's perfect for a casual, "quick outing" on those nights when you "don't want to cook."

Pontevecchio 18 15 18 $28

710 N. 34th St. (Fremont Ave.), 206-633-3989

◪ Those who call Fremont home say this "tiny" Sicilian is a "real neighborhood surprise" – a happy one for some, who "love all the food" and find the atmosphere "cute and fun" and "romantic in a *Lady and the Tramp* sort of way", especially on the nights with free "live entertainment"; "annoyed" adversaries think the "Italian shtick" is laid on pretty thick and the dishes "all taste the same."

Ponti Seafood Grill [S] 23 23 21 $38

3014 Third Ave. N. (Nickerson St.), 206-284-3000

■ It's "a class act", this Northwesterner with a "great setting" "near the Fremont Bridge"; the "relaxing", understatedly "upscale atmosphere" makes an ideal venue for dining on an "imaginative menu" of "wonderful seafood" (from the "justly famous Thai curry penne with crab and scallops" to "ahi with rice that's ahi-some") or enjoying one of the "best happy hours in town"; N.B. on warm, sunny days, the canalside patio is primo.

Poor Italian Cafe [S] 18 17 17 $25

2000 Second Ave. (bet. Lenora & Virginia Sts.), 206-441-4313

◪ A "real trattoria atmosphere" draws Downtowners – the business and shopping crowd by day, Moore Theatre patrons by night – to this casual Italian; there's a "good bar scene" and some say the "food is fine", though others opine it's "too expensive for what you get" and suggest the place "be renamed the Rich Italian Cafe."

Prego ◐ [S] ▽ 19 | 18 | 18 | $38

Renaissance Madison Hotel, 515 Madison St. (6th Ave.), 206-583-0300

■ Applying classic Italian technique to local products, new chef Don Curtiss (ex Assaggio and Andaluca) "has brought his magic" to this "overlooked eatery" high above the Downtown streets; the "very interesting" seasonal menu is embellished by a most urban "city view" from the 28th floor of the Renaissance Madison Hotel.

Primo Grill ▽ 21 | 22 | 21 | $31

601 S. Pine St. (6th Ave.), Tacoma, 253-383-7000

◪ "Upscale food in Tacoma – who knew?" say surveyors who note that this Italian-Med newcomer has "not only set the new benchmark for quality [eats] in the South Sound, it's doing so in style", with a "wide-open" decor that features "painted tables", the work of local art students; a few misers mutter the chic chow arrives "along with Seattle prices."

Provinces [S] ▽ 24 | 17 | 18 | $19

Old Mill Town, 201 Fifth Ave. S. (Maple St.), Edmonds, 425-744-0288

■ "Buried" in Downtown Edmonds' historic Old Milltown, this pastel-colored outpost proves it's no provincial with an array of "flavorful", "superb" "multi-country Asian" fare; the "delicious" dishes range from Bangkok hot-and-sour soup to Mongolian ginger beef.

Pyramid Alehouse [S] 16 | 16 | 16 | $17

91 S. Royal Brougham Way (1st Ave., opp. Safeco Field), 206-682-3377

◪ "*The* place to go before or after a game at Safeco Field" (or anything else that has you down in this SODO 'hood), this large "open warehouse" setting can hold plenty of fans, whether they root for the Mariners or all the "different beers brewed on-premises" served with "good pub grub" and desserts made with Thomas Kemper sodas; spoilsports cry foul, however, over the "so-so food", shrugging "a bar is a bar is a bar."

Queen City Grill [S] 23 | 21 | 21 | $35

2201 First Ave. (Blanchard St.), 206-443-0975

■ Amid the restaurant revolution going on around it, this "stylish" New American still reigns as the "original and continuous heartthrob of Belltown", serving "impeccably prepared grilled seafood and beef", as it has for 14 years (an eon in this trendoid part of town); the "exceptional, friendly service" paired with "great drinks" makes the place a persistent pleaser, though some gripe about the noise level when the popular "bar gets jammed" (think of it as just that "NYC feel").

Queen Mary Tearoom S | 21 | 23 | 20 | $22 |
2912 NE 55th St. (bet. 29th & 30th Aves.), 206-527-2770
◪ The "best tearoom in town" rave royalists about this "charming" Ravenna spot where the gals gather to partake of 20-plus blends, served "very properly" in lovely china pots with all the Anglo accoutrements; it's "wonderful for" "tasty lunches" and "delectable desserts" along with afternoon you-know-what, but the decor, full of feminine flourishes and trinkets, makes dissenters dismiss it as "a ladies' place – a little too quaint."

Racha Noodles & Thai Cuisine S | 20 | 16 | 18 | $17 |
537 First Ave. N. (Mercer St.), 206-281-8883
■ A "great selection of noodles" and "loads of wonderful, fresh vegetarian selections" "at the right price" are what keep this "colorful" lower Queen Anne Thai so "popular" – not to mention its "convenient" proximity to the Seattle Center; advocates also applaud the "recent remodel and expansion", which makes the "pleasant surroundings" even more so.

Raga S | – | – | – | M |
212 Central Way (Lake Washington Blvd.), Kirkland, 425-827-3300
Last summer a devastating fire brought an abrupt halt to the 11-year run of this popular Eastside Indian; but as the *Survey* goes to press, the tandoori ovens are being installed and a fresh coat of paint being applied as this veteran – now relocated to Kirkland – plans a late springtime opening, in a slightly more upscale reincarnation of its previous self.

RAY'S BOATHOUSE S | 23 | 23 | 22 | $34 |
6049 Seaview Ave. NW (Market St.), 206-789-3770
■ Always a "favorite place to take out-of-towners", this Shilshole "landmark" provides patrons with a "complete experience", from the "superb NW seafood" and "stellar wine selections" to the "warm decor" and "an absolutely unbelievable view" overlooking Puget Sound and the Olympic Mountains ("a must-do during summer sunsets"); despite a few of the inevitable "overrated" comments, most deem it that rare thing – "a classic that's as good as it's supposed to be."

Ray's Cafe S | – | – | – | M |
6049 Seaview Ave. NW (Market St.), 206-782-0094
"Dinner and drinks on the deck is what Seattle is about", and it makes this casual, upstairs offspring of Ray's Boathouse almost as much a Shilshole institution as its parent; though you can count on "Ray's-style good food" (including the signature kasu black cod), the menu's flush with more informal and less expensive fare such as salmon burgers and crisp ling cod fish 'n' chips; happy hour's all abuzz with folks going for the "great bargain" of a "bar menu" along with the view.

Red Door Alehouse S   16 13 14 $16
3401 Fremont Ave. N. (34th St.), 206-547-7521

■ This ideal "casual hangout" in the self-styled Center of the Universe has been keeping Fremonters fed for over a decade on "classic pub fare": "good burgers, fries and lots of beer"; N.B. at press time, it was scheduled to move – lock, stock and bar taps – one block west.

Red Mill Burgers S⌀   23 12 15 $11
312 N. 67th St. (Phinney Ave.), 206-783-6362
1613 W. Dravus St. (15th Ave. NW), 206-284-6363

■ The "decor is nothing special, the service is do-it-yourself, but the burgers keep drawing you back" to these twin joints in Phinney Ridge and Magnolia, whose faithful are willing to "drive an hour out of our way" and brave the ubiquitous "intimidating lines" for "smoky-good" patties (special mention: the Verde version, with Anaheim chiles); "don't shortchange your arteries – accompany your order" with "terrific shakes" and "homemade onion rings."

Red Robin S   15 14 16 $16
3272 Fuhrman Ave. NE (Eastlake Ave. E.), 206-323-0918
Pier 55, 1101 Alaskan Way (Spring St.), 206-623-1942
11021 NE Eighth St. (bet. 110th & 112th Aves.), Bellevue, 425-453-9522 ☻
22705 Marine View Dr. S. (227th St.), Des Moines, 206-824-2214
Everett Mall, 1305 SE Everett Mall Way W. (Mall Dr.), Everett, 425-355-7330
1085 Lake Dr. (Pickering Pl.), Issaquah, 425-313-0950
Alderwood Mall, 18410 33rd Ave. W. (184th St. SW), Lynnwood, 425-771-6492
2390 148th Ave NE (bet. 22nd & 24th Sts.), Redmond, 425-641-3810 ☻
Redmond Town Ctr., 7597 170th Ave NE (76th St.), Redmond, 425-895-1870
18029 Garden Way NE (140th Ave.), Woodinville, 425-488-6300

☑ Some locals have been eating at this national American franchise "since there was only one" (it all began with the Furhman Avenue location), and most surveyors say that the "dependable", "fast and friendly" eateries are still bob-bob-bobbin' along with their "specialty burgers", "fun drinks" and those famous "bottomless fries"; "kids love it", but critics carp they're "too old" for "large portions" of "overpriced" "chain food."

Restaurant Zoë S   25 23 25 $37
2137 Second Ave. (Blanchard St.), 206-256-2060

■ This new hot spot has jogged even the most jaded diners with "flavorful food", "fab cocktails", "exceptional service" and a "totally tony" interior, all "in the middle of the action" of Belltown; chef-owner Scott Staples (ex Third Floor Fish Cafe) hits the right notes with a New American menu that's concise and consistently well-executed; no wonder Zoë-goers say they "want more places like this."

Rhododendron Café S   21 17 21 $23
5521 Chuckanut Dr. (Bow Hill Rd.), Bow, 360-766-6667
■ A "great stop" on picturesque Chuckanut Drive, this "sweet little cafe" serves "food that's a surprise" – namely, an earthy eclectic mix of International-NW fare – in a "quaint room"; while it's an "excellent place to know about up north", many sigh "if only it were closer."

Ristorante Paradiso S   21 17 19 $31
120A Park Ln. (Lake Washington Blvd.), Kirkland, 425-889-8601
■ It's common to get "weekly cravings" for the "delicious Italian" cuisine served at this "small" Downtown Kirklander, whose specialties include an aptly named "penne Paradiso" with artichoke hearts in tomato-cream sauce and a veal funghi so good they could "bottle it"; the only question is, "why haven't more people discovered this place?"

Rock Salt Steakhouse   – – – M
on Latitude 47 S
1232 Westlake Ave. N. (Southwest end of Lake Union), 206-284-1047
"Good views" are almost guaranteed at this Lake Union steakhouse in Latitude 47's former digs; led by the rocksalt–encrusted prime rib, bargain-priced beef rules the revamped menu, which has a touch of Southwestern flavor, as do the desert-sunset hues of the refurbished decor.

Romio's Pizza & Pasta S   16 9 14 $15
2001 W. Dravus St. (20th Ave.), 206-284-5420
3242 Eastlake Ave. E. (Fuhrman Ave.), 206-322-4453
917 Howell St. (9th Ave.), 206-622-6878
8523 Greenwood Ave. N. (bet. 85th & 87th Sts.), 206-782-9005
12501 Lake City Way NE (125th St.), 206-362-8080
2020 Maltby Rd. (Thrasher's Corner), Bothell, 425-481-5887
630 Edmonds Way (Paradise Ln.), Edmonds, 425-744-0284
11223 19th Ave. SE (Silver Lake Rd.), Everett, 425-316-0305
2803 Colby Ave. (California St.), Everett, 425-252-0800
16801 Redmond Way (Cleveland St.), Redmond, 425-702-2466
■ Seattle's now got a slew of these "affordable eateries" whose pies come in a "nice variety" of "interesting combos" (the "'GASP' – garlic, artichoke hearts, sun-dried tomatoes, pesto – is the one to get"); though other Italian offerings are available, the "pizza beats the pasta" surveyors say; whatever you choose, "have it delivered."

Rosebud Restaurant & Bar S   ▽ 18 18 17 $21
719 E. Pike St. (Harvard Ave.), 206-323-6636
■ Those in the know "love the cozy, fun atmosphere" at this cafe/lounge in the Pike/Pine section of Capitol Hill, decorated with sleds in homage to *Citizen Kane*; "tasty appetizers" from the Eclectic-American menu go great with the "impressive cocktails" served at the "killer happy hour"; yet oddly enough, this rosebud remains a "well-kept secret" – just like the one in the movie.

Rosita's Mexican Grill S 　　21 | 17 | 21 | $17
7210 Woodlawn Ave. NE (bet. 71st & 72nd Sts.),
206-523-3031
Holman Rd. Sq., 9747 Fourth Ave. NW (Holman Rd.),
206-784-4132

■ The complimentary "fresh corn tortillas are fab and the margaritas are even better" at this pair of "favorite Mexican places", the original in Green Lake ("still a classic" after 20-odd years) and its sib in Crown Hill; both offer "mole with body", "delicious *pollo al carbon*" and "several tasty veggie entrees", along with "fast service for hungry families."

ROVER'S 　　29 | 25 | 28 | $82
2808 E. Madison St. (28th Ave.), 206-325-7442

■ Once again Seattle's No. 1 for Food, and now also for Service, this longtime "champion" in Madison Valley is truly "the tops" for its NW-accented New French "edible art" prepared by chef-owner Thierry Rautureau and presented in "fantastic tasting menus" (including a veggie version) that are "well worth the splurge"; a staff that's "knowledgeable without being stuffy" and a "lovely", "elegant" setting, add up to an "always exceptional" experience, leaving one surveyor to sigh "I'd be a regular if I were Bill Gates."

Roxy's Deli 　　18 | 8 | 10 | $10
1909 First Ave. (Virginia St.), 206-441-6768

■ New Yorkers might quibble (don't they always?), but locals think this Pike Place Market hole-in-the-wall provides slightly "pricey" but highly "yummy" deli sandwiches "East-Coast style", down to the housemade 'kraut mounded on "mouthwatering corned beef" and the crunchy half-sour pickles; N.B. there are only a few stools for noshing on-site, so best get it to go.

Roxy's Diner S 　　▽ 18 | 11 | 11 | $11
1329 First Ave. (Union St.), 206-381-8800

◪ This sit-down sib of Roxy's Deli serves up the same "great pastrami and corned beef", along with some additional Jewish delicacies (i.e. blintzes, latkes with sour cream and applesauce); the "good food at good prices" is enough for some, though others grumble the hot dishes are "ho-hum" and the Downtown digs really "need more atmosphere."

Roy's Seattle S 　　23 | 21 | 22 | $42
Westin Hotel, 1900 Fifth Ave. (Westlake Ave.),
206-256-7697

■ Downtown diners get a "taste of Hawaii" that's "just a delight" at this local outpost of celeb-chef Roy Yamaguchi's empire; the "beautifully presented" menu includes "exotic seafood" ("delicately flavored" ono and "outstanding island ahi") done up in the master's Asian–New American style; ok, so maybe it's "not as great as [the original Roy's on] Kauai – but it's still great."

Roy St. Bistro [S] 20 | 18 | 20 | $32
174 Roy St. (2nd Ave. N.), 206-284-9093
■ "A charming setting" with "fast service and great food" from an eclectic menu makes this self-styled Euro bistro on lower Queen Anne "a perfect pre- or post-theater spot"; being "handy to Seattle Center" means it's "very busy" on performance nights, but it's "quieter" at other times.

Ruth's Chris Steak House [S] 24 | 20 | 23 | $50
800 Fifth Ave. (Columbia St.), 206-624-8524
■ "For the carnivore in you", this Downtown meatery serves up "phenomenal steaks" and some super sides (including "the best potatoes au gratin"); sure, it's "a splurge", but "the service and the quality are fantastic", making those dollars "well worth it"; P.S. "for those who smoke, there's your own cigar room."

Sahib [S] ▽ 23 | 21 | 24 | $23
Edmonds Ferry Dock, 101 Main St. (Sunset Ave.), Edmonds, 425-775-2828
◪ There's a "warm family environment" and "imaginative food" at this "very good Indian" alongside the "Edmonds ferry dock", which also boasts an outdoor deck overlooking the beach; novice nabobs appreciate the "honesty-in-spicing" policy: "a '2' is a '2' and a '5' is an experience."

Saigon Bistro [S] ▽ 22 | 7 | 12 | $14
Asian Plaza, 1032 S. Jackson St. (10th Ave.), 206-329-4939
■ The rather "no-nonsense atmosphere" doesn't deter devotees from this "authentic" eatery in the ID's Little Saigon, which serves up "marvels of Vietnamese cuisine" in "big portions"; though you may be "the only non-local in the place", fear not – they "treat you like family."

Saito's Japanese Cafe & Bar ▽ 25 | 23 | 20 | $22
2122 Second Ave. (bet. Blanchard & Lenora Sts.), 206-728-1333
■ Jumping headlong into the Belltown restaurant blitz, chef-owner Yutaka Saito's new Japanese contribution "shows some real class" with "most excellent sushi" and creative sake-it-to-me cocktails; the sleek, "graceful" setting, accented with splashes of color, offers diners their choice of seats at the "entertaining" bar or streetside tables.

SALISH LODGE DINING ROOM [S] 23 | 26 | 23 | $47
Salish Lodge & Spa, 6501 Railroad Ave. SE (Hwy. 202), Snoqualmie, 425-888-2556
■ When in need of a "special place", this "road-trip restaurant" provides "the ideal escape"; "get ready to be treated royally" in "gorgeous surroundings" (a unique perch above the Snoqualmie Falls) as you sample a "memorable" New French menu, complemented by a winning regional wine list (the "sommelier knows his stuff"); it's "not just a meal, it's an experience", especially if you "go for a romantic overnight" in the lodge.

Salmon Bay Cafe S   16 | 9 | 13 | $13
5109 Shilshole Ave. NW (20th St.), 206-782-5539
■ Starting at 6:30 AM (7 AM on weekends), this American
mainstay forks over "food to fortify" "early-morning" people
(or those who haven't been to bed yet); throw in plenty of
"local Ballard color" (fishermen, etc.) and you see why some
say this is the "best greasy" spoon in town.

Salty's S   19 | 22 | 20 | $33
1936 Harbor Ave. SW (19th St.), 206-937-1600
28201 Beach Dr. S. (280th St.), Redondo, 253-946-0636
☒ A "supremo Sunday brunch" and "fabulous views" of the
Downtown skyline define this Alki and Redondo Beach
seafood duo where throngs congregate "on the deck" ("say
hi to the tourists – they're everywhere"); surveyors sweet
on the experience say the NW-oriented menu "is fine";
but the salty-tongued snap that the "quality of food and
service varies", while their "overpriced" nature does not.

Salumeria on Hudson   – | – | – | I
4918 Rainier Ave. S. (bet. Ferdinand & Hudson Sts.), 206-760-7741
"Sister to La Medusa" just a couple of blocks away, this
Columbia City "grocery-cum-deli is lots of fun and has lots of
heart"; "very good, casual Italian" fare is served over-the-
counter in a big, open urban space with high windows;
select vino, gourmet foods and kitchenware are sold retail,
with wine tastings held on Saturday afternoons.

SALUMI   27 | 14 | 21 | $16
309 Third Ave. S. (bet. Jackson & Main Sts.), 206-621-8772
■ "It's like dining with friends and family, even if you go
alone" to this Pioneer Square "magical lunch spot", thanks
to the communal table at the back of a narrow room; owner
and "master sausage maker" Armandino Batali (papa to
NY chef Mario Batali) shares his "passion" for "true Italian"
flavors in a way that leaves devotees "dreaming of
meatball sandwiches" and other delights; N.B. book ahead –
book way ahead – for the bi-monthly group dinners.

Salute of Bellevue S   19 | 17 | 19 | $29
10134 Main St. (102nd Ave.), Bellevue, 425-688-7613
☒ There's a bifurcated reaction to this Bellevue Italian:
some surveyors salute this "quaint, romantic spot" as a
"terrific value for the money", but insubordinates insist
the "ok food and wine" are "overpriced."

Salute Ristorante Italiano S   22 | 18 | 19 | $28
3426 NE 55th St. (35th Ave.), 206-527-8600
■ Surveyors salute this Ravenna standby for being "always
on the mark" with its "great Italian food", "friendly service"
and "cheery atmosphere"; the pace may not be as frenetic
as when it first opened in the '80s (Seattle had far fewer
ristorantes then), but this "cozy, romantic" spot still brings
plenty of "passion" to its craft ("what more is needed?").

Salvatore Ristorante | 24 | 20 | 22 | $29 |

6100 Roosevelt Way NE (61st St.), 206-527-9301

■ "Comfort for the body and soul" comes easily at this Roosevelt *ristorante*, a "neighborhood institution" where the "engaging staff" serves "consistent quality" cuisine (including "lots of daily specials") that's "good enough to make anyone's Italian grandmother proud"; add in a "great wine list", "warm ambiance" and "reasonable prices" and there's little left to say besides "*molto bene*."

Sand Point Grill [S] | – | – | – | M |

5412 Sandpoint Way NE (55th St.), 206-729-1303

A "warm and cozy" refuge on busy Sandpoint Way, this "great neighborhood restaurant" holds to a well-priced and easygoing style, despite its posh address; the local following ranges from folks who sit at the bar for dinner, shooting the breeze between bites, to those who linger in the colorful dining area; the "small but well-done" menu covers an Eclectic array that includes spring rolls and hush puppies for starters and coriander-crusted tuna and London broil for mains.

SANMI SUSHI [S] | 25 | 18 | 21 | $27 |

Elliott Bay Marina, 2601 W. Marina Pl. (Garfield St.), 206-283-9978

■ Though there's a "nice vista overlooking Elliott Bay Marina" from the main dining room of this "intimate" Japanese in Magnolia, savvy Sanmi-ites head directly to the bar where the only view is of a "nice variety" of "extremely fresh fish" being transformed into "fantastic sushi" before your eyes – in "killer portions" too.

Santa Fe Cafe [S] | 21 | 17 | 19 | $24 |

5910 Phinney Ave. N. (bet. 59th & 60th Sts.), 206-783-9755
2255 NE 65th St. (22nd Ave.), 206-524-7736

■ "Extremely loyal patrons" depend on these Southwestern siblings in Phinney Ridge and Ravenna for "well-executed" fare; so when surveyors say "nothing ever changes", it's clearly a compliment to such "yummy, spicy" goodies as garlic custard and *chile rellenos*, along with "great guac" and the "best and strongest margaritas in town", all delivered by "personable servers" in a "nice, mellow atmosphere."

Sapphire Kitchen & Bar [S] | 21 | 20 | 18 | $28 |

1625 Queen Anne Ave. N. (Blaine St.), 206-281-1931

◪ This Queen Anne Med "sparkles as brightly as its name" according to aficionados who really go for the "sexy atmosphere and unique menu", including the "incredible Chef's Platter antipasti" and "great desserts"; but the dissatisfied complain of service that's "one day great, one day not" and a smoker-friendly bar that, in this small space, can "fill the restaurant with [fumes] during peak hours."

Sazerac [S] 22 23 21 $35
Hotel Monaco, 1101 Fourth Ave. (Spring St.), 206-624-7755
■ "Both the food and the decor have the right amount of spice" at this "swanky" Downtowner where "chef Kevin Davis is cooking up" a "successful take on Southern" cuisine that goes beyond "just fried catfish" (though he does that too, with jalapeño-lime meunière); there's also a "lively bar scene", which leads some to complain this "hip, upbeat spot" gets just "too darn loud" at times; "believe it or not" you can also get an "amazing breakfast" here.

Scarlet Tree [S] 13 8 11 $15
6521 Roosevelt Way NE (66th St.), 206-523-7153
◪ "Friendly" local bar in Roosevelt that's a venue for varying genres of popular music; longtime loyalists find it a "good place to go with a hangover", since the American "breakfast is a real find"; "only for drinking" renegades retort.

Sea Garden [S] 23 13 17 $23
509 Seventh Ave. S. (King St.), 206-623-2100 ◐
200 106th Ave. NE (2nd St.), Bellevue, 425-450-8833
■ A "tasty seafood-oriented menu" that ranges from "basic to exotic" pulls this ID and Bellevue duo "a notch above the typical Chinese restaurant"; the "reasonably priced", "pure-flavored" "crab and fish dishes" belie a "plain setting", however, so if you're "going for atmosphere" – don't.

Seattle Catch Seafood Bistro [S] 18 17 18 $27
460 N. 36th St. (Dayton Ave.), 206-632-6110
◪ This Fremont fish house provides "straightforward seafood" and pasta (which share the plate in the signature *fra diavolo*); fans feel it's a good catch, especially since there's "a valuable parking lot available", but foes feel this Italian-influenced bistro's dropped the ball lately, with food that's "underwhelming", "overcooked and overpriced."

Serafina [S] 23 23 20 $31
2043 Eastlake Ave. E. (Boston St.), 206-323-0807
◪ Loyalists "just want to linger" (on the "lovely garden patio", if they're lucky) at this "cozy, romantic" "dimly lit" Eastlake fave that offers "original", "sophisticated Italian" fare, "supplemented by live jazz" and Latin music; the less-enamored find the "food is sadly inconsistent", the "service spotty" and say it's the "well-stocked [and -tended] bar that's memorable"; N.B. a recent chef change may outdate the above food score.

74th St. Ale House [S] 20 15 17 $18
7401 Greenwood Ave. N. (74th St.), 206-784-2955
■ "Good eats" are on tap alongside the sizable selection of "NW microbrews" at this "great Greenwood pub" where the tavern fare is "far above average" (case in point: the "amazing black-bean burger"); so no surprise it's "always crowded", especially "now that it's all non-smoking."

Shallots **S** | 23 | 18 | 20 | $27 |
2525 Fourth Ave. (Vine St.), 206-728-1888

■ "Beautiful food and surroundings" have bolstered the buzz about this Belltowner, whose "eclectic", "interesting and spicy" Pan-Asian menu (which ranges from "the best calamari" to the "nine-flavor beef, a taste sensation") has earned it comparisons to the mighty Wild Ginger – albeit a "more intimate", less expensive version.

Shamiana **S** | 24 | 18 | 21 | $24 |
Houghton Village, 10724 NE 68th St. (108th Ave.), Kirkland, 425-827-4902

■ "Until the price of a ticket to Pakistan or India comes down", "your best bet" is this "simple but great" "ethnic dining" destination in Kirkland, where a brother-and-sister team demonstrate what they picked up as foreign service brats on the subcontinent; the "mouthwatering food" includes "excellent curried dishes" (the "Major Grey chicken is our favorite") and other "nicely spiced" offerings, accompanied by equally "warm service."

Shanghai Garden **S** | 24 | 11 | 16 | $20 |
524 Sixth Ave. S. (Weller St.), 206-625-1689
80 Front St. N. (Sunset Way), Issaquah, 425-313-3188
Shanghai Cafe **S**
Factoria Sq. Mall, 12708 SE 38th St. (bet. 126th & 128th Aves.), Bellevue, 425-603-1689

■ Ok, so the "ambiance is lacking", but the flavors "haunt the taste buds" at this Chinese triad that shanghais surveyors with "lots of exotic dishes" that have "a healthy angle" ("no MSG", "light sauces" and "always fresh-tasting"); though all the fare's "consistently interesting", it's the "noodles, noodles, noodles", specifically the "great hand-shaven barley green" ones, that ensure a "repeat visit."

Sharp's Roaster & Ale House **S** ▽ | 17 | 14 | 17 | $18 |
18427 Pacific Hwy. S. (188th St., east of Sea-Tac Airport), 206-241-5744

◪ If you're in need of "good food quick" in SeaTac, this American joint is "not a bad option near the airport", just across from the WestCoast Gateway Hotel and a wingspan away from the runways; a south-end sib of the Kirkland Roaster & Ale House, it offers a similar menu of standard meat-and-potatoes fare with plenty of beers on tap.

Shea's Lounge ●**S** ▽ | 24 | 22 | 23 | $33 |
Pike Place Mkt., 94 Pike St. (1st Ave.), 206-467-9990

■ The "no-reservations" alter ego of Chez Shea next door, this equally cozy spot in the Pike Place Market is an "underappreciated place to unwind" after work or to grab a snack of "excellent" NW–New American fare late at night before heading home; the combination of good food and a casual "low-lights" atmo leads lounge lizards to label it "*so* Seattle."

SHIRO'S SUSHI S
26 | 17 | 20 | $35

2401 Second Ave. (Battery St.), 206-443-9844

■ If you're lucky enough to snag a spot at the sushi bar at this Belltowner (hint: be there when it opens), "ignore the menu and have Shiro order for you", because this "master chef" uses only the "highest-grade ingredients" in his "incredible" dishes and he often has "wonderful seasonal surprises" to share; it's "extremely traditional" in decor (some say "stark") and some detractors deem themselves "disappointed", but most maintain it's "worth every yen."

SHOALWATER S
26 | 24 | 23 | $41

Shelburne Inn, 4415 Pacific Hwy. (45th St.), Seaview, 360-642-4142

■ This Long Beach Peninsula destination has provided the region with a "20-year tradition of excellent NW fare", including Willapa Bay oysters and Alaskan halibut, though meat dishes shine as well; the "wine selection is great" and the "service is friendly", making this a solid choice for some of the "best dining on the Washington coast."

Shuckers S
23 | 22 | 21 | $36

Four Seasons Olympic Hotel, 411 University St. (4th Ave.), 206-621-1984

■ "Oysters, oysters, oysters" is the slogan for shell seekers at this "classy-casual" "fun place" Downtown, where "consistency is king" and "service is attentive"; slurp 'em raw, get 'em stewed or pan-fried or choose from plenty of other "great seafood" on the menu; the "wonderful wood decor" makes you "feel like you're in a New England pub."

Shultzy's S
18 | 10 | 15 | $13

4114 University Way NE (bet. 41st & 42nd Sts.), 206-548-9461

■ "Hordes of hungry UW students and faculty" keep this Cajun joint hopping through the day; *bon temps* types "dig the homemade gumbo" and "great fries" served "with a smile"; all the food is big and "easy-on-the-wallet", though a few old-timers think the "new location has less character."

Simpatico S
20 | 20 | 19 | $26

4430 Wallingford Ave. N. (45th St.), 206-632-1000
1313 W. Meeker St. (Washington Ave.), Kent, 253-859-4681

■ "An oasis in a rush-rush world", this "consistent" Wallingford "favorite" offers a "very cozy, laid-back" atmosphere in which to enjoy "savory" Italian food at "affordable" prices; N.B. the Kent location is unrated.

Sisters European Snacks S ⊄
20 | 14 | 15 | $11

Pike Place Mkt., 1530 Post Alley (bet. Pike & Pine Sts.), 206-623-6723

■ Turn your steps toward this "genuine European sidewalk cafe tucked into Post Alley", where the three Jacobi sisters have served up "yummy, creative" sandwiches for a decade, smack dab in the middle of Pike Place Market.

Sit & Spin [S] 13 | 18 | 11 | $12

2219 Fourth Ave. (bet. Bell & Blanchard Sts.), 206-441-9484

■ "Do your laundry, drink beer, take in a show: how perfect is that?" ask multi-taskers who like suds with their duds at this American eatery/laundromat/live music venue in Belltown; serving sandwiches, pizzas and vegetarian offerings, the "laid-back" cafe is also popular for its board games and industrial decor, providing a suitable venue for the "trendy after-hours" spin cycle, when DJs and musicians give it their All.

Six Degrees [S] 16 | 17 | 16 | $22

7900 Green Lake Dr. N. (Ashworth Ave.), 206-523-1600
121 Park Ln. (Kirkland Ave.), Kirkland, 425-803-1766
Redmond Town Ctr., 16551 NE 74th St. (bet. 166th & 168th Aves.), Redmond, 425-869-6686

◪ There's a "comfortable neighborhood feel" at this "casual" trio of American bistros, offering "cleverly disguised comfort food with NW flair" that works well with their "excellent beer selection"; some surveyors separate, however, saying the fare's "hit or miss"; P.S. at the Green Lake and Kirkland outlets, it's "21-and-over only, so no kids."

611 Supreme [S] – | – | – | M

611 E. Pine St. (Boylston St.), 206-328-0292

"You'll swear you died and went to crêpe heaven" when you visit this tiny, "comfortable" Capitol Hill bistro, which does a supreme job with traditional French buckwheat pancakes "inventively" embellished with regional ingredients; though regulars think the "specials are always the best", purists might prefer the more classic dessert varieties.

SkyCity at the Needle [S] 17 | 24 | 18 | $42

Space Needle, 219 Fourth Ave. N. (Broad St.), 206-905-2111

◪ Things are looking up at this 500-foot-high spinner at the Space Needle since last year's makeover; city slickers see a "vast improvement" in the NW fare ("memorable meals" – "wow, what a surprise!"), and of course there's still the same "unsurpassed view"; nevertheless, naysayers needle it for being "overpriced" and regard the extensive renovation as "uninspired."

Sostanza Trattoria 23 | 22 | 22 | $37

1927 43rd Ave. E. (Madison St.), 206-324-9701

■ Though the fare's full of substance (*sostanza*), this "brilliant Madison Park hideaway" is "no meatball joint", but a purveyor of "outstanding Northern Italian cuisine" in "warm, cozy surroundings" decorated with a stylish balcony and fireplace; owner "Lorenzo Cianciusi is a marvelous chef who really cares about his customers", providing them with a "consistently" "classy" dining experience.

Spazzo Mediterranean Grill S   21 | 22 | 19 | $29 |
Key Bank Bldg., 10655 NE Fourth St., 9th fl. (106th Ave.),
Bellevue, 425-454-8255

◰ For "Mediterranean food with a view", Eastsiders head
to the ninth floor of this Bellevue office building for "very
tasty tapas" and "wonderful sangria", which are the
hallmarks – and some would say the extent – of the best
bets here; however, the "good value" gets a nod as well.

Spirit of Washington   18 | 24 | 21 | $55 |
Dinner Train S
625 S. Fourth St. (Burnett Ave.), Renton, 425-227-7245

■ "What a different way to spend dinner" (or weekend
lunch) say spirited types of this vintage train traveling
from Renton to Woodinville and back; it's a "fun", "unique
experience" with a menu of "surprisingly good" NW fare;
"spring for the dome car" ($10 extra) hint those who know
the already-great view is even better from there.

Stalk Exchange S   ▽ 21 | 16 | 18 | $23 |
6711 Greenwood Ave. N (67th St.), 206-782-3911

■ The "interesting menu" of vegetarian-oriented American
food served in a colorful and "quaint atmosphere" (complete
with a "cozy fireplace") makes "a great dining experience"
at this new Greenwooder; the applewood-fired oven
turns out "awesome homemade breads" and other baked
goodies, so the weekend brunches are a "favorite" too.

Stanley & Seafort's S   22 | 22 | 22 | $31 |
115 E. 34th St. (Pacific Ave.), Tacoma, 253-473-7300

■ "A Tacoma favorite for years", this hillside seafooder-and-
steakhouse affords a "great view of Downtown" in a
"handsome setting", where classics like prime rib and
crème brûlée are still house favorites; it's a "terrific place to
meet", whether for a business dinner or a snack in the bar.

Starfish Grill S   – | – | – | M |
Resort at Deer Harbor, 11 Jack & Jill Ln. (Deer Harbor Rd.),
Deer Harbor, Orcas Island, 360-376-2482

Orcas Island star chef Christina Orchid has set up a
second shop across the island; as at her celebrated
Christina's, the menu here makes the most of seasonal
ingredients, though with a more American twist, including
a signature chicken pot pie (this ain't no Swanson's) and
coconut cake, preferably consumed on the "great deck."

St. Clouds S   ▽ 17 | 18 | 18 | $25 |
1131 34th Ave. (Union St.), 206-726-1522

■ In Cool Hand Luke's old Madrona space, this "good new
place" is in formation; the American menu ranges from
simple 'home for dinner' entrees such as roasted chicken
and fancier 'out for dinner' options like fish in a peanut, soy
and ginger sauce; although they may be "working out the
kinks", there's "great potential" for sunny days ahead.

Stella's Trattoria ◑ S   15 14 15 $18
4500 Ninth Ave. NE (45th St.), 206-633-1100
◪ When the evening's plans include "dinner and a movie", this University District all-nighter offers "quick, good Italian" eats – so you're sure to not miss the previews at the multiplex next door; "nothing fancy", certainly, and "not much atmosphere", but a "family spot" that's "reliable" and open seven days a week.

Still Life in   18 17 13 $12
Fremont Coffeehouse S ⊟
709 N. 35th St. (bet. Aurora & Fremont Aves.), 206-547-9850
◼ A "'60s throwback", this "Fremont institution" still draws folks in with "good vegetarian lunches", "wholesome soups" and other "tasty", life-enhancing Eclectic fare; the "relaxing" and "down-to-earth atmosphere" paints a pretty picture for loungers looking to "sit for hours", maybe over "coffee and chess", between mealtime peaks.

Streamliner Diner S ⊟   ▽ 16 9 13 $14
397 Winslow Way (Bijune St.), Bainbridge Island, 206-842-8595
◪ Though some folks still say this diner makes "a nice excuse for a ferry ride" to Bainbridge Island for a "good breakfast and huge muffins" and other American fare, the disgruntled note it's "nothing unique" and "not what it used to be" – an opinion outlined in the downstreamed ratings.

Stumbling Goat S   – – – M
6722 Greenwood Ave. N. (67th St.), 206-784-3535
Those stumbling into this "new bistro in Greenwood" will discover a lush but casual setting in which to enjoy "Eclectic comfort cuisine"; chef Craig Serbousek (ex Herbfarm) offers "exquisitely prepared" items that are "subtly spiced, so you can taste the food"; the wines are selective and well priced, making this an all-around "welcome addition to the neighborhood."

Sunfish S ⊟   ▽ 23 12 16 $11
2800 Alki Ave. SW (62nd Ave.), 206-938-4112
◼ A favorite West Seattle haunt, this "simple" seafood shack "always delights" with its "excellent" "non-greasy fish" 'n' chips, as well as unexpected treats like Greek salad and grilled fish kebabs that some deem "the best deal in town"; there's no booze, but "service is quick" and you get the bonus of a "great view" over the less-bustling end of Alki Beach and beyond.

Sunlight Cafe S   17 12 13 $14
6403 Roosevelt Way NE (64th St.), 206-522-9060
◪ "Another option for Vegetarian fare" say lovers of this long-standing "hippie" hangout in Roosevelt that opened in the '70s and still seems stuck there; the "service is ultra-casual", a nice way of saying that it can take "days to get served"; still, it's "part of the family."

Supreme **S** | – | – | – | E |
1404 34th Ave. (Union St.), 206-322-1974
At this hot new addition to Madrona's burgeoning Restaurant Row, chef Chris Hunter (ex Etta's Seafood) has hit the ground running with a New American menu that gives sophisticated tones to straightforward fare such as a silky chicken liver mousse and oven-roasted cod; desserts, likewise, shine in their simplicity, while the mod, arty decor starkly contrasts with that of previous tenant Plenty Cafe.

SZMANIA'S **S** | 26 | 22 | 24 | $40 |
3321 W. McGraw St. (34th Ave.), 206-284-7305
■ "A great dining experience even if no one can pronounce the name" (hint: the 'z' is silent), this Magnolia "jewel" sparkles, offering "creative NW cuisine with German flair" and some Asian accents; chef-owner Ludger Szmania "does everything right", from "imaginative" dishes like the "awesome Jaeger schnitzel" to the "warm and welcoming atmosphere" and "pampering" service.

Taco Del Mar **S** | 15 | 8 | 12 | $9 |
615 Queen Anne Ave. N. (Mercer St.), 206-281-7420
1520 Broadway (Pike St.), 206-328-4868 ●
90 Yesler St. (1st Ave.), 206-467-5940
Washington State Convention Ctr., 725 Pike St. (7th Ave.), 206-628-8982
1336 First Ave. (Union St.), 206-623-8741
3526 Fremont Pl. N. (35th St.), 206-545-8001
Wallingford Ctr., 1815 N. 45th St. (Wallingford Ave.), 206-545-3720
677 120th Ave. NE (8th St.), Bellevue, 425-646-9041
12551 116th Ave. NE (north of 124th St.), Kirkland, 425-820-5763
13870 NE 175th St. (138th Ave.), Woodinville, 425-398-8183
◪ Seattle is now awash in these Mission-style joints, where the "made-to-order" "fat burritos" are "inexpensive and filling" and the "fish tacos are tasty"; those at sea say the "novelty has worn off" and "lots of beans, lots of rice" just doesn't cut it, though the chain still "works in a pinch."

Tai Tung ●**S** | 18 | 9 | 16 | $20 |
655 S. King St. (Maynard Ave.), 206-622-7372
◪ "Sam Spade might eat here" at this true ID relic, which for nearly 70 years has been serving an "extensive menu" of "authentically good Chinese"; the "plain-Jane interior" is "not much to look at", but with "fair prices", this place still attracts a lot of gumshoes.

Tango **S** | 23 | 20 | 20 | $31 |
1100 Pike St. (Boren Ave.), 206-583-0382
■ It takes two or more to "share and be happy" at this "cool new Pan-Latin place" on Capitol Hill that serves up "fantastic food" including plenty of "imaginative" tapas and "desserts that will make you swoon" (the "chocolate 'El Diablo' is to die for"); the "fun, sassy, sexy" space also has a lively "bar scene" and a selection of top-quality tequilas.

Taqueria Guaymas S | _ | _ | _ | I |
1415 Broadway E. (Union St.), 206-860-3871
1622 SW Roxbury St. (17th Ave.), 206-767-4026
4719 California Ave. SW (Alaska St.), 206-935-8970
5919 196th St. SW (58th Pl. W.), Lynnwood, 425-670-3580
530 Rainer Ave. S. (King St.), Renton, 425-235-2152

Tacos Guaymas S
6808 E. Greenlake Way N. (2nd Ave. NE), 206-729-6563
213 Broadway E. (John St.), 206-860-7345
590 S. Burlington Blvd. (Rio Vista Ave.), Burlington, 360-755-1723
2630 S. 38th St. (Pine St.), Tacoma, 253-471-2224
With "numerous locations", this family of taquerias pleases plenty with its "fresh, light, very flavorful Mexican food" that includes a "whole fried fish special [*pescado dorado*]", a help-yourself bar of zippy salsas and of course a wide variety (including chicken, fish and tongue) of "wonderfully cooked" namesakes; "walk-up service" helps keep the prices down, so the "authentic" fare is also "inexpensive."

Tempero do Brasil S | ▽ 23 | 13 | 20 | $24 |
5628 University Way NE (56th St.), 206-523-6229
■ This University District newcomer is "decidedly Brazilian: delicious, friendly and a lot of fun"; the space is "pretty plain" but "what it lacks in atmosphere it makes up for" with "vibrant food" and live Latin music Tuesday–Sunday.

Ten Mercer ●S | _ | _ | _ | M |
10 Mercer St. (1st Ave. N.), 206-691-3723
Credenzia's Oven is no more, and where its huge wood-burning namesake once stood this newcomer has placed a bar where the lower Queen Anne crowd meets after work or before hitting the Seattle Center; the eclectic New American menu includes local faves such as oven-roasted mussels and pan-roasted chicken, but tosses in some twists with grilled whiskey prawns and bison burgers.

Texas Smokehouse Bar-B-Q S | 17 | 11 | 15 | $13 |
14455 Woodinville-Redmond Rd. (NE 145th St.),
Woodinville, 425-486-1957
■ Woodinville joint that serves "huge", "truly respectable" takes on the usual smoked-meat suspects; but while some surveyors "can't get enough" of the "awesome pork sandwich" and "moist chicken", others offer a more lukewarm opinion ("fine for occasional barbecue") and find the Texas-themed decor "kind of hokey."

Thai on Mercer S | 19 | 12 | 17 | $21 |
7691 27th St. SE (77th Ave.), Mercer Island, 206-236-9990
◪ At this casual, "restful" Thai, the menu "emphasizes lighter selections" (i.e. grilled or poached items), though there's still plenty of rich pan-fried fare, like the halibut with tamarind sauce; while many a Mercer Islander deems the "well-prepared food" a "nice hidden secret", the less-Mercerful mutter "portions are miniscule and overpriced."

That's Amore 🆂
19 | 15 | 19 | $22

1425 31st Ave. S. (Atlantic St.), 206-322-3677

■ Yep, that's *amore* we hear coming from Mt. Baker denizens when they discuss their "simple neighborhood Italian", which offers "great pizza" and other "inexpensive entrees and starters", not to mention "very good service"; equally lovable is the unusual "view of the Seattle skyline."

Third Floor Fish Cafe 🆂
24 | 23 | 22 | $40

205 Lake St. S. (2nd Ave.), Kirkland, 425-822-3553

■ This "trendy" ("for the Eastside" anyway) Kirklander specializes in "superb NW-style seafood with fabulous views" out over Lake Washington ("sunset in summer – wow"); the "wonderfully subdued" and "classy" dining room contrasts with a more lively mood in the piano bar, but there's "gracious service" throughout; some lament that it's "so expensive", but most are willing to pay for a place that's "always predictable", e.g. "consistently great."

13 Coins ⦿🆂
18 | 16 | 19 | $27

18000 Pacific Hwy. S. (opp. Sea-Tac Airport), 206-243-9500
125 Boren Ave. N. (Denny Way), 206-682-2513

☑ The legend lives on at this 30-year-old pair of 24-hour Italian-Americans Downtown and in SeaTac, where "it's heaven to sit in those high-backed chairs at the counter" and watch the kitchen sauté your veal scaloppini or toss your tortellini *della casa* (to name two of the fans' faves); but these veterans are unlucky with the unconverted, who resent paying "too much money for very mediocre food" in a "dated decor" with its "ultimate '70s-Vegas feel" (oh, so that explains the 'steak Sinatra' on the menu).

Three Girls Bakery 🆂
22 | 11 | 16 | $10

Pike Place Mkt., 1514 Pike Pl. (Pine St.), 206-622-1045

■ "Still the best counter in town" rave regulars of this tiny 1912 deli smack in the middle of the Pike Place Market hubbub; you can count on "great soups and generous sandwiches" ("split [the signature] meat loaf, heavy on the horseradish, with a friend"), not to mention "fabulous cookies"; the adjacent bakery doles out a "huge variety of wonderful breads" to take home.

Tia Lou's
– | – | – | M

(fka Mama Lou's)
2218 First Ave. (bet. Bell & Blanchard Sts.), 206-733-8226
Despite its Belltown address, this "undiscovered" newcomer has been riding low on the radar (and a recent re-christening didn't increase its profile); the few who have found it look favorably on its fresh and flavorful Mexican creations, like the signature egg-topped enchiladas in red-chile sauce; the upstairs loft cantina serves up a real lou-lou of a margarita.

Top Gun Seafood ●🅢 | 20 | 10 | 15 | $18 |
668 King St. (bet. Maynard & 7th Aves.), 206-623-6606
■ What's the attraction at this ID "hot spot"? – "it's the dim sum", stupid, served "every day" to the hordes that cruise by for those wonderfully plump dumplings; somewhat "underappreciated" is the rest of the "authentic Chinese" menu, whose specialties include shrimp-stuffed eggplant and crab in black-bean sauce; the only drawback is there's "no decor" to speak of (well, maybe "diner decor").

Torrefazione Italia | 23 | 23 | 20 | $9 |
622 Olive Way (bet. 6th & 7th Aves.), 206-624-1429
Rainier Sq., 1310 Fourth Ave. (University St.),
206-583-8970
Merrill Pl. Bldg., 701 N. 34th St. (Fremont Ave.),
206-545-2721 🅢
320 Occidental Ave. S. (bet. Main & Jackson Sts.),
206-624-5847 🅢
■ In a caffeine-craving city, this now-national chain is for many the coffeehouse of choice – the kind of place you "want to spend all day" in, sipping at the "thickest, most perfectly foamed lattes" and enjoying the "authentic Italian presentation" (in signature imported ceramics); a light pastry-and-panini menu accompanies the java.

Tosoni's | 25 | 16 | 22 | $34 |
14320 NE 20th St. (bet. 140th & 148th Aves.), Bellevue,
425-644-1668
■ "Leave the strip mall behind" and come on in to one of Bellevue's "best", a veteran whose "unassuming location" belies a dining experience reminiscent of "small restaurants in Europe"; chef-owner Walter Walcher's Continental-Eclectic "cuisine beats most of those trendy places Downtown", and the service strikes a perfect balance between "not too chummy and not too aloof."

TOYODA SUSHI 🅢 | 25 | 14 | 21 | $28 |
12543 Lake City Way NE (125th St.), 206-367-7972
■ "A sushi-phile's dream" awaits at this "authentic Japanese" in a "bustling" Lake City locale, because "everything is divine", "insanely fresh" and served in "large portions"; no wonder the "very loyal fans" say it's "worth the drive" to the north end (but you'd "better be there early or expect to wait").

Trapeze Bar & Bistro | – | – | – | I |
Decatur Bldg., 1523 Sixth Ave. (bet. Pike & Pine Sts.),
206-343-0877
"Such a great space" say surveyors of the historic Decatur building Downtown, which once housed the late Theoz but is now home to this American newcomer; by day, the lunch crowd goes for "great grilled sandwiches" and "good pizza" served cafeteria-style; by night, the place swings into more formal sit-down mode.

Trattoria Mitchelli ◐ S   16 | 15 | 15 | $22
84 Yesler Way (bet. 1st & Western Aves.), 206-623-3885
■ There's a good "old-fashioned vibe" at this long-standing Pioneer Square haunt, loved as much for its "late-night" hours (until 4 AM) as for its "many Italian favorites"; though there's "not much ambiance", you do get your choice of the main dining room, the counter (where the "lunch special is an unbeatable bargain") or the bar near the wood-fired pizza oven; oh, and "they serve breakfast too."

Triangle Lounge S   17 | 15 | 15 | $17
3507 Fremont Pl. N. (bet. Fremont Ave. & 35th St.), 206-632-0880
■ A "cool place to meet cool people" – the bar offers a "great nightlife" scene, and the "outdoor seating" can't be beat for watching passerby – this Fremont Med is also "fun" for its "cheap, good" "varied pub food" (from "yummy baked–goat cheese salad" to a "Middle Eastern plate"); the biggest complaint is "flaky service" that can be "painfully slow."

T.S. McHugh's S   15 | 15 | 17 | $21
21 Mercer St. (bet. 1st & Queen Anne Aves. N.), 206-282-1910
◪ The "popular bar and friendly staff" keep wearers o' the green coming back for NW-accented "Irish pub fare", including "wonderful pot pies and soda bread", in a dark-wood interior with plenty of Celtic trinkets; but enemies of the Emerald Isle say the "ho-hum food" only draws because it's so "handy" to Seattle Center destinations.

TULIO RISTORANTE S   24 | 22 | 22 | $36
Hotel Vintage Park, 1100 Fifth Ave. (Spring St.), 206-624-5500
■ "Outstanding", "delightful" and "memorable" are among the raves for this Downtown "white-linen Italian", where the food's so good "it's guaranteed to improve your mood"; "chef-owner Walter Pisano is great", pulling together "imaginative and subtle flavors" (the "sweet-potato gnocchi alone is reason to keep coming back"); a solid standby for "business lunch", it also gets kudos for an "especially good breakfast", making this "definitely the place to be" all day long.

Turkish Delight S ⊘   ▽ 20 | 8 | 16 | $11
Pike Place Mkt., 1930 Pike Pl. (bet. Stewart & Virginia Sts.), 206-443-1387
■ "Delicious Turkish specialties", ranging from savory *borek* pastries to the namesake candy, attract Pike Place Market visitors to this cafeteria; the setting offers little in the way of decor, but there's plenty of personality from the "delightful owners"; N.B. closes at 5:30 PM.

Turntable S　　16 | 17 | 14 | $21
*Experience Music Project, 325 Fifth Ave. N. (Harrison St.),
206-770-2777*

◪ This loud, loudly colored Experience Music Project eatery
serves a mod take on American classics, including a
"terrific Little Richard Bouffant Sundae"(topped with a
toupee-puff of spun sugar), while upstairs at the Liquid
Lounge they shake up a kaleidoscope of cutely named
cocktails (think Blue Suede Booze); clearly, this is not your
typical "museum food" and (critics carp) "not everything
it's hyped to be", but fans say "rock on!"

Two Bells Tavern S　　22 | 16 | 19 | $15
2313 Fourth Ave. (bet. Battery & Bell Sts.), 206-441-3050

■ A couple of blocks from Belltown's main drag, you get a
"mix of artists and businesspeople rubbing shoulders" as
they lift "fat and perfectly cooked" "hand-formed burgers"
and other "great pub food" to their mouths; this "grande
dame of taverns" is also blessed with the "happiest staff"
and, despite new ownership, remains "an old friend."

Typhoon! S　　24 | 21 | 20 | $27
*1400 Western Ave. (Union St.), 206-262-9797
Bella Bottega, 8936 161st Ave. NE (90th St.), Redmond,
425-558-7666*

■ These two "strong newcomers" from Portland have
taken the city by storm with "uncommonly good Thai food"
that's "elegant" and "creative", a "wonderful tea selection"
and "gorgeous" decor; however some blow steam that
the service is "spotty"; N.B. Redmond now has beer and
wine service, while the younger Pike Place Market sib (in
the former Wild Ginger space) features a full bar.

Union Bay Cafe S　　25 | 21 | 23 | $36
*3515 NE 45th St. (bet. Mary Gates Dr. & 36th Ave.),
206-527-8364*

■ "Just plain wonderful, from starters through dessert"
backers bay about this "snazzy" Laurelhurst "find" that
provides diners with "creative" NW–New American fare,
"unobtrusive service" and a "great wine list" in a "simple
but elegant" setting; some unionists even name it one of
the "top underrated restaurants in town."

Union Square Grill S　　23 | 21 | 22 | $40
621 Union St. (7th Ave.), 206-224-4321

■ The Downtown steakhouse scene may be crowded, but
it hasn't sliced into the business of this "dependable and
solid" player with its "classic club look", "gracious waiters"
and "well-prepared meats"; "valet parking" is a plus and
it's "perfect for pre-theater" dining (ACT is across the
street); although the cash-conscious complain it's "pricey",
most would jab back it's "worth it."

Uptown China 🅂　　　　　–　–　–　M
200 Queen Anne Ave. N. (John St.), 206-285-7710
This lower Queen Anne answer to "authentic" multi-
regional Chinese cuisine serves up "great dumplings and
dry sautéed string beans", along with signature crispy
walnut prawns; while it's many a surveyor's "favorite
Sunday night [place] for eat-in or takeout", the quality
lunch is a good bargain as well.

Uptown Espresso 🅂🚭　　　22　17　17　$9
3845 Delridge Way SW (Andover St.), 206-933-9497
2504 Fourth Ave. (Wall St.), 206-441-1084
525 Queen Anne Ave. N. (Mercer St.), 206-281-8669
■ "Love that foam" swoon surveyors about the signature
velvet froth at this trio of oh-so-Seattle coffeehouses
that appeal equally to the "grunge musician and the urban
stockbroker"; serving up "super pastries" and possibly
the "smoothest lattes in town", each offers a "great meeting
[or] reading spot" – though those on-the-go might try the
mobile order system, which lets you call en route and have
your preprogrammed order waiting.

Victor's Coffee Company 🅂🚭　　–　–　–　I
7993 Gilman St. (Cleveland St.), Redmond,
425-881-6451
"Friendly owners" Victor and Jane Harding roast their own
beans in small batches at this "one-of-a-kind coffeehouse"
in Redmond that's a "great local hangout"; Eastsiders
also "love the atmosphere", the "good soups" and "wide
variety of excellent baked goods."

Villa Paradiso 🅂　　　　　–　–　–　M
2220 Queen Anne Ave N. (bet. Boston & McGraw Sts.),
206-285-7949
From the owner of Kirkland's Ristorante Paradiso comes
this cozy cousin, installed in a "quaint" Craftsman house
"atop Queen Anne hill"; chef Tim Clancy (ex Il Terrazzo
Carmine) plays a deft, sophisticated hand with "rich" Italian
classics including *crespelle di spinaci* (spinach crêpes),
fettuccine con vietello (veal with sun-dried tomatoes and
mushrooms) and duck ravioli.

Von's Grand City Cafe 🅂　　15　14　15　$22
WestCoast Roosevelt Hotel, 619 Pine St. (bet. 6th & 7th Aves.),
206-621-8667
◪ Von-derful happy-hour martinis receive a grand reception
from reviewers, who note this Downtowner is "good for
after-work" unwinding and socializing; but the American
fare fares less well: "some things are excellent" (with
special mention for the babyback ribs), but other items
can be "disappointing", even "cafeteria-food–like."

Wasabi Bistro ◐ [S] ▽ 20 | 18 | 17 | $29

2311 Second Ave. (bet. Battery & Bell Sts.), 206-441-6044

◪ This "new sushi joint" has been swelling in popularity among the young Belltown crowd, with its colorful and "fun decor", good "bento box" lunches and some Western touches in the Japanese cuisine (including liberal use of cream cheese) that may not suit the raw-fishionado; heat-seekers hold that the "ambiance is a bit cold" and the staff on the "inexperienced" side.

WATERFRONT [S] 25 | 26 | 23 | $49

Pier 70, 2801 Alaskan Way (Broad St.), 206-956-9171

■ Owner Paul Mackay (El Gaucho) has another hit with this newcomer, whose "wonderful view" from the posh Pier 70 perch is only the opening number; chef Vicky McCaffree (ex Yarrow Bay Grill) assures diners of seafood "cooked to perfection" ("fantastic salt-and-pepper prawns"), while the staff offers "professional, delightful service" in "beautiful surroundings"; though the waterlogged lament that the "gigantic dining room" is pretty "noisy", most declare it "does not get better than this."

Waters, a Lakeside Bistro [S] ▽ 21 | 23 | 18 | $35

Woodmark Hotel, 1200 Carillon Pt. (Lake Washington Blvd.), Kirkland, 425-803-5595

◪ The "ambiance is excellent" at this NW bistro in a lakeside hotel that offers a "fun, lively spot" in Kirkland for enjoying a "great view" across Lake Washington and a striking patio setting when outdoors is an option; despite the varied menu – ranging from salmon hot pot to meat loaf – and "unique presentations", some view-finders feel it "doesn't live up to its waterfront location."

Waypoints [S] ▽ 20 | 22 | 21 | $36

Heron Beach Inn, 1 Heron Rd. (Oak Bay Rd.), Port Ludlow, 360-437-0411

◪ This Port Ludlow resort on the Olympic Peninsula offers a "great view" of the Puget Sound, especially "during the summer", when diners can sup on the wraparound veranda; fans find their way here for one of the "best out-of-city dinners" in the area, consisting of NW seasonal fare blended with eclectically "trendy" influences, but persnickety patrons point to the cuisine's "variable" quality (it's more "good-looking than fine-dining"); a new chef may contribute a consistency not reflected in the current ratings.

Western Vine Caribbean Cafe 18 | 13 | 18 | $26

81 Vine St. (Western Ave.), 206-728-1959

■ "Belltown's best budget meal" comes with a mini-"trip to the Caribbean", where you can get your fill of "spicy, tasty, interesting food" – the jerk chicken's a standout – and, on weekends, some live music to limbo to; the "staff is friendly", though some folks complain of "slow service" (think of it as reflecting a mellow island pace).

WILD GINGER § 26 | 24 | 22 | $36
1401 Third Ave. (Union St.), 206-623-4450

■ Folks are just wild about this Asian (the Seattle *Survey*'s Most Popular), whose "gorgeous" new Downtown digs "don't miss a beat" in satisfying surveyors' craving for the "incredible 'fragrant duck'" and other "fabulous flavors" that make up this "culinary adventure in smells and spices"; anyone hoping the bigger space means "more room for the throngs" will be disappointed, though, because the "hottest place in town" is still "always packed", making it "hard to get a table" ("even with reservations, expect a wait").

Wolfgang Puck Cafe § 16 | 17 | 17 | $27
1225 First Ave. (University St.), 206-621-9653

☒ The puck stops here for "a taste of Wolfgang's Californian cuisine" that, cheerleaders contend, is "surprisingly good" ("better than the critics say" anyway) and served in a "snazzy" setting; but gripers gang up on this New American chain link, complaining that the "blah food" and "tacky interior" ("enough with the broken tile!") equal "all flash, no panache"; no dispute, however, about its "great location" at the top of the Harbor Steps across from SAM.

World Class Chili ⊘ ▽ 23 | 8 | 13 | $9
Pike Place Mkt., 93 Pike St. (1st Ave.), 206-623-3678

■ "If you can find this place" in the midst of Pike Place Market, you're in for some of the "best chili anywhere" (chef-owner Joe Canavan has the blue ribbons behind the counter to prove it), in a variety of traditional and meatless versions; now in its 15th year, this hole-in-the-wall remains "uncorrupted by progress", which means ignore the ambiance (or lack thereof) and concentrate on the vats of long-simmering, well-spiced stew.

Yakima Grill ●§ 17 | 15 | 16 | $27
WestCoast Vance Hotel, 612 Stewart St. (6th Ave.), 206-956-0639

☒ This "cozy, shopper-friendly location" in the Vance Hotel revives weary buyers (and other Downtown types) with a "tasty tapas menu" plus other full-flavored fare that blends South American and Spanish influences; though the bar does its part ("the liquor flows well"), grumblers feel this grill could "be better", especially the "lame service."

Yankee Grill & Roaster § 13 | 12 | 15 | $18
5300 24th Ave. NW (Market St.), 253-475-3006
Holiday Inn Select, 1 S. Grady Way (Rainer Ave.), Renton, 425-255-8543
6812 Tacoma Mall Blvd. (I-5, exit 129), Tacoma, 253-475-3006

☒ Since day one, "huge helpings" have been the hallmark of this American trio, still known as "pot roast/meat loaf/turkey places" despite their new, gentrified name; traditionalists think they "taste like home", which could be why rebels "will not go back."

Yanni's

▽ | 21 | 13 | 20 | $20 |

7419 Greenwood Ave. N. (74th St.), 206-783-6945

■ "Friendly service" helps keep the crowds flocking to this humble Greenwood *taverna* where you'll get "moussaka like grandma's, if grandma was Greek"; so what if "they give you way too much" – just take the leftovers home as part of the "bargain."

Yarrow Bay Beach Cafe S

| 19 | 21 | 18 | $27 |

1270 Carillon Pt. (Lake Washington Blvd.), Kirkland, 425-889-0303

■ This "epitome of a trendy cafe" is where "Kirkland's beautiful people meet to eat" seafood-oriented International cooking and take advantage of the "great happy hour" and "excellent view"("you pay for it too"); though a touch "inconsistent", "when it's good, it's very good" – even "delightful"; P.S. "awesome outdoor seating" in summer.

Yarrow Bay Grill S

| 23 | 23 | 22 | $38 |

1270 Carillon Pt. (Lake Washington Blvd.), Kirkland, 425-889-9052

■ "More elegant" than its downstairs Beach Cafe sib, this Kirklander offers "great seafood" that's "simply prepared but robust in flavor", thanks to diverse International influences; the "sophisticated service" and "outstanding view of Lake Washington" help make this the "place to impress."

Zaina Food, Drink & Friends

▽ | 19 | 9 | 15 | $11 |

108 Cherry St. (1st Ave.), 206-624-5687
1619 Third Ave. (bet. Pine & Stewart Sts.), 206-770-0813 S

■ "When you've just got to have a falafel", come to this Pioneer Square and Downtown duo to tuck into some "flavorful fare" that's a "trip back to the Middle East"; the decor creates a desert oasis amid the concrete jungle.

Zao Noodle Bar S

| – | – | – | I |

University Village, 2590 NE University Village (25th Ave. & 45th St.), 206-529-8278

Smack in the middle of the University Village hubbub, this new noodle shop serves up Asian fare that's easy on both your schedule and your wallet; the selection of noodle and rice dishes is rounded out with specialties such as the ginger-garlic-chili chicken and prawns; it also boasts a full bar with interesting sake cocktails.

Zeek's Pizza S

| 19 | 11 | 14 | $14 |

2108 NE 65th St. (bet. Ravenna Blvd. & 21st St.), 206-525-0250
7900 E. Green Lake Dr. N. (79th St., opp. Green Lake), 206-522-5553
6000 Phinney Ave. N. (60th St.), 206-789-0087
41 Dravus St. (Nickerson St.), 206-285-6046
419 Denny Way (5th Ave.), 206-448-6775

■ "Weird but good" sums up this group of pizzerias whose "unique combos", like the "out-of-this-world Texas Leaguer" (BBQ sauce, chicken, red onion, cilantro), are "inventive" enough to "make you forget all other pizzas."

Seattle Indexes

CUISINES
LOCATIONS
SPECIAL FEATURES

CUISINES

Afghan
Kabul Afghan Cuisine

African
Afrikando

American (New)
Bay Cafe
Bick's Broadview
Bis on Main
Blue Onion Bistro
Earth & Ocean
Eva
Grapes
Jimmy's Table
Jitterbug Cafe
Julia's of Wallingford
Lampreia
Market Street
Mistral
Moonfish
Nell's
Palace Kitchen
Palomino
Queen City Grill
Restaurant Zoë
Roy's Seattle
Shea's Lounge
St. Clouds
Supreme
Ten Mercer
Trapeze Bar
Turntable
Union Bay Cafe
Wolfgang Puck

American (Traditional)
Andy's Diner
Ark
Athenian Inn
Atlas Foods
B&O Espresso
Billy McHale's
Bing's B&G
Blue Onion Bistro
BluWater Bistro
Broadway Grill
Café Soleil
Caffè Minnie's
Chanterelle
Charlie's/Broadway
Circa Neighborhood
CJ's Eatery
Claim Jumper
Crocodile Cafe
Deluxe B&G

Dish
Eggs Cetera's
5 Spot
14 Carrot Cafe
Gordon Biersch
Hattie's Hat
Hillside Manor
Hilltop Ale
Hiram's at the Locks
Hi-Spot Cafe
icon Grill
Kirkland Roaster
Leschi Lakecafe
Lockspot Cafe
Longshoreman's Daughter
Louisa's Cafe
Mae's Cafe
Maggie Bluff's
Maltby Cafe
Meridian
My Friends Cafe
Original Pancake Hse.
Paragon
Pike Pub
Planet Hollywood
Pyramid Alehouse
Red Robin
Rosebud
Salmon Bay Cafe
Scarlet Tree
74th St. Ale
Sharp's Roaster
Sit & Spin
Six Degrees
Stalk Exchange
Starfish Grill
St. Clouds
Streamliner Diner
13 Coins
Turntable
Von's Grand City
World Class Chili
Yankee Grill

Asian
Flying Fish
Mandalay Café
Ohana
Pandasia
Provinces
Roy's Seattle
Szmania's
Wild Ginger
Zao Noodle Bar

Bakery
Ark
Brusseau's
Gelatiamo
Honey Bear Bakery
Il Fornaio
Julia's of Wallingford
La Panzanella
Louisa's Cafe
Macrina Bakery
Three Girls Bakery

Barbecue
Armadillo BBQ
Billy McHale's
Burk's Cafe
Claim Jumper
Dixie's BBQ
Pecos Pit BBQ
Texas Smokehouse BBQ

Bolivian
Copacabana Cafe

Brazilian
Tempero do Brasil

Cajun/Creole
Alligator Soul
Burk's Cafe
Delcambre's Ragin Cajun
New Orleans Creole
Shultzy's

Californian
Wolfgang Puck

Caribbean
Paseo
Western Vine

Chinese
Bamboo Garden
Black Pearl
China Gate
Four Seas
Honey Court
Hong's Garden
House of Hong
Hunan Garden
Judy Fu's
Louie's
Noble Court
Ocean City
Sea Garden
Shanghai Garden
Tai Tung
Top Gun Seafood
Uptown China

Coffeehouse/Dessert
B&O Espresso
Cafe Starbucks
Caffe Ladro
Dilettante Chocolates
Espresso Vivace
Famous Pacific
Gelatiamo
Honey Bear Bakery
Still Life in Fremont
Torrefazione Italia
Uptown Espresso
Victor's Coffee

Coffee Shop/Diner
Andy's Diner
Caffè Minnie's
Hattie's Hat
Luna Park Cafe
Salmon Bay Cafe
Scarlet Tree
Streamliner Diner

Continental
Bis on Main
Café Septieme
Geneva
Kaspar's
Roy St. Bistro
Sisters European
Tosoni's

Croatian
Pogacha

Deli/Sandwich Shop
Bagel Oasis
Bakeman's
Briazz
Brusseau's
Philadelphia Fevre
Roxy's Deli
Roxy's Diner
Salumeria on Hudson
Sisters European
Sit & Spin
Three Girls Bakery

Dim Sum
China Gate
Four Seas
Hong's Garden
House of Hong
Noble Court
Ocean City
Top Gun Seafood

Eclectic/International
Axis
Brad's Swingside Cafe

Bungalow Wine Bar
Cafe Nola
Circa Neighborhood
Cliff House
Coastal Kitchen
Crocodile Cafe
Cyclops
Dahlia Lounge
Eques
Eva
Hilltop Ale
Jimmy's Table
Jitterbug Cafe
Julia's of Wallingford
Limelight Cafe
Maltby Cafe
Maple Leaf Grill
Marco's Supperclub
Moonfish
My Friends Cafe
Palace Kitchen
Pasta Ya Gotcha
Place Pigalle
Ponti Seafood Grill
Rhododendron Café
Rosebud
Sand Point Grill
Still Life in Fremont
Stumbling Goat
Tosoni's
Yarrow Bay Beach
Yarrow Bay Grill

English
Queen Mary

Ethiopian
Café Soleil
Kokeb

French
Barking Frog
Brasserie Margaux
Campagne
Crêpe de Paris
Le Gourmand
Maximilien
Rover's

French (Bistro)
Avenue One
Boat St. Cafe
Cafe Campagne
Cassis
Crêpe de Paris
Figaro Bistro
Le Pichet
Madison Park Cafe
611 Supreme

French (New)
Le Bonaparte
Les Tamales
Mistral
Rover's
Salish Lodge

German
Szmania's

Greek
Bacchus
Byzantion
Costas Greek
Costas Opa
Yanni's

Hamburgers
Belltown Pub
Bing's B&G
Circa Neighborhood
Deluxe B&G
Dick's Drive-In
Grady's Grillhse.
Kidd Valley
Luna Park Cafe
Maggie Bluff's
Planet Hollywood
Red Door Ale
Red Mill Burgers
Red Robin
Shultzy's
Two Bells Tavern

Hawaiian/Polynesian
Luau Polynesian
Ohana
Palisade
Roy's Seattle

Health Food
Café Ambrosia
Cafe Flora
14 Carrot Cafe
Gravity Bar
Green Cat Cafe
Julia's of Wallingford
My Friends Cafe
Stalk Exchange

Hot Dogs
Frankfurter
Matt's Famous Chili Dogs
Shultzy's

Indian
Banjara
Chutney's
Chutney's Bistro
Chutneys Cuisine

Chutneys Grille
India Bistro
India House
Moghul Palace
Raga
Sahib
Shamiana

Irish
Kells Irish
T.S. McHugh's

Italian
(N=Northern; S=Southern;
N&S=Includes both)
Al Boccalino (N&S)
Angelina's Trattoria (N&S)
Assaggio Rist. (N)
Asteroid Cafe (N&S)
Baccano Rist. (N&S)
Belltown Billiards (N&S)
Big Time (N&S)
Bizzarro (N&S)
Buca di Beppo (S)
Buongusto Rist. (N&S)
Cafe Bengodi (N&S)
Cafe Juanita (N)
Cafe Lago (N&S)
Cafe Veloce (N)
Calabria (S)
Ciao Bella (N&S)
Cucina! Cucina! (N&S)
Filiberto's Cucina (N&S)
Firenze (N&S)
Fremont Classic (N&S)
Gaspare's Rist. (S)
Gelatiamo (N&S)
Grazie Rist. (N&S)
Il Bacio (N)
Il Bistro (N)
Il Fornaio (N&S)
Il Gambero (S)
Il Terrazzo Carmine (N)
Isabella Rist. (N&S)
La Fontana Siciliana (S)
La Medusa (S)
Lampreia (N&S)
La Panzanella (N&S)
La Rustica (N)
Lombardi's Cucina (N&S)
Luigi's Grotto (N&S)
Lush Life (N&S)
Machiavelli (N)
Madame K's (N&S)
Mamma Melina (N&S)
Olympia Pizza (N&S)
Palomino (N&S)
Pasta & Co. (N&S)

Pasta Bella (N&S)
Pasta Ya Gotcha (N&S)
Pazzo's (N&S)
Perché No (N&S)
Pink Door (N&S)
Pontevecchio (S)
Poor Italian Cafe (N&S)
Prego (N&S)
Primo Grill (N&S)
Rist. Paradiso (N&S)
Romio's Pizza (N&S)
Salumeria on Hudson (N&S)
Salumi (N&S)
Salute of Bellevue (N&S)
Salute Rist. (N&S)
Salvatore Rist. (N&S)
Seattle Catch (N&S)
Serafina (N&S)
Simpatico (N&S)
Sostanza Trattoria (N)
Stella's Trattoria (N&S)
That's Amore (N&S)
13 Coins (N&S)
Trattoria Mitchelli (N&S)
Tulio Rist. (N&S)
Villa Paradiso (N&S)

Japanese
Aoki Japanese
Bush Garden
Chinoise Café
Eating Factory
I Love Sushi
Izumi
Kikuya
Mashiko
Musashi's
Nara Grill
Nikko
Nishino
Saito's Japanese
Sanmi Sushi
Shiro's Sushi
Toyoda Sushi
Wasabi Bistro

Jewish
Roxy's Diner

Latin American
Bandoleone
Dulces Latin Bistro
Fandango
Paseo
Tango

Lebanese
Karam's Lebanese
Mediterranean Kitchen

Malaysian
Malay Satay Hut

Mediterranean
Adriatica
Andaluca
Bistro Pleasant Bch.
Brasa
Cafe Langley
Capitol Club
Dulces Latin Bistro
El Greco
Hunt Club
Macrina Bakery
Mediterranean Kitchen
Mona's Bistro
Neo Bistro
96 Union
Phoenecia at Alki
Primo Grill
Sapphire Kitchen
Spazzo Mediterranean Grill
Triangle Lounge

Mexican/Tex-Mex
Agua Verde Cafe
Azteca
Burrito Loco
Cactus
Chevys
Chile Pepper
El Camino
El Niño
El Puerco Lloron
Galerias
Gordito's
Jalisco Mexican
Les Tamales
Mama's Mexican
Pesos Kitchen
Rosita's Mexican
Taco Del Mar
Taqueria Guaymas
Tia Lou's

Middle Eastern
Kabul Afghan Cuisine
Karam's Lebanese
Mediterranean Kitchen
Phoenecia at Alki
Zaina

Moroccan
Bella Rosa Bistro

Noodle Shop
Fremont Noodle Hse.
Krittika Noodles
Noodle Ranch

Noodle Studio
Ocean City
Pho Thân Bros.
Racha Noodles
Zao Noodle Bar

Pacific Northwest
Ark
Arnies
Barking Frog
Bell St. Diner
Belltown Pub
Brasserie Margaux
Bridges on Eastlake
Calcutta Grill
Canlis
Cascadia
Chez Shea
Christina's
Circa Neighborhood
Coho Café
Dahlia Lounge
Dimitriou's Jazz
Foghorn
Fullers
Geneva
Georgian Room
Herbfarm
Hunt Club
Inn at Langley
Ivar's Mukilteo Landing
Kaspar's
Lampreia
Oyster Bar/Chuckanut
Oyster Creek Inn
Painted Table
Place Pigalle
Ponti Seafood Grill
Ray's Boathouse
Ray's Cafe
Rhododendron Café
Rover's
Salty's
Shea's Lounge
Shoalwater
Six Degrees
SkyCity/Needle
Spirit of Washington
Szmania's
Third Floor Fish Cafe
T.S. McHugh's
Union Bay Cafe
Waters
Waypoints

Pakistani
Shamiana

Pan-Asian
Asian Wok & Grill
Chinoise Café
Dragonfish
Nara Grill
Noodle Ranch
Provinces
Roy's Seattle
Shallots
Wild Ginger

Pizza
Axis
Belltown Billiards
Big Time
Cafe Lago
Coyote Creek
Delfino's
Fremont Classic
Gordon Biersch
Grazie Rist.
Il Fornaio
Isabella Rist.
La Medusa
Madame K's
Mad Pizza
Olympia Pizza
Pagliacci Pizza
Palomino
Pazzo's
Pegasus Pizza
Piecora's
Pogacha
Romio's Pizza
Salumeria on Hudson
Sit & Spin
That's Amore
Trapeze Bar
Trattoria Mitchelli
Zeek's Pizza

Pub Food
Charlie's/Broadway
Circa Neighborhood
Gordon Biersch
Grady's Grillhse.
Hale's Ales
Hilltop Ale
Kells Irish
Nickerson St. Saloon
Pike Pub
Pyramid Alehouse
Red Door Ale
74th St. Ale
Triangle Lounge
T.S. McHugh's
Two Bells Tavern

Russian
My Favourite Piroshky

Seafood
Anthony's
Anthony's Pier 66
Ark
Arnies
Bay Cafe
Bell St. Diner
Bistro Pleasant Bch.
Brooklyn Seafood
Canlis
Chandler's Crabhse.
Chinook's/Salmon Bay
Coho Café
Crab Cracker
Cutters Bayhouse
Dash Point
Duke's Chowder Hse.
Elliott's Oyster Hse.
Emmett Watson's
Etta's Seafood
Falling Waters
Flying Fish
Foghorn
F.X. McRory's
Greenlake B&G
Hiram's at the Locks
Ivar's Acres of Clams
Ivar's Mukilteo Landing
Ivar's Salmon House
Jack's Fish Spot
Lake Washington
Leschi Lakecafe
Matt's in the Market
McCormick & Schmick's
McCormick & Schmick's Harbor
McCormick's Fish Hse.
Oyster Bar/Chuckanut
Oyster Creek Inn
Palisade
Ponti Seafood Grill
Queen City Grill
Ray's Boathouse
Ray's Cafe
Roy's Seattle
Salty's
Sea Garden
Seattle Catch
Shoalwater
Shuckers
Stanley & Seafort's
Sunfish
Third Floor Fish Cafe
Top Gun Seafood
Waterfront

Yarrow Bay Beach
Yarrow Bay Grill

Senegalese
Afrikando

South American
Copacabana Cafe
Tempero do Brasil
Yakima Grill

Southern/Soul
Alligator Soul
Catfish Corner
Ezell's Famous Chicken
Jimmy's Table
Kingfish
Sazerac

Southwestern
Cactus
Desert Fire
Santa Fe Cafe

Spanish
Dulces Latin Bistro
Harvest Vine
Marcha Tapas
Yakima Grill

Steakhouse
BluWater Bistro
Brooklyn Seafood
Canlis
Daniel's Broiler
DC's Steakhse.
El Gaucho
Fleming's Prime
F.X. McRory's
JaK's Grill
Lake Washington
Metropolitan Grill
Morton's of Chicago
Rock Salt Steakhse.
Ruth's Chris
Stanley & Seafort's
Union Square Grill

Tapas
Andaluca
Bandoleone

Cactus
Harvest Vine
Marcha Tapas
Spazzo Mediterranean Grill
Tango
Yakima Grill

Tearoom
Queen Mary

Thai
Angel's Thai
Ayutthaya
Bahn Thai
Bai Tong
Fremont Noodle Hse.
Krittika Noodles
Mae Phim Thai
Noodle Studio
Pon Proem
Racha Noodles
Thai on Mercer
Typhoon!

Turkish
Turkish Delight

Vegetarian
(Most Chinese, Indian and
Thai restaurants usually offer
vegetarian dishes; * vegan)
Bamboo Garden
Café Ambrosia*
Cafe Flora
Carmelita
Gravity Bar
Green Cat Cafe
Julia's of Wallingford
Rover's
Sit & Spin
Stalk Exchange
Still Life in Fremont
Sunlight Cafe

Vietnamese
Café Huê
Monsoon
Pho Thân Bros.
Saigon Bistro

LOCATIONS

Bainbridge Island
Bistro Pleasant Bch.
Cafe Nola
Moonfish
Streamliner Diner

Ballard/Shilshole
Anthony's
Azteca
Burk's Cafe
Grapes
Hattie's Hat
Hiram's at the Locks
India Bistro
Le Gourmand
Lockspot Cafe
Lombardi's Cucina
Louie's
Madame K's
Market Street
Pasta Bella
Ray's Boathouse
Ray's Cafe
Salmon Bay Cafe
Yankee Grill

Beacon Hill/Mt. Baker
That's Amore

Bellevue
Azteca
Billy McHale's
Bis on Main
Briazz
Calcutta Grill
Chutneys Cuisine
Coyote Creek
Cucina! Cucina!
Daniel's Broiler
Dixie's BBQ
Duke's Chowder Hse.
Eating Factory
Eques
Firenze
Frankfurter
Grazie Rist.
Hunan Garden
I Love Sushi
Kidd Valley
Matt's Famous Chili Dogs
Mediterranean Kitchen
Moghul Palace
My Favourite Piroshky
Noble Court
Pasta & Co.
Pogacha

Red Robin
Salute of Bellevue
Sea Garden
Shanghai Garden/Cafe
Spazzo Mediterranean Grill
Taco Del Mar
Tosoni's

Belltown
Afrikando
Axis
Baccano Rist.
B&O/Cherry St.
Belltown Billiards
Belltown Pub
Brasa
Cascadia
CJ's Eatery
Crocodile Cafe
Cyclops
El Gaucho
Falling Waters
Fandango
Flying Fish
Il Gambero
La Fontana Siciliana
Lampreia
Lush Life
Macrina Bakery
Mama's Mexican
Marco's Supperclub
Mistral
Noodle Ranch
Ohana
Queen City Grill
Restaurant Zoë
Saito's Japanese
Shallots
Shiro's Sushi
Sit & Spin
Tia Lou's
Two Bells Tavern
Uptown Espresso
Wasabi Bistro
Western Vine

Bothell/Kenmore/Maltby
Grazie Rist.
Hillside Manor
Jalisco Mexican
Kidd Valley
Lake Washington
Maltby Cafe
Romio's Pizza

Capitol Hill

Angel's Thai
Aoki Japanese
Asian/B'way Wok
Ayutthaya
Bacchus
B&O Espresso
Broadway Grill
Byzantion
Café Septieme
Caffè Minnie's
Capitol Club
Cassis
Charlie's/Broadway
Chutneys Grille
Coastal Kitchen
Deluxe B&G
Dick's Drive-In
Dilettante Chocolates
El Greco
Espresso Vivace/To Go
Galerias
Gravity Bar
Green Cat Cafe
Jalisco Mexican
Karam's Lebanese
Kidd Valley
Kingfish
Kokeb
La Panzanella
Machiavelli
Med. Kitchen/Express
Monsoon
My Favourite Piroshky
Noodle Studio
Olympia Pizza
Pagliacci Pizza
Pho Thân Bros.
Piecora's
Romio's Pizza
Rosebud
611 Supreme
Taco Del Mar
Tango
Taq. Guaymas/Tacos

Central District

Catfish Corner
Ezell's Famous Chicken

Columbia City/ Seward Park

La Medusa
Salumeria on Hudson

Crown Hill

Burrito Loco
Dick's Drive-In
Rosita's Mexican

Downtown

Andaluca
Assaggio Rist.
Brasserie Margaux
Briazz
Brooklyn Seafood
Cafe Starbucks
Caffe Ladro
Crêpe de Paris
Dahlia Lounge
Desert Fire
Dimitriou's Jazz
Dragonfish
Earth & Ocean
El Niño
Fleming's Prime
Frankfurter
Fullers
Gelatiamo
Georgian Room
Gordon Biersch
icon Grill
Il Fornaio
Isabella Rist.
Mae Phim Thai
Marcha Tapas
McCormick & Schmick's
McCormick's Fish Hse.
Metropolitan Grill
Morton's of Chicago
Nara Grill
Nikko
Painted Table
Palace Kitchen
Palomino
Planet Hollywood
Poor Italian Cafe
Prego
Roxy's Diner
Roy's Seattle
Ruth's Chris
Sazerac
Shuckers
Taco Del Mar
13 Coins
Torrefazione Italia
Trapeze Bar
Tulio Rist.
Union Square Grill
Von's Grand City
Wild Ginger
Wolfgang Puck

Yakima Grill
Zaina

Edmonds/Shoreline
Anthony's
Arnies
Black Pearl
Brusseau's
Chanterelle
Neo Bistro
Provinces
Romio's Pizza
Sahib

Everett/Mukilteo
Alligator Soul
Anthony's
Arnies
Ivar's Mukilteo Landing
Lombardi's Cucina
Red Robin
Romio's Pizza

First Hill
Geneva
Hunt Club
Mad Pizza

Fremont/Wallingford
Asian Wok & Grill
Asteroid Cafe
Bagel Oasis
Bizzarro
Brad's Swingside Cafe
Bungalow Wine Bar
Caffe Ladro
Chile Pepper
Chutney's Bistro
Costas Opa
Dick's Drive-In
Dish
Eggs Cetera's
El Camino
Fremont Classic
Fremont Noodle Hse.
Hale's Ales
Jitterbug Cafe
Julia's of Wallingford
Kabul Afghan Cuisine
Longshoreman's Daughter
Mad Pizza
Mandalay Café
Musashi's
Nickerson St. Saloon
Olympia Pizza
Paseo
Pontevecchio

Ponti Seafood Grill
Red Door Ale
Seattle Catch
Simpatico
Still Life in Fremont
Taco Del Mar
Torrefazione Italia
Triangle Lounge
Zeek's Pizza

Green Lake/
Greenwood/Phinney Ridge
Bick's Broadview
Carmelita
Duke's Chowder Hse.
Eva
Gordito's
Greenlake B&G
Kidd Valley
Krittika Noodles
Luau Polynesian
Mae's Cafe
Mona's Bistro
My Friends Cafe
Nell's
Pho Thân Bros.
Red Mill Burgers
Romio's Pizza
Rosita's Mexican
Santa Fe Cafe
74th St. Ale
Six Degrees
Stalk Exchange
Stumbling Goat
Taq. Guaymas/Tacos
Yanni's
Zeek's Pizza

International District
Bush Garden
China Gate
Chinoise Café
Four Seas
Honey Court
House of Hong
Malay Satay Hut
Ocean City
Saigon Bistro
Sea Garden
Shanghai Garden
Tai Tung
Top Gun Seafood

Issaquah/Sammamish
Cucina! Cucina!
DC's Steakhse.

JaK's Grill
Lombardi's Cucina
Pogacha
Red Robin
Salish Lodge
Shanghai Garden

Kent/Des Moines/Burien

Anthony's
Azteca
Filiberto's Cucina
Le Bonaparte
Red Robin
Salty's
Simpatico

Kirkland

Anthony's
Azteca
Cafe Juanita
Cafe Veloce
Calabria
Coyote Creek
Crab Cracker
Cucina! Cucina!
Foghorn
Izumi
Jalisco Mexican
Kidd Valley
Kirkland Roaster
Original Pancake Hse.
Pasta Ya Gotcha
Pegasus Pizza
Piecora's
Raga
Rist. Paradiso
Shamiana
Six Degrees
Taco Del Mar
Third Floor Fish Cafe
Waters
Yarrow Bay Beach
Yarrow Bay Grill

Lake City/North Seattle/Northgate

Azteca
Dick's Drive-In
Frankfurter
Gaspare's Rist.
Jalisco Mexican
Kidd Valley
Romio's Pizza
Toyoda Sushi

Lake Forest Park/ Mountlake Terrace

Firenze/Il Capo
Honey Bear Bakery

Lake Union/Eastlake

Adriatica
Azteca
Bandoleone
BluWater Bistro
Bridges on Eastlake
Café Ambrosia
Canlis
Chandler's Crabhse.
Cucina! Cucina!
Daniel's Broiler
Duke's Chowder Hse.
14 Carrot Cafe
I Love Sushi
Ivar's Salmon House
Louisa's Cafe
McCormick & Schmick's Harbor
Meridian
Pazzo's
Red Robin
Rock Salt Steakhse.
Romio's Pizza
Serafina

Laurelhurst/Sand Point

Sand Point Grill
Union Bay Cafe

Leschi/Madrona

Café Soleil
Daniel's Broiler
Dulces Latin Bistro
Hi-Spot Cafe
Leschi Lakecafe
St. Clouds
Supreme

Lynnwood

Billy McHale's
Buca di Beppo
Chevys
Ezell's Famous Chicken
Red Robin
Taqueria Guaymas

Madison Park/ Madison Valley

Bing's B&G
Cactus
Cafe Flora
Cafe Starbucks
Chinoise/Madison
Harvest Vine
Jimmy's Table

Madison Park Cafe
Mad Pizza
Nishino
Philadelphia Fevre
Rover's
Sostanza Trattoria

Magnolia/Interbay
Chinook's/Salmon Bay
Limelight Cafe
Maggie Bluff's
Palisade
Pandasia
Red Mill Burgers
Romio's Pizza
Sanmi Sushi
Szmania's

Maple Leaf/Roosevelt
Ciao Bella Too
Judy Fu's
Maple Leaf Grill
Salvatore Rist.
Scarlet Tree
Sunlight Cafe

Mercer Island
Pon Proem
Thai on Mercer

Mill Creek/Snohomish
Azteca

Montlake
Cafe Lago
Grady's Grillhse.

NW Washington
Billy McHale's
Oyster Bar/Chuckanut
Oyster Creek Inn
Rhododendron Café
Taq. Guaymas/Tacos
Waypoints

Olympia
Anthony's

Pike Place Market
Athenian Inn
Avenue One
Cafe Campagne
Campagne
Chez Shea
Copacabana Cafe
Cutters Bayhouse
Delcambre's Ragin Cajun
El Puerco Lloron
Emmett Watson's
Etta's Seafood
Il Bistro

Jack's Fish Spot
Kells Irish
Le Pichet
Matt's in the Market
Maximilien
96 Union
Pike Pub
Pink Door
Place Pigalle
Roxy's Deli
Shea's Lounge
Sisters European
Three Girls Bakery
Turkish Delight
Typhoon!
World Class Chili

Pioneer Square/SODO
Al Boccalino
Andy's Diner
Bakeman's
B&O/Cherry St.
Cafe Bengodi
Café Huê
F.X. McRory's
Honey Bear Bakery
Il Terrazzo Carmine
Luigi's Grotto
Matt's Famous Chili Dogs
New Orleans Creole
Pecos Pit BBQ
Pyramid Alehouse
Salumi
Taco Del Mar
Torrefazione Italia
Trattoria Mitchelli
Zaina

Queen Anne/ Seattle Center
Bahn Thai
Bamboo Garden
Banjara
Buca di Beppo
Buongusto Rist.
Caffe Ladro
Caffè Minnie's
Chinoise Café
Chutney's
Dick's Drive-In
Famous Pacific
Figaro Bistro
5 Spot
Frankfurter
Hilltop Ale
Jalisco/Taqueria
Kaspar's
Kidd Valley

Mediterranean Kitchen
Olympia Pizza
Pagliacci Pizza
Paragon
Pasta & Co.
Pasta Bella
Perché No
Pesos Kitchen
Racha Noodles
Roy St. Bistro
Sapphire Kitchen
SkyCity/Needle
Taco Del Mar
Ten Mercer
T.S. McHugh's
Turntable
Uptown China
Uptown Espresso
Villa Paradiso
Zeek's Pizza

Ravenna/Wedgwood
Bagel Oasis
Black Pearl
Kidd Valley
Queen Mary
Salute Rist.
Santa Fe Cafe
Zeek's Pizza

Redmond
Big Time
Billy McHale's
Claim Jumper
Coho Café
Cucina! Cucina!
Desert Fire
Il Bacio
Kikuya
Red Robin
Romio's Pizza
Six Degrees
Typhoon!
Victor's Coffee

Renton
Billy McHale's
Ezell's Famous Chicken
Hong's Garden
Kidd Valley
Pegasus Pizza
Spirit of Washington
Taqueria Guaymas
Yankee Grill

San Juan Islands
Bay Cafe
Christina's
Starfish Grill

SeaTac/Tukwila
Azteca
Bai Tong
Claim Jumper
Cucina! Cucina!
Grazie Rist./Pizza
Sharp's Roaster
13 Coins

Seattle Waterfront
Anthony's Pier 66
Bell St. Diner
Elliott's Oyster Hse.
Frankfurter
Ivar's Acres of Clams
Red Robin
Waterfront

South Seattle
Frankfurter
Jalisco Mexican

SW Washington Coast
Ark
Shoalwater

Tacoma/Federal Way
Anthony's
Azteca
Billy McHale's
Chevys
Cliff House
Cucina! Cucina!
Dash Point/S.
Primo Grill
Stanley & Seafort's
Taq. Guaymas/Tacos
Yankee Grill

University District/ University Village
Agua Verde Cafe
Atlas Foods
Bella Rosa Bistro
Blue Onion Bistro
Boat St. Cafe
Burrito Loco
Ciao Bella
Costas Greek
Delfino's
India House
Mamma Melina
Pagliacci Pizza
Pasta & Co.
Pho Thân Bros.
Shultzy's
Stella's Trattoria
Tempero do Brasil
Zao Noodle Bar

West Seattle
Angelina's Trattoria
Caffe Ladro
Circa Neighborhood
JaK's Grill
La Rustica
Les Tamales
Luna Park Cafe
Mashiko
Pegasus Plzza
Phoenecia at Alki
Salty's
Sunfish

Taqueria Guaymas
Uptown Espresso

Whidbey Island
Cafe Langley
Inn at Langley

Woodinville
Armadillo BBQ
Barking Frog
Herbfarm
Red Robin
Taco Del Mar
Texas Smokehouse BBQ

SPECIAL FEATURES

Breakfast
(All hotels and the
following standouts)
Athenian Inn
Atlas Foods
Bacchus
B&O Espresso
Broadway Grill
Brusseau's
Byzantion
Cafe Campagne
Café Septieme
Café Soleil
Cafe Starbucks
Caffè Minnie's
Chanterelle
Chutneys Grille
CJ's Eatery
Coastal Kitchen
Costas Greek
Costas Opa
Crocodile Cafe
Dish
Eggs Cetera's
5 Spot
14 Carrot Cafe
Green Cat Cafe
Hi-Spot Cafe
Honey Bear Bakery
Jitterbug Cafe
Julia's of Wallingford
Le Pichet
Longshoreman's Daughter
Louisa's Cafe
Luna Park Cafe
Macrina Bakery
Mae's Cafe
Maltby Cafe
My Friends Cafe
Original Pancake Hse.
Queen Mary
Salmon Bay Cafe
Scarlet Tree
Sisters European
Stella's Trattoria
Still Life in Fremont
Streamliner Diner
13 Coins

Brunch
(Best of many)
Anthony's
Ark
Arnies

Bay Cafe
Boat St. Cafe
Cafe Bengodi
Cafe Flora
Cafe Nola
Calcutta Grill
Chandler's Crabhse.
Chinook's/Salmon Bay
Circa Neighborhood
Coho Café
Cutters Bayhouse
Dash Point/S.
El Greco
Etta's Seafood
Ivar's Mukilteo Landing
Ivar's Salmon House
Kingfish
Madison Park Cafe
Maximilien
Palisade
Paragon
Ponti Seafood Grill
Rock Salt Steakhse.
Rosebud
Roxy's Diner
Roy's Seattle
Salty's
Sapphire Kitchen
SkyCity/Needle
Stalk Exchange
St. Clouds
Sunlight Cafe
Two Bells Tavern
Yarrow Bay Grill

Buffet
(Check prices, days
and times)
Angel's Thai
Banjara
Calabria
Calcutta Grill
Chutney's
Chutney's Bistro
Chutneys Cuisine
Chutneys Grille
Eating Factory
Four Seas
Kabul Afghan Cuisine
La Rustica
Mamma Melina
My Friends Cafe
Paseo
Phoenecia at Alki
Raga

Roy's Seattle
Shallots
Shamiana
Starfish Grill
Tosoni's

Business Dining
Al Boccalino
Andaluca
Anthony's Pier 66
Assaggio Rist.
Avenue One
Brasa
Cafe Juanita
Calcutta Grill
Campagne
Canlis
Cliff House
Daniel's Broiler
Earth & Ocean
El Gaucho
Eques
Etta's Seafood
Fleming's Prime
Fullers
Geneva
Georgian Room
Hunt Club
Il Fornaio
Il Terrazzo Carmine
Kaspar's
Lampreia
McCormick & Schmick's
McCormick & Schmick's Harbor
McCormick's Fish Hse.
Metropolitan Grill
Morton's of Chicago
Nikko
96 Union
Painted Table
Palisade
Palomino
Ponti Seafood Grill
Prego
Ray's Boathouse
Rock Salt Steakhse.
Rover's
Roy's Seattle
Ruth's Chris
Salish Lodge
Sazerac
Shuckers
Sostanza Trattoria
Stanley & Seafort's
Third Floor Fish Cafe
Tulio Rist.
Union Square Grill

Waypoints
Yarrow Bay Grill

Caters
(Best of many)
Afrikando
Ark
Bahn Thai
Bandoleone
Bella Rosa Bistro
Bis on Main
Blue Onion Bistro
Brad's Swingside Cafe
Burk's Cafe
Cactus
Cafe Langley
Café Soleil
Calcutta Grill
Carmelita
Cascadia
Christina's
Dahlia Lounge
Daniel's Broiler
Delcambre's Ragin Cajun
Dixie's BBQ
Dulces Latin Bistro
Elliott's Oyster Hse.
Etta's Seafood
Fullers
Gelatiamo
Grapes
Hillside Manor
Il Fornaio
Il Terrazzo Carmine
India Bistro
Isabella Rist.
Jimmy's Table
Kabul Afghan Cuisine
Karam's Lebanese
Kaspar's
Kokeb
La Fontana Siciliana
La Medusa
La Rustica
Limelight Cafe
Luau Polynesian
Madison Park Cafe
Mandalay Café
Marcha Tapas
McCormick & Schmick's Harbor
Nell's
96 Union
Nishino
Ohana
Palace Kitchen
Paragon
Paseo

Pasta Bella
Phoenecia at Alki
Ponti Seafood Grill
Primo Grill
Provinces
Queen City Grill
Ray's Boathouse
Rover's
Sahib
Saito's Japanese
Salish Lodge
Salty's
Salumeria on Hudson
Sand Point Grill
Sazerac
Sea Garden
Serafina
Shallots
Shiro's Sushi
Simpatico
Stalk Exchange
Starfish Grill
Szmania's
Tai Tung
Texas Smokehouse BBQ
Tia Lou's
Top Gun Seafood
Tosoni's
Typhoon!
Union Square Grill
Wild Ginger
Yarrow Bay Grill
Zao Noodle Bar

Cigar Friendly

Baccano Rist.
Bandoleone
Bridges on Eastlake
Calcutta Grill
Cascadia
Daniel's Broiler
Duke's Chowder Hse.
Dulces Latin Bistro
El Gaucho
Firenze
Fullers
F.X. McRory's
Il Bistro
Kirkland Roaster
McCormick & Schmick's
McCormick & Schmick's Harbor
McCormick's Fish Hse.
Metropolitan Grill
Mona's Bistro
Morton's of Chicago
96 Union
Palomino

Pike Pub
Ruth's Chris
Texas Smokehouse BBQ
13 Coins
Trattoria Mitchelli
Union Square Grill
Waterfront
Waypoints

Delivers*/Takeout

(Nearly all Asians, coffee shops, delis, diners and pasta/pizzerias deliver or do takeout; here are some interesting possibilities; D=delivery, T=takeout; *call to check range and charges, if any)
Afrikando (T)
Al Boccalino (T)
Alligator Soul (T)
Andaluca (T)
Angelina's Trattoria (T)
Ark (T)
Armadillo BBQ (T)
Assaggio Rist. (T)
Atlas Foods (T)
Baccano Rist. (D,T)
Bacchus (D,T)
Bay Cafe (T)
BluWater Bistro (T)
Brad's Swingside Cafe (T)
Brasserie Margaux (T)
Buca di Beppo (T)
Bungalow Wine Bar (T)
Cafe Bengodi (T)
Cafe Lago (T)
Calcutta Grill (T)
Chutney's (D)
Chutney's Bistro (D)
Chutneys Cuisine (D,T)
Chutneys Grille (T)
Cliff House (T)
Crêpe de Paris (T)
Dahlia Lounge (D,T)
Daniel's Broiler (T)
Dash Point (T)
El Greco (T)
Elliott's Oyster Hse. (T)
Falling Waters (T)
Fleming's Prime (T)
Flying Fish (T)
Gordito's (T)
Gordon Biersch (T)
Grady's Grillhse. (T)
Hattie's Hat (T)
Hillside Manor (D,T)

Hiram's at the Locks (T)
Hi-Spot Cafe (T)
Il Fornaio (T)
Il Gambero (T)
Ivar's Salmon House (T)
Jimmy's Table (T)
Kells Irish (D,T)
La Rustica (T)
Les Tamales (T)
Lush Life (T)
Maggie Bluff's (T)
Maltby Cafe (T)
Mamma Melina (T)
Marcha Tapas (T)
Marco's Supperclub (T)
Market Street (T)
Meridian (T)
Moonfish (T)
Nickerson St. Saloon (T)
Nikko (T)
Ohana (T)
Palace Kitchen (D,T)
Paseo (T)
Philadelphia Fevre (T)
Pike Pub (T)
Pogacha (D,T)
Prego (T)
Primo Grill (T)
Pyramid Alehouse (T)
Ruth's Chris (T)
Saito's Japanese (T)
Salute Rist. (T)
Sazerac (T)
Simpatico (T)
Stalk Exchange (T)
Starfish Grill (T)
St. Clouds (T)
Still Life in Fremont (T)
Tango (T)
Tempero do Brasil (T)
Texas Smokehouse BBQ (T)
That's Amore (D)
Third Floor Fish Cafe (T)
Tia Lou's (T)
Trapeze Bar (D,T)
Turntable (T)
Union Bay Cafe (T)
Union Square Grill (T)
Waterfront (T)
Western Vine (T)
Wolfgang Puck (T)
Yakima Grill (D,T)

Dessert/Ice Cream
Ark
B&O Espresso
Brusseau's

Cafe Nola
Café Septieme
Caffe Ladro
Dilettante Chocolates
Famous Pacific
Gelatiamo
Honey Bear Bakery
La Panzanella
Louisa's Cafe
Macrina Bakery
Queen Mary
Still Life in Fremont
Uptown Espresso

Dining Alone
(Other than hotels, coffee
shops, sushi bars and places
with counter service)
Angel's Thai
Ayutthaya
Bai Tong
Black Pearl
Cafe Flora
Café Septieme
Café Soleil
Coastal Kitchen
Elliott's Oyster Hse.
Emmett Watson's
Etta's Seafood
14 Carrot Cafe
Fremont Noodle Hse.
Grazie Rist.
Green Cat Cafe
Harvest Vine
Il Fornaio
Jitterbug Cafe
Julia's of Wallingford
Le Pichet
Longshoreman's Daughter
Macrina Bakery
Mae's Cafe
Maggie Bluff's
Malay Satay Hut
Maple Leaf Grill
Marco's Supperclub
Matt's in the Market
Mona's Bistro
Noodle Ranch
Palace Kitchen
Paseo
Philadelphia Fevre
Salumi
Seattle Catch
Shallots
Shamiana
Spazzo Mediterranean Grill
St. Clouds

Stella's Trattoria
Sunlight Cafe
Szmania's
Trattoria Mitchelli
Two Bells Tavern
Typhoon!
Wild Ginger
Wolfgang Puck
Zaina

Entertainment

(Check days, times and performers for entertainment; D=dancing; best of many)
Alligator Soul (blues)
Avenue One (jazz)
Axis (jazz)
Baccano Rist. (guitar/jazz)
Bandoleone (Latin)
Belltown Billiards (D/jazz)
Brad's Swingside Cafe (folk/jazz)
Broadway Grill (jazz)
Bush Garden (karaoke)
Calabria (varies)
Calcutta Grill (piano)
Canlis (piano)
Cascadia (piano)
Chutney's Bistro (sitar)
Ciao Bella (opera/piano)
Cliff House (piano)
Crêpe de Paris (cabaret)
Crocodile Cafe (bands)
Daniel's Broiler (jazz/piano)
Dimitriou's Jazz (blues/jazz)
Dulces Latin Bistro (jazz/Latin)
El Gaucho (D/piano/jazz)
El Niño (Spanish guitar)
Fremont Noodle Hse. (jazz)
Georgian Room (piano)
Grazie Rist. (jazz)
Herbfarm (guitar)
Hillside Manor (jazz)
Hunt Club (piano)
Il Terrazzo Carmine (guitar)
Isabella Rist. (guitar)
Julia's/Wallingford (jazz/piano)
Kabul Afghan Cuisine (sitar)
Kells Irish (folk/Irish)
Mamma Melina (opera/piano)
Marcha Tapas (D/salsa)
Mona's Bistro (jazz)
Neo Bistro (blues/jazz)
New Orleans (D/blues/jazz)
96 Union (opera/piano)
Ohana (Hawaiian)
Palomino (jazz)
Paragon (blues/jazz/R&B)

Pegasus Pizza (comedy/rock)
Perché No (guitar/piano)
Pink Door (varies)
Planet Hollywood (D/DJ)
Pontevecchio (opera/tango)
Provinces (varies)
Rock Salt Steakhse. (D/DJ)
Salty's (jazz)
Salute/Bellevue (classical/opera)
Scarlet Tree (varies)
Seattle Catch (jazz)
Serafina (jazz/Latin)
Shamiana (sitar/tabla)
Sit & Spin (varies)
St. Clouds (varies)
Tempero do Brasil (Brazilian)
Third Floor Fish Cafe (piano)
13 Coins (piano/vocals)
T.S. McHugh's (Irish)
Turntable (varies)
Waterfront (piano)
Western Vine (Caribbean)
Wolfgang Puck (jazz)

Fireplace

(* check locations)
Angelina's Trattoria
Ark
Avenue One
Barking Frog
Bay Cafe
BluWater Bistro
Bungalow Wine Bar
Buongusto Rist.
Cafe Juanita
Cafe Starbucks*
Cafe Veloce
Calcutta Grill
Canlis
Cascadia
Christina's
Claim Jumper
Daniel's Broiler
Desert Fire
Duke's Chowder Hse.*
Dulces Latin Bistro
Eques
Foghorn
Gordito's
Grady's Grillhse.
Herbfarm
Hillside Manor
Hilltop Ale
Hiram's at the Locks
Hunt Club
Il Fornaio
Inn at Langley

Ivar's Salmon House
Judy Fu's
Leschi Lakecafe
Lockspot Cafe
Lombardi's Cucina*
Madison Park Cafe
Mandalay Café
Maple Leaf Grill
McCormick & Schmick's Harbor
Moonfish
Neo Bistro
96 Union
Oyster Bar/Chuckanut
Paragon
Pasta Bella
Pogacha*
Ponti Seafood Grill
Salish Lodge
Salty's*
Salute of Bellevue
Sostanza Trattoria
Stalk Exchange
Starfish Grill
Szmania's
T.S. McHugh's
Waypoints
Yarrow Bay Grill
Zao Noodle Bar

Game in Season
Asteroid Cafe
Blue Onion Bistro
Brad's Swingside Cafe
Brasserie Margaux
Bungalow Wine Bar
Campagne
Cascadia
Christina's
Dahlia Lounge
Earth & Ocean
El Gaucho
Etta's Seafood
Georgian Room
Herbfarm
Hillside Manor
Hunt Club
Le Bonaparte
Le Gourmand
New Orleans Creole
Palace Kitchen
Place Pigalle
Primo Grill
Queen City Grill
Stumbling Goat
Szmania's
Tosoni's

Union Bay Cafe
Yarrow Bay Grill

Historic Interest
(Year opened; *building)
1800s Madame K's*
1889 Cascadia*
1890 Brooklyn Seafood*
1896 Shoalwater*
1898 Dash Point*
1908 Copacabana Cafe*
1908 Hunt Club*
1909 Athenian Inn
1910 China Gate*
1912 Chez Shea*
1912 Matt's in the Market*
1912 Shea's Lounge*
1912 Three Girls Bakery
1913 Avenue One*
1916 Hillside Manor*
1916 Salish Lodge
1920 Lockspot Cafe
1921 Chanterelle*
1921 Provinces*
1922 Noodle Studio*
1922 Oyster Creek Inn
1922 Trapeze Bar*
1924 Georgian Room
1924 Shuckers*
1925 Cliff House
1926 Wild Ginger*
1930s Blue Onion Bistro*
1930 Christina's*
1930 Oyster Bar/Chuckanut
1934 Maltby Cafe*
1935 Tai Tung
1937 Spirit of Washington*
1938 Ivar's Acres of Clams
1949 Andy's Diner
1950 Ark
1950 Canlis

Hotel Dining
Alexis Hotel
    Painted Table
Four Seasons Olympic Hotel
    Georgian Room
    Shuckers
Heron Beach Inn
    Waypoints
Holiday Inn Select
    Yankee Grill
Hotel Monaco
    Sazerac
Hotel Vintage Park
    Tulio Rist.
Hyatt Regency Hotel
    Eques

Inn at Langley
  Inn at Langley
Mayflower Park Hotel
  Andaluca
Oyster Creek Inn
  Oyster Creek Inn
Paramount Hotel
  Dragonfish
Renaissance Madison Hotel
  Prego
Resort at Deer Harbor
  Starfish Grill
Salish Lodge & Spa
  Salish Lodge
Shelburne Inn
  Shoalwater
Sheraton Seattle
  Fullers
Sorrento Hotel
  Hunt Club
Warwick Hotel
  Brasserie Margaux
WestCoast Roosevelt
  Von's Grand City
WestCoast Vance Hotel
  Yakima Grill
Westin Hotel
  Nikko
  Roy's Seattle
W Hotel
  Earth & Ocean
Willows Lodge
  Barking Frog
  Herbfarm
Woodmark Hotel
  Waters

"In" Places

Barking Frog
Blue Onion Bistro
Brasa
Cafe Juanita
Cafe Lago
Capitol Club
Cascadia
Cassis
Dahlia Lounge
Earth & Ocean
El Gaucho
Fandango
Flying Fish
Harvest Vine
Kingfish
Le Pichet
Luau Polynesian
Marcha Tapas
Market Street

Ohana
Palace Kitchen
Restaurant Zoë
Saito's Japanese
Salumeria on Hudson
Salumi
Sapphire Kitchen
Stumbling Goat
Tango
Typhoon!
Waterfront
Wild Ginger

Late Late – After 12:30
(All hours are AM;
* check locations)
Asian/B'way Wok (2)
Belltown Billiards (1)
BluWater Bistro (1)
Broadway Grill (1:30)
Caffè Minnie's (24 hrs.)
Charlie's/Broadway (2)
China Gate (1:30)
Dick's Drive-In (2)
Dragonfish (1)
El Gaucho (1)
Fandango (1)
Flying Fish (1)
Honey Court (2)
Palace Kitchen (1)
Pegasus Pizza (1)*
Pesos Kitchen (1)
Red Robin (1)*
Sea Garden (2)
Stella's Trattoria (24 hrs.)
13 Coins (24 hrs.)
Top Gun Seafood (3)
Trattoria Mitchelli (4)
Wasabi Bistro (1)
Yakima Grill (2)

Meet for a Drink
(Most top hotels and the
following standouts)
Adriatica
Agua Verde Cafe
Anthony's Pier 66
Athenian Inn
Atlas Foods
Avenue One
Axis
Bandoleone
Belltown Billiards
BluWater Bistro
Brasa
Bridges on Eastlake
Brooklyn Seafood

Bungalow Wine Bar
Bush Garden
Cactus
Capitol Club
Chandler's Crabhse.
Charlie's/Broadway
Chutneys Grille
Coho Café
Crocodile Cafe
Cucina! Cucina!
Cutters Bayhouse
Cyclops
Dahlia Lounge
Daniel's Broiler
Dash Point
Deluxe B&G
Duke's Chowder Hse.
Dulces Latin Bistro
El Camino
El Gaucho
Elliott's Oyster Hse.
El Niño
Etta's Seafood
Fandango
Fleming's Prime
Flying Fish
Greenlake B&G
Hattie's Hat
Il Bistro
Il Gambero
Il Terrazzo Carmine
Jimmy's Table
Jitterbug Cafe
Kaspar's
Kells Irish
Le Pichet
Les Tamales
Luau Polynesian
Lush Life
Machiavelli
Mama's Mexican
Marcha Tapas
Marco's Supperclub
Market Street
McCormick & Schmick's Harbor
Metropolitan Grill
Mona's Bistro
Neo Bistro
New Orleans Creole
Ohana
Palace Kitchen
Palisade
Palomino
Paragon
Pink Door
Place Pigalle
Primo Grill

Queen City Grill
Ray's Cafe
Restaurant Zoë
Rosebud
Ruth's Chris
Saito's Japanese
Salty's
Santa Fe Cafe
Sapphire Kitchen
Scarlet Tree
Seattle Catch
Serafina
Shea's Lounge
Six Degrees
Sostanza Trattoria
Spazzo Mediterranean Grill
Stanley & Seafort's
Tango
Ten Mercer
Third Floor Fish Cafe
13 Coins
Triangle Lounge
Turntable
Typhoon!
Waterfront
Wild Ginger
Yarrow Bay Beach

Noteworthy Newcomers (19)

Barking Frog
Blue Onion Bistro
Café Ambrosia
Falling Waters
Fandango
Fleming's Prime
Greenlake B&G
Le Pichet
Market Street
Mistral
Restaurant Zoë
Saito's Japanese
Starfish Grill
St. Clouds
Stumbling Goat
Supreme
Tango
Wasabi Bistro
Waterfront

Offbeat

Afrikando
Alligator Soul
Armadillo BBQ
Asteroid Cafe
Bizzarro
Brad's Swingside Cafe
Buca di Beppo

Capitol Club
Crocodile Cafe
Dixie's BBQ
Dragonfish
Earth & Ocean
Gravity Bar
Green Cat Cafe
Luau Polynesian
Luna Park Cafe
Madame K's
Mae's Cafe
Mama's Mexican
Mashiko
New Orleans Creole
Ohana
Paseo
Pecos Pit BBQ
Pink Door
Pontevecchio
Salumi
Shultzy's
Sit & Spin
Tempero do Brasil
Turntable
Western Vine

Outdoor Dining

(G=garden; P=patio;
S=sidewalk; T=terrace;
W=waterside; best of many)
Agua Verde Cafe (P,W)
Alligator Soul (G)
Angelina's Trattoria (P,S)
Anthony's (G,P,T,W)
Anthony's Pier 66 (P,W)
Ark (T,W)
Arnies (P,W)
Axis (P,S)
Bandoleone (P)
Barking Frog (P)
Bay Cafe (W)
Bell St. Diner (P,W)
Bick's Broadview (T)
Bing's B&G (P)
Blue Onion Bistro (P)
BluWater Bistro (P,W)
Boat St. Cafe (G,P)
Brad's Swingside Cafe (G,P)
Bridges on Eastlake (P,W)
Broadway Grill (S)
Buongusto Rist. (P)
Café Ambrosia (P,W)
Cafe Flora (P)
Cafe Juanita (G,P)
Cafe Nola (P)
Café Septieme (S)
Calcutta Grill (P,T)

Campagne (P)
Capitol Club (T)
Carmelita (G,P,T)
Cascadia (P)
Cassis (P)
Chandler's Crabhse. (P,W)
Chinoise Café (G,P)
Chinook's/Salmon Bay (P,W)
Christina's (T,W)
Copacabana Cafe (T)
Cucina! Cucina! (P,W)
Daniel's Broiler (P,W)
Dash Point (T,W)
Deluxe B&G (S)
Dixie's BBQ (P)
Duke's Chowder Hse. (P,W)
El Camino (P)
Elliott's Oyster Hse. (P)
Emmett Watson's (P)
Filiberto's Cucina (P)
Flying Fish (P)
Fremont Classic (P)
F.X. McRory's (P)
Galerias (T)
Green Cat Cafe (S)
Greenlake B&G (P,S)
Hale's Ales (P)
Hillside Manor (G)
Hiram's at the Locks (P,T,W)
Hi-Spot Cafe (G,P)
Il Bistro (T)
I Love Sushi (W)
Il Terrazzo Carmine (T)
India Bistro (S)
Ivar's Mukilteo Landing (P,W)
Ivar's Salmon House (G,P,W)
Kells Irish (P)
Kirkland Roaster (P,S,W)
La Fontana Siciliana (P)
Lake Washington (W)
La Rustica (G,P,W)
Le Pichet (S)
Leschi Lakecafe (P,W)
Les Tamales (S)
Limelight Cafe (P)
Lush Life (G)
Madame K's (G,P)
Madison Park Cafe (P)
Maggie Bluff's (P,W)
Maple Leaf Grill (P)
Marco's Supperclub (P)
McCormick/Schmick's Harb. (P,W)
Moonfish (P,W)
New Orleans Creole (P,S)
Oyster Bar/Chuckanut (P,W)
Palisade (W)
Pecos Pit BBQ (G,P)

Pegasus Pizza (S)
Pink Door (G,P,T)
Place Pigalle (P)
Ponti Seafood Grill (P,W)
Pyramid Alehouse (P)
Ray's Cafe (P)
Red Door Ale (P)
Rist. Paradiso (S)
Rock Salt Steakhse. (P,W)
Rosebud (P)
Rover's (P)
Sahib (W)
Salish Lodge (P)
Salty's (P,T,W)
Salute of Bellevue (P,S)
Sapphire Kitchen (T)
Serafina (G)
Shallots (S)
Shoalwater (P)
Simpatico (P)
Sisters European (P,S)
Sostanza Trattoria (P)
Stalk Exchange (G,P)
Stanley & Seafort's (P)
Starfish Grill (T,W)
St. Clouds (P)
Still Life in Fremont (S)
Triangle Lounge (P)
Two Bells Tavern (P)
Union Bay Cafe (P)
Waterfront (P,W)
Waters (P,W)
Waypoints (T,W)
Yarrow Bay Beach (P,W)
Yarrow Bay Grill (P,W)

Oyster Bar

(* check locations)
Brooklyn Seafood
Chandler's Crabhse.
Daniel's Broiler*
Elliott's Oyster Hse.
Emmett Watson's
F.X. McRory's
Ivar's Acres of Clams
Jack's Fish Spot
McCormick & Schmick's Harbor
McCormick's Fish Hse.
Ray's Boathouse

Parking/Valet

(V=valet parking;
*=validated parking)
Andaluca (V)*
Anthony's Pier 66 (V)*
Assaggio Rist. (V)
Axis (V)
Bandoleone*

Bell St. Diner (V)*
BluWater Bistro (V)*
Brasserie Margaux (V)*
Brooklyn Seafood (V)
Byzantion*
Cafe Campagne*
Cafe Starbucks (V)
Calcutta Grill (V)
Campagne*
Canlis (V)
Cascadia (V)*
Chandler's Crabhse. (V)*
Chez Shea (V)*
Cucina! Cucina!*
Cutters Bayhouse*
Dahlia Lounge (V)
Daniel's Broiler (V)*
Dilettante Chocolates*
Dimitriou's Jazz*
Duke's Chowder Hse. (V)*
Earth & Ocean (V)
El Gaucho (V)*
Elliott's Oyster Hse.*
Eques (V)*
Fleming's Prime (V)*
Four Seas (V)
Fullers (V)*
Geneva*
Georgian Room (V)*
Gravity Bar*
Hillside Manor (V)
House of Hong*
Hunt Club (V)
Il Bistro (V)*
I Love Sushi (V)
Il Terrazzo Carmine (V)
Isabella Rist. (V)
Jack's Fish Spot*
Lake Washington (V)
Maximilien (V)*
McCormick/Schmick's Harbor*
Metropolitan Grill (V)
Morton's of Chicago (V)
Nikko (V)*
96 Union*
Palisade (V)
Palomino*
Perché No (V)
Pike Pub*
Pink Door (V)
Place Pigalle (V)*
Ponti Seafood Grill (V)
Prego (V)*
Pyramid Alehouse*
Raga*
Ray's Boathouse (V)*
Red Robin (V)

Rock Salt Steakhse. (V)
Roxy's Diner*
Roy's Seattle (V)*
Ruth's Chris (V)
Saigon Bistro*
Salish Lodge (V)
Salty's (V)
Sazerac (V)
Shea's Lounge (V)*
SkyCity/Needle (V)
Spazzo Mediterranean Grill*
Tulio Rist. (V)*
Union Square Grill (V)*
Waterfront (V)
Waters (V)*
Wild Ginger (V)
Yakima Grill (V)
Yarrow Bay Beach (V)*
Yarrow Bay Grill (V)*

Parties & Private Rooms

(Any nightclub or restaurant
charges less at off-times;
* indicates private rooms
available; best of many)
Adriatica
Afrikando
Al Boccalino*
Alligator Soul*
Andy's Diner*
Angelina's Trattoria
Anthony's*
Ark
Armadillo BBQ
Asian Wok & Grill
Assaggio Rist.*
Athenian Inn
Atlas Foods
Avenue One*
Axis*
Baccano Rist.*
Bacchus*
Bakeman's
B&O Espresso
Bandoleone
Banjara*
Bella Rosa Bistro
Big Time
Bis on Main
BluWater Bistro*
Brasa*
Brasserie Margaux
Brooklyn Seafood*
Buca di Beppo
Bush Garden*
Cafe Bengodi*
Cafe Flora*

Café Huê
Cafe Juanita*
Cafe Veloce
Calabria*
Calcutta Grill*
Canlis*
Capitol Club*
Carmelita*
Cascadia*
Chandler's Crabhse.
Chanterelle
Chevys
Chez Shea*
China Gate
Chinook's/Salmon Bay*
Chutneys Grille
CJ's Eatery
Cliff House*
Coastal Kitchen
Coho Café
Costas Opa
Crab Cracker
Cutters Bayhouse*
Dahlia Lounge*
Daniel's Broiler*
Dash Point*
Deluxe B&G
Desert Fire*
Dimitriou's Jazz
Dragonfish*
Duke's Chowder Hse.*
Dulces Latin Bistro*
Eggs Cetera's
El Gaucho*
Elliott's Oyster Hse.
El Niño
Emmett Watson's
Etta's Seafood*
Falling Waters*
Figaro Bistro*
Firenze*
5 Spot*
Fleming's Prime*
Flying Fish*
Four Seas*
Fullers*
F.X. McRory's
Galerias
Gaspare's Rist.
Geneva
Georgian Room*
Gordon Biersch*
Grapes
Grazie Rist.*
Hale's Ales
Harvest Vine
Herbfarm*

Hillside Manor*
Hiram's at the Locks*
Honey Court
House of Hong*
icon Grill*
Il Fornaio*
Il Terrazzo Carmine
India House
Isabella Rist.
Ivar's Acres of Clams*
Ivar's Salmon House*
Julia's of Wallingford
Kabul Afghan Cuisine
Kaspar's
Kells Irish*
Kirkland Roaster*
Kokeb
La Fontana Siciliana*
Lake Washington
Le Bonaparte*
Le Gourmand
Lombardi's Cucina*
Luigi's Grotto*
Macrina Bakery
Madison Park Cafe*
Mae's Cafe
Maggie Bluff's
Malay Satay Hut
Maximilien*
McCormick & Schmick's*
McCormick/Schmick's Harb.*
McCormick's Fish Hse.
Meridian*
Metropolitan Grill*
Monsoon
Moonfish*
Morton's of Chicago*
My Friends Cafe
Nara Grill*
Neo Bistro
New Orleans Creole*
Nickerson St. Saloon
Nikko*
96 Union*
Ohana*
Oyster Bar/Chuckanut*
Painted Table*
Palace Kitchen*
Palomino*
Pandasia*
Paragon
Pasta Bella
Pegasus Pizza
Perché No
Piecora's*
Pike Pub
Place Pigalle

Planet Hollywood*
Pogacha*
Pontevecchio
Ponti Seafood Grill*
Prego
Provinces
Pyramid Alehouse
Queen City Grill
Ray's Boathouse*
Rock Salt Steakhse.*
Romio's Pizza*
Rosebud
Rover's*
Roy's Seattle*
Roy St. Bistro*
Ruth's Chris*
Salty's*
Salute of Bellevue
Sanmi Sushi*
Sazerac*
Sea Garden*
Seattle Catch
Shanghai Garden*
Sharp's Roaster
Shoalwater*
Simpatico
Sostanza Trattoria*
Spazzo Mediterranean Grill*
Spirit of Washington*
Stalk Exchange
Stella's Trattoria
Szmania's*
Tai Tung*
Tango*
Third Floor Fish Cafe*
13 Coins*
Tia Lou's*
Top Gun Seafood
Trattoria Mitchelli
T.S. McHugh's*
Tulio Rist.*
Typhoon!*
Union Square Grill*
Villa Paradiso*
Von's Grand City*
Wasabi Bistro*
Waterfront*
Waypoints*
Western Vine
Wild Ginger*
Yakima Grill
Yankee Grill*
Yanni's*
Yarrow Bay Grill*
Zeek's Pizza

People-Watching

Assaggio Rist.
Athenian Inn
Axis
Belltown Billiards
Broadway Grill
Café Septieme
Coastal Kitchen
Copacabana Cafe
Cyclops
Deluxe B&G
Dilettante Chocolates
El Gaucho
Etta's Seafood
Fandango
Flying Fish
Gordon Biersch
Gravity Bar
Jack's Fish Spot
Le Pichet
Longshoreman's Daughter
Macrina Bakery
Mama's Mexican
Marcha Tapas
Noodle Ranch
Ohana
Palace Kitchen
Queen City Grill
Restaurant Zoë
Sazerac
Sisters European
Tango
Three Girls Bakery
Triangle Lounge
Waterfront
Wild Ginger

Power Scene

Brooklyn Seafood
Campagne
Canlis
Daniel's Broiler
El Gaucho
Georgian Room
Il Terrazzo Carmine
McCormick & Schmick's
McCormick's Fish Hse.
Metropolitan Grill
Morton's of Chicago
Rover's
Ruth's Chris
Sazerac
Shuckers
Union Square Grill
Waterfront

Pub/Bar/Microbrewery

Belltown Pub
Circa Neighborhood
Eggs Cetera's
F.X. McRory's
Gordon Biersch
Grady's Grillhse.
Hale's Ales
Hilltop Ale
Kells Irish
Kirkland Roaster
Leschi Lakecafe
Maple Leaf Grill
Nickerson St. Saloon
Paragon
Pike Pub
Pyramid Alehouse
Red Door Ale
74th St. Ale
Sharp's Roaster
Six Degrees
T.S. McHugh's
Two Bells Tavern

Quiet Conversation

Adriatica
Al Boccalino
Ark
Avenue One
Bacchus
Boat St. Cafe
Bungalow Wine Bar
Cafe Juanita
Café Soleil
Campagne
Chez Shea
Christina's
Cliff House
Dash Point
Dulces Latin Bistro
Eques
Eva
Figaro Bistro
Fullers
Geneva
Georgian Room
Hunt Club
Il Bistro
Il Gambero
Il Terrazzo Carmine
Isabella Rist.
Kaspar's
La Fontana Siciliana
Lampreia
La Rustica
Le Bonaparte
Le Gourmand

Madison Park Cafe
Matt's in the Market
Maximilien
Mistral
Nell's
Painted Table
Ponti Seafood Grill
Prego
Queen Mary
Rover's
Ruth's Chris
Salish Lodge
Shea's Lounge
Shoalwater
Sostanza Trattoria
Stumbling Goat
Szmania's
Union Bay Cafe
Waypoints

Romantic

Adriatica
Al Boccalino
Andaluca
Assaggio Rist.
Avenue One
Bandoleone
Bella Rosa Bistro
Boat St. Cafe
Brasa
Cafe Campagne
Cafe Juanita
Campagne
Canlis
Cassis
Chez Shea
Christina's
Ciao Bella
Dulces Latin Bistro
El Gaucho
Eva
Figaro Bistro
Geneva
Hunt Club
Il Bistro
Il Gambero
Il Terrazzo Carmine
Isabella Rist.
La Fontana Siciliana
La Rustica
Le Gourmand
Luigi's Grotto
Lush Life
Madison Park Cafe
Marco's Supperclub
Matt's in the Market
Maximilien

Mona's Bistro
Painted Table
Perché No
Place Pigalle
Ponti Seafood Grill
Prego
Queen City Grill
Rover's
Salish Lodge
Salvatore Rist.
Sapphire Kitchen
Serafina
Shea's Lounge
Shoalwater
Sostanza Trattoria
Spirit of Washington
Szmania's
Waypoints
Yarrow Bay Grill

Senior Appeal

Andy's Diner
Ark
Arnies
Calcutta Grill
Chanterelle
Chinook's/Salmon Bay
Cliff House
Crab Cracker
Dash Point
Foghorn
Geneva
Georgian Room
Hiram's at the Locks
Hunt Club
Ivar's Acres of Clams
Ivar's Mukilteo Landing
Ivar's Salmon House
McCormick & Schmick's Harbor
Meridian
Original Pancake Hse.
Palisade
Provinces
Queen Mary
Ray's Boathouse
Salish Lodge
Salmon Bay Cafe
Shoalwater
SkyCity/Needle
Spirit of Washington
Stanley & Seafort's
Streamliner Diner
13 Coins
Yankee Grill

Singles Scene

Axis
Bandoleone

Belltown Billiards
BluWater Bistro
Broadway Grill
Brooklyn Seafood
Cactus
Capitol Club
Crocodile Cafe
Cucina! Cucina!
Cutters Bayhouse
Cyclops
Deluxe B&G
Duke's Chowder Hse.
Earth & Ocean
El Niño
F.X. McRory's
Gordon Biersch
Gravity Bar
Grazie Rist.
Green Cat Cafe
Hale's Ales
Hattie's Hat
Hilltop Ale
Il Bistro
Kells Irish
Kirkland Roaster
Leschi Lakecafe
Luau Polynesian
Machiavelli
Madame K's
Mama's Mexican
Maple Leaf Grill
Marcha Tapas
Marco's Supperclub
New Orleans Creole
Noodle Ranch
Ohana
Palace Kitchen
Paragon
Pike Pub
Pyramid Alehouse
Queen City Grill
Ray's Cafe
Red Door Ale
Restaurant Zoë
Rosebud
Salty's
Sapphire Kitchen
Sazerac
74th St. Ale
Sit & Spin
Tango
Trattoria Mitchelli
Triangle Lounge
T.S. McHugh's
Turntable
Two Bells Tavern
Union Square Grill

Von's Grand City
Wasabi Bistro
Western Vine
Wild Ginger
Yakima Grill
Yarrow Bay Beach

Sleepers
(Good to excellent food,
but little known)
Bella Rosa Bistro
Bistro Pleasant Bch.
Christina's
Falling Waters
Firenze
Geneva
Grapes
Hong's Garden
Karam's Lebanese
Kikuya
Kokeb
Krittika Noodles
La Fontana Siciliana
Malay Satay Hut
Mandalay Café
Market Street
Mashiko
Moghul Palace
Nara Grill
Philadelphia Fevre
Pon Proem
Primo Grill
Provinces
Sahib
Saigon Bistro
Saito's Japanese
Shea's Lounge
Stalk Exchange
Sunfish
Tempero do Brasil
Waters
World Class Chili
Yanni's

Teenagers & Other Youthful Spirits
Armadillo BBQ
Billy McHale's
Bing's B&G
Buca di Beppo
Cafe Veloce
Caffè Minnie's
Chevys
Claim Jumper
Coyote Creek
Cucina! Cucina!
Desert Fire
Dick's Drive-In

Eating Factory
Frankfurter
Gordito's
Gravity Bar
Grazie Rist.
Jalisco Mexican
Jitterbug Cafe
Kidd Valley
Lake Washington
Luna Park Cafe
Mad Pizza
Mama's Mexican
Mediterranean Kitchen
Olympia Pizza
Pagliacci Pizza
Paseo
Pasta Ya Gotcha
Pazzo's
Pecos Pit BBQ
Pegasus Pizza
Planet Hollywood
Red Mill Burgers
Red Robin
Romio's Pizza
Roxy's Deli
Roxy's Diner
Scarlet Tree
Sharp's Roaster
Sit & Spin
Spazzo Mediterranean Grill
Stella's Trattoria
Still Life in Fremont
Streamliner Diner
Sunfish
Taco Del Mar
Taqueria Guaymas
Tempero do Brasil
Texas Smokehouse BBQ
Three Girls Bakery
Trattoria Mitchelli
Turntable
Wolfgang Puck
World Class Chili
Yankee Grill
Zaina
Zeek's Pizza

Teflons

(Get lots of business, despite
so-so food, i.e. they have
other attractions that prevent
criticism from sticking)
Azteca
Billy McHale's
Briazz
Broadway Grill
Cafe Starbucks

Caffè Minnie's
Deluxe B&G
Dimitriou's Jazz
Planet Hollywood
Yankee Grill

Theme Restaurant

Andy's Diner
Baccano Rist.
Billy McHale's
Buca di Beppo
Cafe Veloce
Claim Jumper
Desert Fire
Luau Polynesian
Madame K's
Ohana
Planet Hollywood
Spirit of Washington
Turntable

Visitors on Expense Account

Adriatica
Anthony's Pier 66
Avenue One
Barking Frog
Brasa
Brooklyn Seafood
Campagne
Canlis
Cascadia
Chandler's Crabhse.
Dahlia Lounge
Daniel's Broiler
Earth & Ocean
El Gaucho
Fleming's Prime
Fullers
Geneva
Georgian Room
Hunt Club
Il Terrazzo Carmine
Kaspar's
Lampreia
Le Gourmand
McCormick's Fish Hse.
Metropolitan Grill
Mistral
Morton's of Chicago
Nell's
Nikko
Nishino
Painted Table
Palisade
Prego
Ray's Boathouse
Rover's

Roy's Seattle
Ruth's Chris
Salish Lodge
Sazerac
SkyCity/Needle
Szmania's
Third Floor Fish Cafe
Tulio Rist.
Union Square Grill
Waterfront
Wild Ginger
Yarrow Bay Grill

Wine/Beer Only
(* check locations)
Alligator Soul
Angelina's Trattoria
Aoki Japanese
Armadillo BBQ
Ayutthaya
Bacchus
Bahn Thai
Bai Tong
B&O Espresso*
Banjara
Bella Rosa Bistro
Bis on Main
Bistro Pleasant Bch.
Bizzarro
Black Pearl
Blue Onion Bistro
Boat St. Cafe
Brad's Swingside Cafe
Bungalow Wine Bar
Burk's Cafe
Burrito Loco
Café Ambrosia
Cafe Flora
Café Huê
Cafe Nola
Cafe Starbucks
Cafe Veloce
Caffè Minnie's
Carmelita
Chanterelle
Chinoise Café
Ciao Bella
Circa Neighborhood
CJ's Eatery
Copacabana Cafe
Costas Greek
Coyote Creek
Crêpe de Paris
Delcambre's Ragin Cajun
Delfino's
Dilettante Chocolates
Eating Factory

Eggs Cetera's
El Greco
Emmett Watson's
Eva
14 Carrot Cafe
Fremont Classic
Fremont Noodle Hse.
Gaspare's Rist.
Gordito's
Grapes
Green Cat Cafe
Hale's Ales
Harvest Vine
Herbfarm
Hilltop Ale
Hi-Spot Cafe
Honey Bear Bakery*
Honey Court
Hunan Garden
Il Bacio
India Bistro
Inn at Langley
Izumi
Julia's of Wallingford
Kabul Afghan Cuisine
Karam's Lebanese
Kikuya
Kingfish
Kokeb
La Fontana Siciliana
La Medusa
La Rustica
Longshoreman's Daughter
Luna Park Cafe
Macrina Bakery
Madame K's
Mad Pizza
Malay Satay Hut
Maltby Cafe
Mandalay Café
Maple Leaf Grill
Mashiko
Matt's in the Market
Mediterranean Kitchen
Monsoon
Musashi's
Noodle Ranch
Olympia Pizza
Oyster Bar/Chuckanut
Oyster Creek Inn
Pandasia
Pasta Bella
Pegasus Pizza
Perché No
Philadelphia Fevre
Phoenecia at Alki
Piecora's

Pogacha
Pon Proem
Pontevecchio
Pyramid Alehouse
Queen Mary
Racha Noodles
Red Door Ale
Rhododendron Café
Rist. Paradiso
Romio's Pizza
Roxy's Diner
Saigon Bistro
Salmon Bay Cafe
Salumeria on Hudson
Salumi
Salute of Bellevue
Salvatore Rist.
74th St. Ale
Shamiana
Shanghai Garden
Shultzy's
Simpatico
Six Degrees
Stalk Exchange
Starfish Grill
Still Life in Fremont
Stumbling Goat
Sunlight Cafe
Taqueria Guaymas
Texas Smokehouse BBQ
Thai on Mercer
That's Amore
Tosoni's
Toyoda Sushi
Two Bells Tavern
Typhoon!
Union Bay Cafe
Western Vine
World Class Chili
Zaina
Zeek's Pizza

Winning Wine List

Adriatica
Ark
Assaggio Rist.
Avenue One
Axis
Brasa
Brasserie Margaux
Bungalow Wine Bar
Cafe Campagne
Cafe Juanita
Cafe Lago
Campagne
Canlis
Cascadia

Christina's
Dahlia Lounge
Daniel's Broiler
Dulces Latin Bistro
El Gaucho
Etta's Seafood
Fleming's Prime
Flying Fish
Foghorn
Fullers
Georgian Room
Grapes
Harvest Vine
Herbfarm
Hunt Club
Il Bistro
Il Terrazzo Carmine
Inn at Langley
Kaspar's
Lampreia
Le Gourmand
Le Pichet
Metropolitan Grill
Mistral
Oyster Bar/Chuckanut
Painted Table
Palace Kitchen
Place Pigalle
Ponti Seafood Grill
Prego
Queen City Grill
Ray's Boathouse
Rover's
Ruth's Chris
Salish Lodge
Shoalwater
Szmania's
Tulio Rist.
Waterfront
Waypoints
Wild Ginger
Yarrow Bay Grill

Worth a Trip

Bainbridge Island
    Bistro Pleasant Bch.
Bow
    Oyster Bar/Chuckanut
    Oyster Creek Inn
    Rhododendron Café
Deer Harbor, Orcas Island
    Starfish Grill
Eastsound, Orcas Island
    Christina's
Langley, Whidbey Island
    Inn at Langley

Lopez Island
  Bay Cafe
Maltby
  Maltby Cafe
Nahcotta
  Ark
Port Ludlow
  Waypoints
Seaview
  Shoalwater
Snoqualmie
  Salish Lodge

Young Children

(Besides the normal fast-food
places; * indicates children's
menu available)
Angelina's Trattoria*
Anthony's*
Anthony's Pier 66*
Arnies*
Atlas Foods*
Azteca*
Baccano Rist.
Bacchus*
Bay Cafe*
Bell St. Diner*
Belltown Pub*
Bick's Broadview*
Big Time*
Billy McHale's*
Bridges on Eastlake*
Broadway Grill*
Brusseau's
Buca di Beppo
Burk's Cafe
Burrito Loco*
Cafe Flora*
Cafe Langley*
Cafe Nola*
Cafe Starbucks*
Cafe Veloce
Calabria*
Carmelita*
Cascadia*
Chandler's Crabhse.*
Chanterelle*
Chevys*
Chinook's/Salmon Bay
CJ's Eatery*
Claim Jumper*
Coho Café*
Crab Cracker*
Cucina! Cucina!*
Cutters Bayhouse*
Dish*
Duke's Chowder Hse.*

Elliott's Oyster Hse.*
Emmett Watson's*
Etta's Seafood*
5 Spot*
F.X. McRory's*
Galerias*
Gordito's*
Hale's Ales*
Hillside Manor
Hiram's at the Locks*
Honey Bear Bakery
Ivar's Acres of Clams*
Ivar's Salmon House*
Jitterbug Cafe*
Julia's of Wallingford*
Kirkland Roaster*
Leschi Lakecafe*
Lockspot Cafe*
Lombardi's Cucina*
Luna Park Cafe*
Maggie Bluff's
Maltby Cafe*
My Friends Cafe*
Original Pancake Hse.*
Pandasia*
Pasta Bella*
Pazzo's
Pike Pub*
Planet Hollywood*
Primo Grill*
Provinces*
Ray's Boathouse*
Red Robin*
Rhododendron Café*
Rist. Paradiso*
Rock Salt Steakhse.*
Rosita's Mexican*
Salish Lodge*
Santa Fe Cafe*
Sharp's Roaster*
Shoalwater*
Simpatico*
Spirit of Washington*
Stanley & Seafort's*
Starfish Grill*
St. Clouds*
Stella's Trattoria*
Szmania's*
Texas Smokehouse BBQ*
That's Amore
Tia Lou's*
Trattoria Mitchelli*
T.S. McHugh's*
Turntable*
Wolfgang Puck*
Yankee Grill
Yarrow Bay Beach*

Portland

Portland's Most Popular

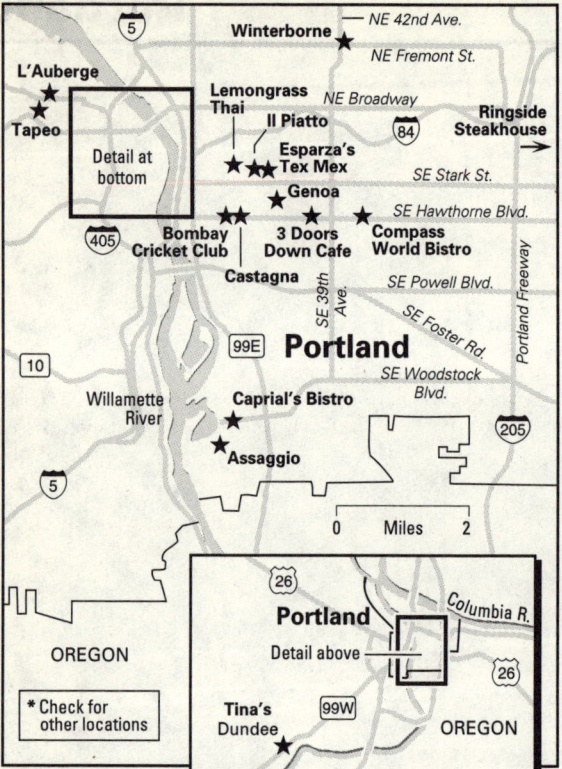

Winterborne — NE 42nd Ave.
NE Fremont St.
L'Auberge
NE Broadway
Tapeo
Lemongrass Thai
Il Piatto
Ringside Steakhouse
Detail at bottom
Esparza's Tex Mex
SE Stark St.
Genoa
Bombay Cricket Club
3 Doors Down Cafe
SE Hawthorne Blvd.
Compass World Bistro
Castagna
SE Powell Blvd.
SE Foster Rd.
Portland
SE Woodstock Blvd.
Willamette River
Caprial's Bistro
Assaggio

0   Miles   2

Portland
Detail above
Columbia R.
Tina's Dundee
OREGON
Willamette River
* Check for other locations

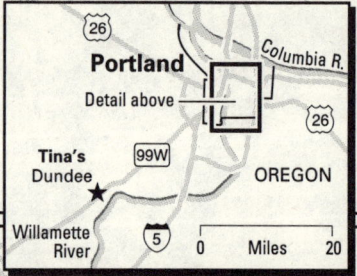

0   Miles   20

Wildwood
Paley's Place
Caffe Mingo
Tuscany Grill
NW Lovejoy St.
Cafe des Amis
NW Broadway
Lucy's Table
Fratelli
Laslow's Northwest
¡Oba! Restaurante
NW Glisan St.
Typhoon!
Le Bouchon
Il Fornaio
Bluehour
Cafe Azul
Saucebox
W Burnside St.
Ringside Steakhouse
El Gaucho
Typhoon! on Broadway
Portland Steak
Jake's Famous Crawfish
McCormick & Schmick's
SW Salmon St.
Pazzo Ristorante
Mother's Bistro
Couvron
Southpark Seafood
Higgins
The Heathman
SW Market St.
Downtown Portland

142   www.zagat.com

Portland's Most Popular

Each of our reviewers has been asked to name his or her five favorite restaurants. The 40 spots most frequently named, in order of their popularity, are:

1. Genoa
2. Wildwood
3. Higgins
4. Paley's Place
5. Castagna
6. Caffe Mingo
7. Caprial's Bistro
8. Cafe des Amis
9. Couvron
10. Jake's Famous Crawfish
11. Bluehour
12. Heathman, The
13. 3 Doors Down Cafe
14. Assaggio
15. Typhoon!
16. ¡Oba! Restaurante
17. Le Bouchon
18. Southpark Seafood
19. Cafe Azul
20. Esparza's Tex Mex*
21. Il Piatto
22. Ringside Steakhouse
23. Lucy's Table
24. Il Fornaio
25. Pazzo Ristorante
26. Tapeo
27. L'Auberge
28. Saucebox
29. Portland Steak
30. Tina's*
31. El Gaucho
32. Fratelli
33. McCormick & Schmick's*
34. Compass World Bistro
35. Lemongrass Thai*
36. Mother's Bistro*
37. Winterborne*
38. Bombay Cricket Club
39. Laslow's Northwest
40. Tuscany Grill

It's obvious that many of the restaurants on the above list are among the most expensive, but if popularity were calibrated to price, we suspect that a number of other restaurants would join the above ranks. Thus, for frugal gourmets, we have listed 80 Best Buys on page 150.

---

* Tied with the restaurant listed directly above it.

Top Ratings

Top lists exclude restaurants with low voting.

Top Food Ranking

28 Genoa
Paley's Place
Tina's
27 Joel Palmer House
Cafe des Amis
Couvron*
Pearl Bakery
Wildwood
26 Saburo's Sushi
Castagna
Winterborne
Red Hills Provincial
Restaurant Murata
Higgins
Heathman, The
25 Typhoon!
3 Doors Down Cafe
Lemongrass Thai
Laslow's Northwest
Caprial's Bistro

Sungari
Tapeo
Caffe Mingo
Cafe Azul
24 Nicholas'
Nick's Italian Cafe
Bluehour
William's on 12th
John Street Cafe
Bugatti's Ristorante
Morton's of Chicago
Hands on Café
Jake's Famous Crawfish
Clarke's
Ruth's Chris
Pho Van Vietnamese
Original Pancake Hse.
Plainfields' Mayur
23 Le Bouchon
Compass World Bistro

Top Food by Cuisine

American (New)
24 Clarke's
23 Lucy's Table
22 Papa Haydn West
Besaw's Cafe
20 Little Wing Cafe

American (Traditional)
23 Mother's Bistro
22 Bijou Cafe
Jake's Grill
21 Hall Street Grill
Red Star Tavern

Bakery
27 Pearl Bakery
22 Grand Central Bakery
21 Pazzoria
20 Il Fornaio
19 Tully's Coffee

Cafe
24 John Street Cafe
Hands on Café
22 Zell's
21 Cadillac Cafe
19 Beaterville Cafe

Chinese
25 Sungari
22 Thien Hong
21 Fong Chong
20 Legin
19 FuJin

Deli/Sandwich Shop
22 Grand Central Bakery
21 Good Dog/Bad Dog
20 Little Wing Cafe
19 Tully's Coffee
Kornblatt's Deli

Dessert
27 Pearl Bakery
26 Heathman, The
23 L'Auberge
Mother's Bistro
22 Papa Haydn East

Eclectic/International
24 John Street Cafe
Hands on Café
23 Compass World Bistro
22 Wild Abandon
Oritalia

* Tied with the restaurant listed directly above it.

Top Food

French
28 Tina's
27 Couvron
26 Castagna
   Winterborne
   Heathman, The

French (Bistro)
27 Cafe des Amis
24 William's on 12th
23 Le Bouchon
   L'Auberge
21 Esplanade

Indian
24 Plainfields' Mayur
23 Bombay Cricket Club
21 India House
20 Swagat

Italian
28 Genoa
25 Caffe Mingo
24 Nick's Italian Cafe
   Bugatti's Ristorante
23 Pazzo Ristorante

Japanese
26 Saburo's Sushi
   Restaurant Murata
23 Obi Japanese
20 Koji Osakaya
   Uogashi

Mediterranean
25 3 Doors Down Cafe
   Tapeo
24 Bluehour
23 Lucy's Table
21 Southpark Seafood

Mexican/Tex-Mex
25 Cafe Azul
22 El Burrito Loco
   Esparza's Tex Mex
20 La Calaca Comelona
19 Chez Jose

Middle Eastern
24 Nicholas'
23 Bombay Cricket Club
22 Al-Amir
21 Abou Karim
18 Hoda's

Northwest (Contemporary)
26 Red Hills Provincial
   Higgins
25 Caprial's Bistro
22 Dundee Bistro
21 Hudson's Bar & Grill

Northwest (Traditional)
28 Paley's Place
   Tina's
27 Joel Palmer House
   Wildwood
25 Laslow's Northwest

Pizza
22 Pizzicato
21 Pazzoria
   Escape From N.Y.
   Accuardi's
20 Hot Lips Pizza

Seafood
26 Winterborne
24 Jake's Famous Crawfish
23 McCormick's Fish Hse.
   McCormick & Schmick's
22 Jake's Grill

Southern/Soul
22 Delta Cafe
21 Bernie's
   Three Sq. Grill
20 Tennessee Red's
   Doris' Cafe

Steakhouse
24 Morton's of Chicago
   Ruth's Chris
23 El Gaucho
22 Jake's Grill
   Portland Steak

Thai
25 Typhoon!
   Lemongrass Thai
22 Thai Orchid
   Thanh Thao
20 Misohapi

Top Food

Top Food by Special Feature

Breakfast*
24 Original Pancake Hse.
23 Mother's Bistro (wknds.)
22 Bijou Cafe
   Besaw's Cafe
21 Cadillac Cafe

Brunch
27 Wildwood
26 Heathman, The
23 Compass World Bistro
   London Grill
22 Papa Haydn East

Hotel Dining
26 Heathman, The
   Heathman Hotel
23 Pazzo Ristorante
   Hotel Vintage Plaza
   London Grill
   Benson Hotel
22 Oritalia
   Westin Portland
21 Red Star Tavern
   Fifth Ave. Suites

Newcomers/Rated
25 Laslow's Northwest
   Sungari
24 Bluehour
23 El Gaucho
21 Fratelli

Newcomers/Unrated
   Cafe Castagna
   Grant House
   Sweet Basil
   Taqueria Nueve
   Ya Hala

Offbeat
22 Counter Culture
   Delta Cafe
   Esparza's Tex Mex
21 Salvador Molly's
20 Tao of Tea

People-Watching
24 Bluehour
   Jake's Famous Crawfish
23 ¡Oba! Restaurante
22 Bijou Cafe
21 Veritable Quandary

Worth a Trip
28 Tina's
   Dundee
27 Joel Palmer House
   Dayton
26 Red Hills Provincial
   Dundee
24 Nick's Italian Cafe
   McMinnville
21 Columbia River Court
   Hood River

---

* Other than hotels.

Top Food by Location

Downtown
- **26** Higgins
  - Heathman, The
- **25** Sungari
- **23** Pazzo Ristorante
  - El Gaucho

Hawthorne
- **26** Castagna
- **25** 3 Doors Down Cafe
- **23** Compass World Bistro
  - Bombay Cricket Club
- **22** Casablanca

Lloyd Center/NE Broadway
- **23** Paparazzi Pastaficio
- **22** Grand Central Bakery
- **21** Cadillac Cafe
  - Metronome
- **20** Koji Osakaya

Northwest Portland
- **28** Paley's Place
- **27** Wildwood
- **25** Typhoon!
  - Laslow's Northwest
  - Caffe Mingo

Pearl District
- **25** Cafe Azul
- **24** Bluehour
- **23** Le Bouchon
  - ¡Oba! Restaurante
- **22** Giorgio's

Westmoreland/Sellwood
- **26** Saburo's Sushi
- **25** Caprial's Bistro
- **22** Papa Hadyn East
  - Assaggio
  - Pizzicato

Wine Country
- **28** Tina's
- **27** Joel Palmer House
- **26** Red Hills Provincial
- **24** Nick's Italian Cafe
- **22** Dundee Bistro

Top Decor Ranking

27 Bluehour	Plainfields' Mayur
26 Oritalia	Jake's Famous Crawfish
25 Columbia River Court	Serratto
¡Oba! Restaurante	Pazzo Ristorante
Casablanca	Huber's
Joel Palmer House	**22** Southpark Seafood
24 London Grill	Tina's
Hudson's Bar & Grill	Red Hills Provincial
Tao of Tea	Castagna
Heathman, The	Il Fornaio
Genoa	Dundee Bistro
Brazen Bean	Harborside
Esplanade	Tuscany Grill
Marrakesh	L'Auberge
Higgins	Brasserie Montmartre
El Gaucho	Lucy's Table
23 Wildwood	Jo Bar & Rotisserie
Paley's Place	Alexander's
Morton's of Chicago	Il Piatto
Cafe des Amis	Red Star Tavern

Dramatic Interior

Bluehour	Hudson's Bar & Grill
Cafe Azul	¡Oba! Restaurante
El Gaucho	Oritalia
Heathman, The	Serratto
Higgins	Wildwood

Outdoor

Beaches	Harborside
Compass World Bistro	L'Auberge
Esplanade	Riccardo's
Grant House	Sweet Basil
Hall Street Grill	Tara Thai House
Hands on Café	Veritable Quandary

Romantic

Brazen Bean	La Catalana
Cafe des Amis	L'Auberge
Casablanca	Oritalia
Couvron	Paley's Place
El Gaucho	Pazzo Ristorante
Genoa	Red Hills Provincial
Giorgio's	Tina's
Higgins	William's on 12th

View

Alexander's	Esplanade
Beaches	Harborside
Columbia River Court	McMenamins/Columbia

Top Service Ranking

28 Genoa

26 Paley's Place
Cafe des Amis

25 Couvron
Castagna
Tina's
Higgins

24 London Grill
Joel Palmer House
Heathman, The
El Gaucho
Winterborne
Wildwood
John Street Cafe
Laslow's Northwest

23 Morton's of Chicago
Compass World Bistro
Ruth's Chris
Nick's Italian Cafe
Red Hills Provincial

3 Doors Down Cafe
William's on 12th
Jake's Famous Crawfish
L'Auberge
Alexander's

22 Caffe Mingo
Bugatti's Ristorante
Clarke's
Cafe Azul
Lucy's Table*
Counter Culture
Plainfields' Mayur
Giorgio's
Caprial's Bistro
Mother's Bistro
Chameleon
Casablanca
McCormick's Fish Hse.
Sungari
Columbia River Court

---

* Tied with the restaurant listed directly above it.

Best Buys

Top Bangs for the Buck

This list is derived by dividing the cost of a meal into its combined ratings.

1. Dog House
2. Big Dan's
3. El Burrito Loco
4. Pearl Bakery
5. Good Dog/Bad Dog
6. Escape From N.Y.
7. Grand Central Bakery
8. Tao of Tea
9. Beaterville Cafe
10. Tully's Coffee
11. Fuller's Coffee Shop
12. Fat City Cafe
13. J & M Cafe
14. John Street Cafe
15. Pazzoria
16. Anne Hughes Kitchen
17. Original Pancake Hse.
18. Hot Lips Pizza
19. Byways Cafe
20. Nicholas'
21. Pho Van Vietnamese
22. Hands on Café
23. Hungry Dog Burrito
24. Cup & Saucer Cafe
25. Accuardi's
26. Horn of Africa
27. Delta Cafe
28. Cadillac Cafe
29. Bijou Cafe
30. Stanich's
31. Maya's Taqueria
32. Macheezmo Mouse
33. Counter Culture
34. Garbonzos
35. Pasta Veloce
36. Pizzicato
37. Stickers Asian Cafe
38. Dot's Cafe
39. Misohapi
40. Thien Hong

Additional Good Values

Moderately priced restaurants that give you your money's worth.

Alameda Brewhouse
Alameda Cafe
Besaw's Cafe
Brazen Bean
BridgePort Ale House
BridgePort Brew Pub
Buster's
Campbell's Bar-B-Q
Daily Cafe
Doris' Cafe
Esparza's Tex Mex
Foothill Broiler
Fusion
Gustav's Bier Stube
Henry's Cafe
Hoda's
Ken's Home Plate
Kornblatt's Deli
La Buca
La Calaca Comelona

La Cruda
Little Wing Cafe
Marco's Cafe
Milo's City Cafe
Noho's Hawaiian Cafe
Old Spaghetti Factory
Old Wives' Tales
Pambiche
Produce Row Cafe
Red Electric Cafe
Salvador Molly's
Siam
Taqueria La Sirenita
Tennessee Red's
Thai Kitchen
Thai Orchid
Thai Touch
Thanh Thao
Yen Ha
Zell's

Portland
Restaurant Directory

Portland

F	D	S	C

Abou Karim S
21 | 15 | 19 | $19

221 SW Pine St. (bet. 2nd & 3rd Aves.), 503-223-5058

■ This "always busy" but "low-key" Downtown Middle Eastern has served up "healthy, fresh" fare that's been "consistent for 25 years"; for a "great light lunch", loyalists elect the "lovely meze plate", an "assortment of Lebanese dishes" that includes "wonderful hummus" and pita, all leavened by "delightful service."

Accuardi's Old Town Pizza S
21 | 19 | 16 | $14

226 NW Davis St. (bet. 2nd & 3rd Aves.), 503-222-9999

■ "The perfect place for pizza!" cry townies about this Old Town institution, which has been slinging pies for over 25 years; regulars recommend the "classic Dragon Lady" version (artichokes and sun-dried tomatoes) and are devoted to the "Victorian-style", "funky atmosphere" that's a "jumble of cozy furniture"; however, this parlor's popularity may mean "finding a seat is a challenge."

Alameda Brewhouse S
16 | 17 | 16 | $16

4765 NE Fremont St. (47th Ave.), 503-460-9025

☑ Hopheads hail the homemade "epic bevs" at this Beaumont microbrewery "that's a cut above average", though the American pub grub served in "HUGE portions" underwhelms some, who call it "uneven" and "ordinary"; the "industrial setting" is "strangely attractive", if a bit "chilly due to the high ceilings", but "one sip of the stout shake" will warm you up.

Alameda Cafe, The S
17 | 17 | 18 | $16

4641 NE Fremont St. (47th Ave.), 503-284-5314

☑ Regulars are reluctant "to tell others how much they love" this American-Eclectic in Beaumont, known for its "great breakfasts", lunchtime sandwiches and innovative dinner specials; the "cute", "comfy" digs create a "neighborhood hangout", though some protest it's no more than an "overpriced," "upscale coffee shop"; N.B. a new chef may outdate the above food rating.

Al-Amir S
22 | 19 | 21 | $22

223 SW Stark St. (bet. 2nd & 3rd Aves.), 503-274-0010

■ For "elegance in Middle Eastern food", this "festive favorite" in the historic Bishop's House Downtown sets "the standard": the chef's way with "seasonings is the stuff of legend" and the "lamb and chicken are always cooked right"; it's "fun with a group" on weekends, offering "entertaining belly dancing."

Alessandro's – | – | – | M

301 SW Morrison St. (3rd Ave.), 503-222-3900

Popular at lunch with Downtown suits and shoppers, this traditional Italian serves penne Gorgonzola, oysters almondine and various veal dishes; it elevates its beneath-a-parking-garage perch by dressing up Mediterranean-style: wicker, wood and red, white and green tablecloths.

Alexander's 21 | 22 | 23 | $34

Hilton Portland, 921 SW Sixth Ave. (bet. Salmon & Taylor Sts.), 503-226-1611

◪ Atop the Downtown Hilton, this NW's panoramic "great view" and piano music don't distract diners from the "outstanding food" and the attentions of the maitre d', which are "worth the price of admission"; a few dissenters decry the tariff, warning "bring the platinum", and carp it's "a corporate cookie-cutter version of upscale."

Alexis Restaurant 21 | 17 | 21 | $23

215 W. Burnside St. (bet. 2nd & 3rd Aves.), 503-224-8577

■ For "traditional Greek", this family-run taverna on the edge of Old Town elicits a chorus of raves, especially for the "best calamari" and "hearty portions"; its "old-world look", "fun belly dancing" and "perky service" have made it "great for special occasions" for over 20 years, but a few independents insist it "seems to be skating" on its reputation.

Anne Hughes Kitchen Table Cafe 💳 18 | 15 | 14 | $11

400 SE 12th Ave. (Oak St.), 503-230-6977

■ For "the kitchen table and family you wish you had", home in on this "charming" Eastsider featuring traditional American breakfast and lunch; "perfectly prepared soup and salad", the "best sandwiches" (including an "amazing egg salad") and "good cookies" vie for your inner child's attention in this spot with "funky '60s flair", but a few prodigals pout "there's no whipped cream for the cocoa."

ASSAGGIO 22 | 21 | 21 | $28

7742 SE 13th Ave. (Lambert St.), 503-232-6151

◪ "Every meal is an aria" at this "classy" Sellwood Italian that packs 'em in with its "inventive", largely "vegetarian-friendly" cuisine; fans recommend the "terrific" *assaggio di pasta* (translated as a 'sampling' of three noodle dishes), washed down by "great" vinos (which you can also order at the "hip" wine bar); counter-tenors complain it's a "spot to be seen in but not heard", and the long wait–producing "no-reservations" policy is "a hassle."

Bamboos [S] 18 | 12 | 17 | $16

103 NW 21st Ave. (Davis St.), 503-241-8122

◪ This "typical Chinese" in Northwest serves "basic fare" (surveyors single out the sesame beef) in "generous portions" for "good prices"; the bamboozled find "no surprises, no big hits" and boo the less-than-friendly service.

Baobab [S] | 19 | 16 | 16 | $19 |

42 NW Eighth Ave. (bet. Flanders & Glisan Sts.), 503-241-0390

◪ "Once you find" this Senegalese sapling in the Pearl District, it's "worth it" for the "interesting menu", especially the chicken in mustard sauce, as well as the "cute" atmosphere and "outdoor tables" that allow for canine customers; non–tree-huggers say the "food presentation is somewhat crude" and the fiery "spices spoil the palate", but others douse the fire with African beer and wine.

Bastas Trattoria [S] | 20 | 18 | 19 | $26 |

410 NW 21st Ave. (Flanders St.), 503-274-1572

◪ One of several "solid" Italians in Northwest, where the "great collection of Italian wines" and "huge portions" of "excellently prepared" "unusual" pastas – some hop for the "rabbit" version – are all "reasonably priced"; those who like livin' *la dolce vita* dig its "trendy" setting in a "converted fast-food joint", but others opine the setting's "odd" and say *basta* to the "uneven service."

Beaches Restaurant & Bar [S] | 17 | 19 | 20 | $22 |

Murray Scholls Town Ctr., 14550 Murray Scholls Dr. (bet. Murray Blvd. & Scholls Ferry Rd.), Beaverton, 503-579-3737

1919 SE Columbia River Dr. (1 mi. east of I-5), Vancouver, WA, 503-222-9947

■ Go coastal at this "upbeat" Vancouver American that provides a "great riverside view", as well as "something for everyone": parents sail in for "consistently good food", including "excellent ribs", kiddies clamor for pizza and "buckets of toys" while singles surf the "great happy hour" scene; a few landlubbers lament this "crowded" beach is "too loud"; N.B. comb their new shoreline in Beaverton.

Beaterville Cafe [S]⊘ | 19 | 19 | 16 | $11 |

2201 N. Killingsworth St. (bet. Gay & Omaha Aves.), 503-735-4652

◪ "Breakfast freaks" beat a path to this "quirky", "comfy" American in North Portland known for its "kitschy decor"; beatniks dig the "tasty omelets" and "delicious burgers" served by a "delightfully insane staff", but a few hotheads contend they're "too cool to care about customers."

Berbati ◐ | 18 | 15 | 17 | $19 |

19 SW Second Ave. (bet. Ankeny & Burnside Sts.), 503-226-2122

■ For a "rock 'n' roll dinner", bop on over to this Downtown Greek eatery serving "exotic and delicious" fare as a warm-up act for a "hell of a music venue" (Berbati's Pan, located in the back of the restaurant) that "starts hopping after 9 PM"; other attractions include "ping-pong", "amazing happy-hour deals" and "nice owners."

Berlin Inn German Restaurant & Bakery S
21 | 16 | 19 | $21

3131 SE 12th Ave. (Powell Blvd.), 503-236-6761

■ Diners say *danke* for this Eastside Deutschlander, where the "delightful", "reasonably priced food" "like your German grandma makes" is "not for dieters" (there are, however, vegetarian options); the brunch bunch says it's best in "summer when you can eat outside" in the "beer garden" as an alternative to the occasionally "cramped converted-house" setting; P.S. try the bakery for "good desserts" and imported comestibles.

Bernie's Southern Bistro
21 | 20 | 20 | $24

2904 NE Alberta St. (29th Ave.), 503-282-9864

■ Serving Southern "comfort food" in Northeast Portland, this "welcome addition" to an "up-and-coming" nabe offers "hospitality" to "homesick" diners; its confederates march for the "charming" atmosphere, and belles ring for the "best buttermilk fried chicken", "catfish done right", "fabulous fried green tomatoes" and "lavish drinks", even though a few rebels yell "is everything fried?"

Besaw's Cafe S
22 | 17 | 20 | $19

2301 NW Savier St. (23rd Ave.), 503-228-2619

■ Since 1903 breakfast buffs have "stormed the doors" at this NW-American "small place with big food ideas" in Northwest; "loyal customers" tuck into "fluffy eggs" and salmon Benedict and move on to "tasty appetizers", "the best meat loaf sandwiches" and other "consistent" choices for lunch and dinner; though it's "dizzyingly busy", the "fun visible kitchen" and "superb service" keep it "hustlin' and bustlin'."

Big Dan's West Coast Bento ⊅
23 | 8 | 18 | $7

2346 NW Westover Rd. (23rd Pl.), 503-227-1779

■ "Get it to go" is the way to dine at this pared-down Japanese longtime lunch stop in Northwest with "limited options" but "prime" and "dependable" chicken dressed with a "fun selection of sauces"; "no-frills" means quick service even during the busy midday crush.

Bijou Cafe S
22 | 17 | 20 | $15

132 SW Third Ave. (Pine St.), 503-222-3187

■ This Downtown Contemporary American gem offers "rock-solid, perfectly prepared wholesome breakfast" and lunch using mostly "organic, local ingredients"; corn-flour pancakes, the "freshest eggs" and "standout snapper hash" all shine, served in a "simple wainscoted interior"; the repeat cast includes the "quintessential" Portland elite – "politicians, lawyers, architects and urban planners", who all "gather and gossip" here.

Billy Reed's Restaurant & Bar S   15 | 17 | 17 | $19
2808 NE Martin Luther King Jr. Blvd. (Graham St.), 503-493-8127
☑ This Traditional American "hoppin' pub" rocks its "cool" restored 1927 dairy building in North Portland with "great music" and a "hot atmosphere"; the "broad menu" stars Kentucky bourbon chicken and "lots o' meat", but a few foes say the newcomer's "fun feels prefab."

Bistro 921 S   16 | 17 | 16 | $22
Hilton Portland, 921 SW Sixth Ave. (Taylor St.), 503-220-2685
☑ For casual dining with a NW emphasis, this Downtown Hilton bistro offers "above-average hotel fare" that's "okay for a quick fix"; the menu rotates, as do the chefs, and opponents opine the service suffers in the shuffle.

BLUEHOUR   24 | 27 | 22 | $42
250 NW 13th Ave. (Everett St.), 503-226-3394
■ "Wear black and you'll fit in" at this "instant hit" in the Pearl, serving "inventive" but "surprisingly unpretentious" French-Italian-Med cuisine; the dishes are "elegant from start to finish", ranging from "celestial salmon tartare" and seasonal "pumpkin ravioli that's a taste of fall" to "unforgettable chocolate pudding", all "superbly served" in "lovely surroundings" (voted No. 1 in Portland for Decor) with high ceilings and drapes that create intimate areas; P.S. it's red-"hot, hot, hot", so make reservations.

Bombay Cricket Club Restaurant S   23 | 17 | 20 | $22
1925 SE Hawthorne Blvd. (bet. 19th & 20th Aves.), 503-231-0740
■ Bowlers and batsmen team up at this Hawthorne "new-wave Indian" that also serves Middle Eastern dishes, where you can "catch a cricket match" on the telly and a buzz from "strong mango margaritas"; "complex curries" and "delicious lamb masala" are "spiced just right", and though the "Raj theme may be a bit un–PC", the "lively scene" means it's "difficult to get a table."

Brasilia Restaurant & Bar   15 | 13 | 17 | $23
6401 SW Macadam Ave. (Dakota St.), 503-293-2219
☑ Samba to Johns Landing for dinner at this Brazilian known for its "coffeeshop-meets-the-tropics" setting; its signature dish is feijoada (a national specialty of black beans, pork, rice and greens), but to be really happy "you'd better like coconut and plantains", and you can blame it on Rio if it gets "too noisy."

Brasserie Montmartre ●S   20 | 22 | 19 | $27
626 SW Park Ave. (bet. Alder & Morrison Sts.), 503-224-5552
■ Boulevardiers swarm this long-running French bistro Downtown ("within walking distance of cultural" attractions) known as a "great date place"; the "fly-you-to-the-moon seafood bisque" and "wonderful pâté" are outdone only by twice-weekly magicians and "live jazz", but some snipe the Tou-louse ambiance is "more interesting than the menu."

Brazen Bean ◑
18 | 24 | 17 | $18

2075 NW Glisan St. (21st Ave.), 503-294-0636

■ Those who've bean there, done that know about the "yummy $3" libations during "the best happy hour" at this hip Eclectic in Northwest, serving starters, snacks and desserts; the "novel", "intimate atmosphere" is perfect for a "rainy-night" repast of "great chocolate martinis", smoked salmon and fondue, but a few advise: "watch out for cigars."

Bread & Ink Cafe S
21 | 17 | 18 | $22

3610 SE Hawthorne Blvd. (bet. 36th & 37th Aves.), 503-239-4756

■ "Wild and witty wall hangings" adorn this "relaxed" Hawthorne Eclectic "classic" where everyone from hipsters to "old hippies" comes to loaf; the flour power's in the homemade "perfect baguettes" and "divine cheese blintzes" (they're famous for their "fabulous Yiddish brunch") as well as an "imaginative" lunch and dinner menu; though it's "reliable and reasonably priced", a few ink-stained wretches report "it needs a new-millennium injection."

BridgePort Ale House S
17 | 18 | 16 | $16

3632 SE Hawthorne Blvd. (bet. 36th & 37th Aves.), 503-233-6540

■ "Bring your beer buddies" to this Hawthorne "haven" serving American pub food: "luscious burgers", "great pizza" and pasta, with "potent" brews; some dig the "nice digs", but a few find the "sterile" decor ails 'em.

BridgePort Brew Pub S
16 | 17 | 15 | $14

1313 NW Marshall St. (bet. 13th & 14th Aves.), 503-241-3612

■ This "always hopping" ivy-covered Pearl District brewpub is Portland's oldest, pumping out "authentic bevs", soups, sandwiches and "claim-to-fame pizza" with crust fashioned with unfermented beer wort; for those "in need of recalling college days", it's a "fun place to hang out with friends", play "darts" and "slum it", although English majors find the laid-back service an "oxymoron."

Bugatti's Caffe & Pizzeria S
– | – | – | I

1885 Blankenship Rd. (10th St.), West Linn, 503-557-8686

With a special kids' menu, you can take the whole family to this bright, shiny Italian newcomer in West Linn (next to its popular, larger, longtime big brother, Bugatti's), serving pizzas, panini, gourmet burgers and 18 beers on tap.

Bugatti's Ristorante S
24 | 20 | 22 | $30

18740 Willamette Dr. (Fairview Way), West Linn, 503-636-9555

■ "Worth the trip to West Linn", this family-owned Southern Italian offers "elegant", "romantic" dining (particularly in the "great courtyard"); the "modestly priced" fare is "fantastic from starters to dessert", including "excellent Caesar salad", "pasta with crab" and "yummy profiteroles", though some regulars request "changes in the menu, please."

Burgerville USA S   – | – | – | 1
*1135 NE Martin Luther King Jr. Blvd. (Multnomah St.),
503-235-6858*
1122 SE Hawthorne Blvd. (11th Ave.), 503-230-0479
3432 SE 25th Ave. (Powell Blvd.), 503-239-5942
16211 SE Division St. (162nd Ave.), 503-762-1648
429 SE 122nd St. (Stark St.), 503-253-0553
8218 NE Glisan St. (82nd Ave.), 503-255-2815
4229 NE 122nd Ave. (Sandy Blvd.), 503-252-1804
3504 SE 92nd Ave. (Powell Blvd.), 503-777-7078
307 E. Mill Plain Blvd. (3rd St.), Vancouver, WA, 360-693-8801
*7401 E. Mill Plain Blvd. (Morrison Rd.), Vancouver, WA,
360-694-4971*
Dairy queens "couldn't live without the real-milk milk
shakes" (with fresh fruit) at this citywide chain built on
serving locally-inspired fast food such as Tillamook
cheeseburgers, Walla Walla onion rings, berry desserts
and espresso drinks in "spotlessly clean" surroundings,
some with '50s-themed decor; N.B. those in a hurry can
always use the drive-through.

Bush Garden S   19 | 21 | 19 | $27
900 SW Morrison St. (9th Ave.), 503-226-7181
*8290 SW Nyberg St. (Tualatin-Sherwood Rd.), Tualatin,
503-691-9744*

Bush Soba S
*10500 SW Beaverton-Hillsdale Hwy. (bet. 107th &
Western Aves.), Beaverton, 503-469-9077*
◪ "Take your shoes off" when you dine in the "authentic
tatami rooms" at these Japanese "jewels" that are
"picturesque and serene for the taste buds as well";
debate swirls around the price and dependability of the
sushi, though an entertaining counter chef is a sure thing;
N.B. the Tualatin offshoot is unrated.

Buster's Texas-Style Barbecue S   18 | 13 | 14 | $15
1355 NE Burnside Rd. (Division St.), Gresham, 503-667-4811
*17883 SE McLoughlin Blvd. (bet. Boardman & Jennings Aves.),
Milwaukie, 503-652-1076*
11419 SW Pacific Hwy. (65th Ave.), Tigard, 503-452-8384
1118 NE 78th St. (13th Ave.), Vancouver, WA, 360-546-2439
◪ "Thanks, Texas" for this "folksy" family-owned minichain
made for barbeque wranglers "in the mood to get messy";
the 'cue is "basic, brawny" and "hard to beat", with a
"variety of sauces" and "good-value side dishes", but
traditionalists caution "it doesn't compare" to Lone Star fare.

Byways Cafe S   17 | 15 | 16 | $11
1212 NW Glisan St. (12th Ave.), 503-221-0011
◪ This Pearl District American diner is a "popular breakfast
spot" that also attracts hungry travelers with its "awesome
burgers and shakes"; the "fun decor" with its road trip
theme includes Viewmasters at each table, but a few
stay-at-homes insist "once is enough."

Cadillac Cafe S 　　　　21 | 15 | 18 | $14
914 NE Broadway (9th Ave.), 503-287-4750
■ "There's a reason the line is always long" outside this Northeast "Pepto-pink" diner serving American fare; auto-mates marvel at the "divine breakfasts" that include hazelnut French toast, as well as "excellent burgers" and "fabulous Reubens" for lunch, and "comfortable staff and atmosphere" make it easy to see why "it's worth the wait."

CAFE AZUL 　　　　25 | 21 | 22 | $33
112 NW Ninth Ave. (bet. Couch & Davis Sts.), 503-525-4422
◪ "Haute Mexican" that would make "Diane Kennedy proud" transforms this Pearl spot into a "sophisticated" experience; "homemade chips and salsa" are hard to resist, and the "vibrantly flavored" "mole is darn close to what you'd find in Oaxaca"; though the "service is impeccable" and the "ambiance lovely", a few gringos gripe it's "too expensive" and "overly noisy."

Cafe Castagna S 　　　　– | – | – | M
1758 SE Hawthorne Blvd. (18th Ave.), 503-231-9959
This casually chic Italian-French bistro in Hawthorne shares a kitchen and strong international wine list with its upscale next-door parent, Castagna, turning out traditional roast chicken, cassoulet, pizza and homemade sorbets in a spare gray space just right for equally chic crowds.

CAFE DES AMIS 　　　　27 | 23 | 26 | $40
1987 NW Kearney St. (20th Ave.), 503-295-6487
■ A "long-standing favorite" of Francophiles, this Gallic "classic" in the Northwest District features a "charming setting" that's the backdrop for "intimate dining"; its many friends say *encore* to "satiny soups", the "duck with blackberry sauce" and an "excellent wine list" but save loud cheers for the "superior service"; N.B. they've added a new franc-friendly bistro menu.

CAFFE MINGO S 　　　　25 | 21 | 22 | $29
807 NW 21st Ave. (bet. Johnson & Kearney Sts.), 503-226-4646
■ "A tiny room full of Tuscan sunshine" keeps the *famiglia* growing at this trattoria in Northwest that's a "crowded" pleaser; the chef's "maniacal passion for fine food" produces "fabulous risotto" and the "best pasta around"; *paesani* appreciate the "jolly, 'peasanty' atmosphere" and "good value", but even regulars regard the "no-reservations policy" for parties under six as "a real problem."

Campbell's Bar-B-Q 　　　　22 | 9 | 17 | $16
8701 SE Powell Blvd. (bet. 87th & 88th Aves.), 503-777-9795
■ "Test your spice quotient" at this suburban Southeast family-friendly spot where patrons "pig out" on "Texas-size servings" of "tasty and tender" pork with "zingy sauces"; though the ambiance is "budget country", city slickers find it "worth the drive" for the "best 'cue in town, y'all."

CAPRIAL'S BISTRO   25   21   22 $34
7015 SE Milwaukie Ave. (Bybee Blvd.), 503-236-6457
■ Devotees of the "seasonal" NW fare served at PBS chef Caprial Pence's "premier place" in Westmoreland say it's "as good as her cookbooks"; the recently "enlarged" "lovely new space" sets the stage for "creative", "beautifully presented" dishes with a "slight Asian accent", and the "reasonably priced" 250-choice "wall of wine" provides another "grand" reason to celebrate here; stargazers "like seeing [the owner] work with her staff."

CASABLANCA MOROCCAN   22   25   22 $24
RESTAURANT Ⓢ
2221 SE Hawthorne Blvd. (22nd Ave.), 503-233-4400
■ "You'll feel like you've entered another country" at this family-run Hawthorne Moroccan where "exotic divans", brass tables and billowing fabric ceilings almost "upstage" the "lovely couscous", baklava and other "wonderful" dishes; P.S. you must remember this: "make sure the belly dancer is scheduled."

Cassidy's ◗Ⓢ   17   16   18 $23
1331 SW Washington St. (bet. 13th & 14th Aves.),
503-223-0054
■ Regulars have hopped along to this Downtown Northwest "solid standby" for over 20 years, attracted by its "cool atmosphere" that feels both "homey" and "classic"; featuring NW cuisine, the "changing menu" is "always interesting" and perfect "pre-play or -movie", but even its partisans agree: "it's a bar with a restaurant attached."

CASTAGNA   26   22   25 $41
1752 SE Hawthorne Blvd. (18th Ave.), 503-231-7373
■ This Hawthrone French newcomer that is an embodiment of the "clear vision" of husband-and-wife owners Kevin Gibson ("former Genoa chef") and Monique Siu (ex Zefiro), where the kitchen "artistically" creates "spectacular scallops, duck and rack of lamb" using "clean, pure flavors [that] echo the minimalist decor" (though a few find it "sterile"); with a "varied, affordable wine list" and "gracious service", it's a "chic place for clients" and out-of-towners.

Caswell ◗   16   17   15 $21
533 SE Grand Ave. (Washington St.), 503-232-6512
▧ Diners divide on this "comfortable", "romantic" Eastside bistro on a busy arterial, serving Eclectic-American fare from steaks to pizzas that fans call "the big yum" and appreciate even more for its late-night availability and "money's-worth" prices; foes, however, find there's a "long wait from the sleepy kitchen" under new ownership.

Cedar's Lebanese   ▽ 21 | 14 | 19 | $18

*Johns Landing Shopping Ctr., 5331 SW Macadam Ave.,
503-224-4695*

■ Those in the know say this family-owned Johns Landing
Lebanese's location in a commercial building is "the best-
kept secret in town", serving "good-value, quality" dishes
like meze (with "to-die-for hummus"), kebabs and baklava.

Celadon S   21 | 17 | 19 | $26

1203 NW 23rd Ave. (Northrup St.), 503-464-9222

■ Adventurers discover "Pan-Asian perfection" at this
"difficult-to-find" Northwest "hidden treasure" where you
have to step down from the sidewalk on a busy avenue into
a cool, celadon-hued setting; offering a mainly Japanese
and Korean menu that stars "decadent, melt-in-your-mouth
sushi" and bibimbop, it's "different from the standard."

Chameleon Restaurant & Bar   21 | 18 | 22 | $28

2000 NE 40th Ave. (Sandy Blvd.), 503-460-2682

■ "Almost invisible but worth finding", this Northeast
Eclectic is considered by some to be the "most underrated
restaurant in town"; its "unique menu" with "fusion
instincts" is "elegantly presented" in a "marvelous
atmosphere", and though the wowed wonder "why they
don't get more business", a few feel a "broader menu"
might improve its karma.

Chevys Fresh Mex S   16 | 15 | 16 | $17

8400 SW Nimbus Ave. (Hall Blvd.), Beaverton, 503-626-7667
*Clackamas Promenade, 12520 SE 93rd Ave. (Sunnyside Rd.),
Clackamas, 503-654-1333*
1951 NW 185th Ave. (Cornell Rd.), Hillsboro, 503-690-4524
*14991 SW Bangy Rd. (Meadows Rd.), Lake Oswego,
503-620-7700*
*4315 NE Thurston Way (Hwy. 500), Vancouver, WA,
360-256-6922*

☑ "Great for kids who get to watch the tortilla machine"
(aka the "hokey" El Machino), this chain also attracts
adult amigos with "simple, fun Mexican" fare, especially
the "fresh fajitas" and "flawless chips and salsa"; a few
with road rage growl that the grub's "average at best"
and the crowds make 'em "feel like cattle."

Chez Grill ◑S   18 | 18 | 18 | $20

*2229 SE Hawthorne Blvd. (bet. 22nd & 23rd Aves.),
503-239-4002*

■ Homies head to this Hawthorne hot spot for "upscale"
Southwestern basics such as "fish tacos" that are a "step
up from ordinary"; it's doubly distinguished for its "hip"
and "knowledgeable" bar that slings "superb" "fresh-fruit
margaritas", making this a "great place for a summer
evening" or a "perfect break in a gray Portland winter."

Chez Jose East S　　　　19 | 17 | 18 | $18
2200 NE Broadway (22nd Ave.), 503-280-9888
Chez Jose West S
8502 SW Terwilliger Blvd. (Taylors Ferry Rd.),
503-244-0007
■ "Kid-friendly to the max", this Mex in Northeast has been
in full fiesta mode for 10 years, especially since "moms
love the margaritas" and the "all-you-can-eat chips and
salsa"; the "quick and inexpensive" fare includes "lime-
chicken enchiladas" and "interesting specials" while
the Day-of-the-Dead decor features "plastic bugs and
skeletons"; N.B. its Southwest twin is unrated.

Chez What? S　　　　－|－|－| l
2203 NE Alberta St. (22nd Ave.), 503-281-1717
Join the young and the pierced for a thick 'Laguna Tuna'
with avocado on crusty bread at this hoppin' American
cafe along the Alberta corridor in Northeast with "funky
decor" (notably ceramic poodles) and "spunky waitresses"
who deliver breakfast all day, as well as "greasy-spoon"
hamburgers and veggie specials; Tuesday nights feature
'Basketti Madness' – all-you-can-eat spaghetti and garlic
bread for six bucks.

Clarke's　　　　24 | 18 | 22 | $33
455 Second St. (bet. A & B Aves.), Lake Oswego,
503-636-2667
◩ Acolytes assert that this spacious "neighborhood cafe"
run by Jonathan and Laurie Clarke in Lake Oswego delivers
"wonderful" New American, French and Northern Italian
dishes, "excellent service" and "beautiful ambiance", as
well as 100 wine choices; however, a few heretics deem
the dishes "overrated", adding they "need flavor."

Colosso ◖S　　　　18 | 19 | 17 | $19
1932 NE Broadway (bet. 19th & 21st Aves.), 503-288-3333
■ Go "to be seen" at this Northeast Broadway Iberian
"hipster haven", whose "piquant menu" includes "authentic
tapas" and the "best Spanish coffees" made with espresso
to fuel the "late-night dining" crowd; admittedly, "it costs
a lot to fill up here", but the "cool" environs, including a "bar
top made from a bowling alley lane", make it worthwhile.

COLUMBIA RIVER COURT　　21 | 25 | 22 | $35
DINING ROOM S
Columbia Gorge Hotel, 4000 Westcliff Dr. (I-84, exit 62),
Hood River, 541-386-5566
◩ "Ask for a window seat" at this "romantic", historic
(circa 1921) hotel "charmer", "scenically located" on the
Columbia River; some love to gorge on the NW cuisine that
uses "local foods" (the "fit-for-a-queen" "farm breakfast"
especially is "worth the drive"), but homebodies harrumph
that the "great atmosphere" calls for "much better" dining.

Compass World Bistro S　　　23 │ 21 │ 23 │ $28
4741 SE Hawthorne Blvd. (48th Ave.), 503-231-4840

■ "The compass points to a different direction, and with it, the menu changes" every three months at this Hawthorne "secret", a "cool concept" that produces "innovative", Eclectic-International fare in "surprising combinations"; the "thoughtful wine list" reflects the global reach of the cuisine, and the "homey, parlor-like" setting and "magical patio" outdoors make this a year-round "favorite."

Counter Culture S　　　22 │ 16 │ 22 │ $16
3000 NE Killingsworth St. (30th Ave.), 503-249-3799

■ "Hooray! upmarket vegan" cheer the cultured of this "exceptional" Northeast oasis that serves "inventive" Eclectic-Kosher dishes using no animal products, where cultured types opt for "amazing" specials like the seitan satay, "great salads" and other "high-quality dishes"; in this "stylish" atmosphere, the only squares are the dinner-time meals and weekend brunches.

COUVRON　　　27 │ 22 │ 25 │ $66
1126 SW 18th Ave. (bet. Madison & Salmon Sts.), 503-225-1844

■ "Every bite is truly delicious" at this "tiny", "elegant" Westside Contemporary French – the crème de la crème in local "haute cuisine", famed for its "fanatical devotion" to "world-class" flavors, "architectural presentations" and "personalized service"; featuring five-, seven- and nine-course "amazing prix fixe" meals only (the "vegetarian offering brings tears" to some eyes), it's an "expensive splurge", but go ahead – "sell the family jewels and enjoy."

Cozze S　　　20 │ 16 │ 21 │ $27
1205 SE Morrison St. (bet. 12th & 13th Aves.), 503-232-3275

■ Known for its "well-thought-out *Big Night*" Monday dinners, where they recreate the menu from the movie, this Southeast Italian is "so cozy, comforting and caring" that folks "let the chef" make the decisions; regulars "love the booths" and order "excellent Caesar salads", "very good" *cozze* (mussels) and "seafood lasagna in a bowl."

Cup & Saucer Cafe S ⌿　　　19 │ 14 │ 15 │ $12
3566 SE Hawthorne Blvd. (bet. 35th & 36h Aves.), 503-236-6001

◪ "The lines never slacken" at this "funky" Hawthorne American cafe dishing up "cheap", "filling breakfast" all day and into the evening, washed down by "lots of java"; famed for any-way-you-want-'em home fries, they also offer "out-of-this-world vanilla scones" and "vegan goodies", though a few find cracks in the crockery, citing big "crowds" and "slow service."

Daily Cafe @ Rejuvenation [S] ▽ 23 | 19 | 19 | $11

Rejuvenation House Parts, 1100 SE Grand Ave. (Taylor St.), 503-234-8189

Daily Cafe in the Pearl [S]

902 NW 13th Ave. (bet. NW Kearney & NW Lovejoy St.), 503-242-1916

■ Life's literally chock-full of nuts and bolts at this Eclectic "dandy little lunch spot" located in Southeast's Rejuvenation House Parts; do-it-yourselfers "love the cute Italian" panini, "homemade soups", the "best cookies" and "great coffee" after browsing the "cool" hardware and handcrafted furniture in the store, and the "good prices" and "nice people" help make this "a rejuvenating experience"; N.B. at press time, a new location is set to open in the Pearl.

Dan & Louis' Oyster Bar [S] 17 | 20 | 18 | $19

208 SW Ankeny St. (bet. 2nd & 3rd Aves.), 503-227-5906

◪ This Downtown seafooder, a Portland "landmark", has been luring them in since 1907, and the "Gay Nineties shipboard atmosphere" and walls "adorned with nautical artifacts" make for a "great piece of history"; its maties maintain it's "wonderful for oysters, no matter how you order them" and their "fried shrimp is the best in the world", but a few landlubbers lament the "so-so" food at this "tourist trap."

Delta Cafe [S]≠ 22 | 18 | 17 | $14

4607 SE Woodstock Blvd. (46th Ave.), 503-771-3101

■ "Down-home Southern cooking meets pink hair and piercings" at this Woodstock Soul Fooder near Reed College; the "hick chic" say "you get a lot for your money", including "killer fried chicken", "sublime catfish" and "heavenly succotash", but there's "no need to order salad – it's all there in the Bloody Mary"; P.S. regulars rave about a recent remodel: "looks great – less wait."

Dog House, The [S]≠ 20 | 12 | 20 | $7

2845 E. Burnside St. (bet. 28th & 29th Aves.), 503-239-3647

■ "Hardworking, honest dogs" are man's best friend at this parking lot–located Northeast wiener hut that also offers bratwurst and kielbasa at "good value" (it's Portland's No. 1 Bang for the Buck), though if you relish a "veggie" version, "get there early"; its faithful companions hunker down at "picnic tables when it's sunny" and otherwise opt for the "terrific service" at the drive-through.

Doris' Cafe [S] 20 | 13 | 17 | $16

325 NE Russell St. (MLK Jr. Blvd.), 503-287-9249

■ "Bring your bib" to this soul-ful Northeast "homey" joint with a thick Southern accent, and "go hungry" 'cuz it's "good and filling"; Dixie chicks declare "fried chicken rules", along with "first-rate ribs", the "best BBQ" and "wonderful yams"; a few Yankees yell about the "snail's-pace service."

Dot's Cafe ●S⌿ 17 | 19 | 15 | $14
2521 SE Clinton St. (bet. 25th & 26th Aves.), 503-235-0203
■ "Hepcats and insomniacs" groove at this Southeast
Eclectic serving "comfort food with funk"; it may be "dark"
inside, but "scenesters" don't lose any sleep choosing the
"cheap cheddar fries" and 'burrito in a bowl', while
java jivers jump for "great high-carb breakfasts"; a few
establishment types cough it's "too smoky."

Dragonfish Asian Cafe S – | – | – | M
Paramount Hotel, 909 SW Park Ave. (Taylor St.), 503-243-5991
In the new Paramount Hotel Downtown, this Pan-Asian
(with a Seattle sib) is slaying the crowds with 'dragonfire'
chicken, dragon rolls as well as a five-spice chocolate cake;
plum-colored booths, red lamps, aquariums and bamboo
appointments add exotic flair; fire-breathers fancy the
late-night hours too.

Dragonfly Restaurant S 19 | 18 | 17 | $18
1411 NE Broadway (bet. 14th & 15th Aves.), 503-288-3960
■ This "cool" Northeast Pan-Asian "pleases every palate"
with a "fusion of flavors" and "spicy tastes", mostly Thai
and Chinese; its "creative menu" includes "fun invent-
your-own stir-fries" served in a "converted old house"
habitat that makes for "intimate dining"; a few prod that
"the portions are too small for the price."

Dundee Bistro S 22 | 22 | 19 | $29
100 SW Seventh St. (Hwy. 99), Dundee, 503-554-1650
◪ Oenophiles exult in this "attractive, bright" new NW bistro
in a "lifesaver location" in Dundee's pinot noir country;
owned by pioneering Oregon vintners Nancy and Dick Ponzi,
it offers Willamette Valley ingredients and 200 wines –
50 percent of which are Oregonian; but a few whiners are
woeful about "unexceptional food" and "spotty service."

El Burrito Loco S 22 | 8 | 16 | $7
1942 N. Portland Blvd. (Denver Ave.), 503-735-9505
3126 NE 82nd Ave. (Siskiyou St.), 503-252-1343
18238 SE Division St. (182nd Ave.), Gresham, 503-669-1253
■ Amigos advise "take the chile-relleno burrito to go"
because you get "no amenities" in this "hole-in-the-wall"
"family-owned" Mexican minichain; however, you will find
"friendly service" and "fantastic" "comfort food"; to make
a long, crazy story short: "it's cheap, fast and authentic."

Eleni's Estiatorio S – | – | – | M
7712 SE 13th Ave. (Malden St.), 503-230-2165
This "elegant" Hellenic yearling in Sellwood serves upscale
fare with a Cretan accent, including a "delicious" 'small
plate' menu of stuffed eggplant, *saganaki* and baklava, plus
specialties like slow-cooked rabbit, as well as "a nice
Greek wine list"; warm colors, an open kitchen and a
friendly bar help create an hospitable atmosphere.

El Gaucho ◗ 🅂   23 | 24 | 24 | $52

Benson Hotel, 319 SW Broadway (bet. Oak & Stark Sts.),
503-227-8794

■ Bypass the pampas and go Downtown to "the new kid on the block" in the Benson Hotel where visiting Presidents bunk and buckaroos bet on "big portions" of "fabulous steaks", including "excellent" classics such as Châteaubriand followed by "bananas Foster to rival Brennan's", served by a staff that "bends over backward to make you happy"; however, a number of el grouchos grumble it's "overpriced."

Escape From N.Y. Pizza 🅂⊘   21 | 11 | 14 | $9

622 NW 23rd Ave. (bet. Hoyt & Irving Sts.), 503-227-5423

■ "Faux Big Apple-tude doesn't spoil the best pizza" at this Northwest "hole-in-the-wall" where instead of "la-di-da toppings", youse get "huge slices" with "great, crispy" crusts and the "best sauce"; it's a "cheap eat", but nostalgic New Yawkers sigh "if only the service were more surly."

ESPARZA'S TEX MEX CAFE   22 | 21 | 18 | $20

2725 SE Ankeny St. (28th Ave.), 503-234-7909

■ "Where Lyle Lovett would eat", this "funky", "boisterous" Southeast cantina and "tequila shrine" speaks fluent Tex-Mex with a "bold" accent; "fabulous BBQ'd brisket" and "luscious lamb enchiladas" seem almost tame compared to "exotic" ostrich and alligator selections, and while the "amusingly quirky decor" with "marionettes on the ceiling" is equally song-worthy, be prepared for a "long wait."

Esplanade Restaurant 🅂   21 | 24 | 21 | $38

RiverPlace Hotel, 1510 SW Harbor Way (Montgomery St.),
503-295-6166

■ "The river view is mesmerizing" at this "understated and outstanding" Downtown French bistro with NW accents; the "elegant, interesting cuisine" includes sea scallops with lobster and "excellent homemade ice cream", delivered by a "crisp staff", but the "beautiful Willamette" still steals the show, so "have a drink on the terrace" after dinner.

Fat City Cafe 🅂   19 | 15 | 19 | $11

7820 SW Capitol Hwy. (35th Ave.), 503-245-5457

■ "No calorie counters, please" pronounce the plump and pleased of this 30-year-old diner in Multnomah specializing in "great, big cheap breakfasts" and lunches with a side of "witty banter"; favorites include the "best cinnamon rolls ever" and "artery-clogging but to-die-for hash browns."

Fernando's Hideaway [S] 20 | 19 | 19 | $27

824 SW First Ave. (bet. Taylor & Yamhill Sts.), 503-248-4709

◪ Scenesters say Latin dancing and a lively bar scene create a "party atmosphere" at this "romantic" two-story Downtown Spanish offering "wonderful tapas" with "great Rioja"; owner "Fernando makes you feel like royalty", though a few hiders hint it's "too dark" and "noisy."

Fong Chong [S] 21 | 9 | 16 | $16

301 NW Fourth Ave. (Everett St.), 503-220-0235

◪ Advocates anticipate "dim sum heaven" at lunch and "delicious potstickers" and "good noodles" at night at this Cantonese "institution" in Old Town, near the new Chinese Garden; while angels appreciate its "classic cheesy ambiance", devils declare "they need a serious decorator."

Foothill Broiler ⊄ 16 | 11 | 13 | $12

Uptown Shopping Ctr., 33 NW 23rd Pl. (Burnside St.), 503-223-0287

■ The frugal don't mind footing the bill at this "cafeteria-style" American "oasis of cheap food" in Northwest; though it's under new ownership, you can expect the same "traditions", including the "best deviled-egg sandwich anywhere" and a "good selection of pies."

Fratelli [S] 21 | 20 | 19 | $31

1230 NW Hoyt St. (bet. 12th & 13th Aves.), 503-241-8800

■ An "arty, sophisticated venue" with a "rustic, warm feel", this Italian in the Pearl keeps the dishes "inventive" and seasonal with a "rotating" menu; the chef's "subtly flavored" food is "cooked with passion" and "a lot of thought" and the wine list includes "hard-to-get bottles" (all from Italy) at "reasonable" prices; a few, however, give the boot to the service, calling it "distracted."

FuJin 19 | 10 | 16 | $16

3549 SE Hawthorne Blvd. (bet. 35th & 36th Aves.), 503-231-3753

◪ "Crispy eggplant" are the buzzwords at this Hawthorne Chinese where the service is so fast "you'll swear they bugged your table"; it offers a relatively "small selection" of "cheap", "tasty food" that "hits the spot", but aesthetes who find the decor "depressing" urge "get it to go."

Fuller's Coffee Shop ⊄ 18 | 15 | 18 | $11

136 NW Ninth Ave. (Davis St.), 503-222-5608

■ "Step back in time" to this "old-fashioned" all-American counter-only diner, serving "the Pearl District's last working-man's breakfast" (available all day), including "excellent German pancakes and eggs", and a lunch that's also a "good value for hungry guys" and dolls; as its filled-up followers say, "if your fanny fits the stool", sit there.

Fusion
21 | 21 | 19 | $20

4100 SE Division St. (41st Ave.), 503-233-6950

■ This Eclectic Southeast "local eatery" creatively fuses "underpriced" "innovative" fare with a "funky", "chrome-and-Formica" secondhand-store setting; the "chef surprises with a new perspective on international flavors", including an "amazing bread pudding", all served by "caring staff" (no cold fusion here).

Garbonzos S
17 | 11 | 14 | $11

922 NW 21st Ave. (Lovejoy St.), 503-227-4196 ☾
3433 SE Hawthorne Blvd. (bet. 34th & 35th Aves.), 503-239-6087 ☾
6341 SW Capitol Hwy. (Sunset Blvd.), 503-293-7335

■ Featuring "falafel on the go" in a "fast-food atmosphere", these Middle Eastern walk-ins are "dependable" for a "quick lunch" or "late-night emergency"; pea-pickers praise the "yummy hummus", "healthy tabbouleh" (and other "good veggie salad plates") and "spicy, tender kebabs" – "cheap eats" all; N.B. the Sunset location doesn't stay up as late as its sibs.

GENOA
28 | 24 | 28 | $63

2832 SE Belmont St. (bet. 28th & 29th Aves.), 503-238-1464

■ Portland's No. 1 for Food and Service as well as Most Popular, this 30-year-old "world-class" Belmont Italian is "a sublime experience", whether for the "gastronomic euphoria" of the seven-course prix fixe dinner or the service where "no detail is overlooked" or a setting that's "opulent without being stuffy"; three-hour meals and a "hugely expensive" tab put off a few, who say "if not the best, easily the longest experience in town", but most concur: "it's worth every penny" and minute.

Gino's Restaurant & Bar S
21 | 15 | 19 | $24

8051 SE 13th Ave. (bet. Spokane & Tacoma Sts.), 503-233-4613

■ This "totally unpretentious" family-run Italian is "a find" in Sellwood, thanks to "huge servings" of "reasonably priced" pastas, salads and tiramisu and an "incredible" 500-strong wine selection, "cheerful service" and a "homey feel"; regulars recommend eating "in the cozy bar booths for privacy", even though others complain it's "smoke filled."

Giorgio's
22 | 21 | 22 | $33

1131 NW Hoyt St. (12th Ave.), 503-221-1888

■ A "wonderful addition" to the Pearl, this "charming" Northern Italian serves a "limited menu" focusing on "simple and pure" dishes such as tagliatelle with duck ragout and "great desserts"; owner Giorgio Kawas "goes out of his way to keep people happy" in the small dining room or bar, where ceiling fans blow in a "European atmosphere."

Good Day Restaurant [S] ▽ 21 | 10 | 15 | $17

312 NW Couch St. (bet. 3rd & 4th Aves.), 503-223-1393

■ "There's no ambiance, so close your eyes and enjoy" this Cantonese in Chinatown where "authentic" tastes help make the "crispy" chicken legendary; day-trippers (and take-outers) tip for notable noodles at nice prices.

Good Dog/Bad Dog [S] 21 | 15 | 17 | $9

708 SW Alder St. (Broadway), 503-222-3410

■ "No bad dogs!" opine the obedient of this "kick-back Downtown people-watching" wienery where your canine companions are welcome "at outdoor tables"; multi-national, "succulent sausages" with "multiple toppings" and "great chili and baked beans" make for "satisfyingly messy" wolfing, but a few bark "the buns leave much to be desired."

Goose Hollow Inn [S] – | – | – | I

1927 SW Jefferson St. (19th Ave.), 503-228-7010

This Southwest cafe, owned by Portland's legendary former mayor Bud Clark, serves up an American menu of soups, pizzas and sandwiches; the deck fills up in the summer with politicos and Downtowners longing for a microbrew or a sip of – and chat with – Bud.

Grand Central Bakery & Cafe [S] 22 | 15 | 17 | $10

1444 NE Weidler St. (15th Ave.), 503-288-1614

■ This "clean, bright and cheery" Northeast bakery/cafe attracts dough-hemians with its "homemade", "high-quality" goods; loafers love the "nice selection of artisanal breads", "super sandwiches" and "divine soups" while the sweet-toothed bite into the "best scones" and would even "kill for a jammer" (flaky pastry filled with jam).

Grant House [S] – | – | – | M

1101 Officers Row (south of Mill Plain Blvd.), Vancouver, WA, 360-696-1727

Standing at attention in Vancouver's Officers Row in the beautifully restored 1849 Ulysses S. Grant House, this Eclectic cafe is on the upswing under yet another new chef and owner, who hope you'll march over for bistro-style sandwiches at lunch and rack of lamb at dinner; an outdoor garden, porch seating and the next-door folk art museum should make this a destination.

Gustav's Bier Stube [S] 21 | 19 | 19 | $19

5035 NE Sandy Blvd. (50th Ave.), 503-288-5503

Gustav's German Pub & Grill [S]

12605 SE 97th Ave. (Sunnyside Rd.), Clackamas, 503-653-1391

■ You, too might cry "*achtung,* baby – awesome German food!" about these "comfy" Northeast and Clackamas pubs, celebrated for sausages, "amazing cheese fondue" and a "great beer selection"; the "jovial atmosphere" includes a "mandatory sing-along" that can get "chaotic", but with "great prices", parents, *kinder* and "grandma will be happy."

Hall Street Grill S | 21 | 19 | 20 | $28 |

3775 SW Hall Blvd. (Center St.), Beaverton, 503-641-6161
■ "When you want something nice and easy without much ado", haul yourself to this "casual" American-NW "oasis in Beaverton", where families, "business diners" and singles mingle for "wonderful coconut shrimp", "great steaks" and cedar-planked salmon; "early-bird specials are a great value", "happy hour is a pleasure" (especially on the patio) and though "it can get crowded", it "never lets you down."

Hands on Café S⇗ | 24 | 18 | 18 | $14 |

Oregon College of Arts & Crafts, 8215 SW Barnes Rd. (Leahy Rd.), 503-297-1480
■ "Art + food = fun" at this Eclectic college eatery in Southwest, where "fresh", "creative" daily-changing specials (including authentic curries) at "extraordinary prices" are "imaginatively presented" on "hand-thrown pottery" in a "homey" interior or on the patio; the "restful and beautiful" grounds, perfect for a pre-brunch stroll, have some "wishing they were students" again.

Harborside Restaurant S | 20 | 22 | 19 | $31 |

RiverPlace Marina, 309 SW Montgomery St. (Harbor Dr.), 503-220-1865
■ "Every table has a view" of the Willamette River at this "dependable" McCormick & Schmick–owned NW-seafooder in Southwest that's "a well-kept secret for uncrowded lunches" served by an "impeccable" staff; singles and hopheads head for the Pilsner Room where Full Sail beer is brewed onsite, and when the weather is fair, everyone tacks to the sidewalk tables.

Hayden Island Steak House S | – | – | – | E |

DoubleTree Hotel, 909 N. Hayden Island Dr. (I-5), 503-978-4595
This "hidden pleasure" steakhouse, a North Portland newcomer in a Jantzen Beach hotel, boasts "beautiful" Columbia River views and a menu of prime rib, "fresh fish" and salads with tableside preparations; prices are lower than those at most beef palaces.

HEATHMAN RESTAURANT, THE S | 26 | 24 | 24 | $41 |

Heathman Hotel, 1001 SW Broadway (Salmon St.), 503-241-4100
■ Normandy-born chef Philippe Boulot is the "outstanding" presiding force at this "dependably excellent" Downtown NW-French landmark where "elegance and class" define setting, service, food and wine; added attractions include "power breakfast and lunch", afternoon tea or a rendezvous by the bar's fireplace for "heavenly crab cakes and Irish coffee"; N.B. under new management since October 2000, the menu now offers a wider price range.

Henry's Cafe 🅂 ▽ 23 21 19 $20
2508 SE Clinton St. (bet. 25th & 26th Aves.), 503-236-8707
■ "Quality's the name of the game" at this "smart" Eclectic cafe with a French twist set on a busy corner of a hip street in Southeast; the first inning features "great breakfasts", while the tomato-sauced polenta hits a home run for the "fresh, delicious" lunch and dinner fare; a "we-always-feel-welcome" experience keeps players coming back.

HIGGINS 🅂 26 24 25 $39
1239 SW Broadway (Jefferson St.), 503-222-9070
■ Local, organic "ingredients combined with the freshest imagination" are the hallmark of this Downtown NW "foodies' paradise", notable for "Mr. Natural" (chef Greg Higgins), whose "flawless execution" elicits repeat visits from carnivores and vegheads alike, not to mention fans of the 400-bottle wine list; the busy bar serves a "great hamburger", and the Broadway "location, location, location" makes it a magnet for theater- or concert-goers.

Hoda's Middle Eastern Cuisine 🍴 18 11 19 $14
3401 SE Belmont St. (34th Ave.), 503-236-8325
■ Falafel followers find this "cheap, friendly" Middle Eastern in Belmont "authentic", with its "steaming-hot" pita bread, "great hummus" and other "fresh, spicy dishes" served in a "pleasant dining room" by an "attentive crew"; with its "neighborhood atmosphere", this offspring of Nicholas' Restaurant is a "welcome addition."

Horn of Africa 21 13 19 $13
3939 NE Martin Luther King Jr. Blvd. (bet. Failing & Shaver Sts.), 503-331-9844
■ "Go for the exotic tastes", "excellent spongy bread" and "tender meats" at this family-owned East African in Northeast, where "flavors and spices explode in your mouth"; though the decor is "modest" and the MLK Boulevard location off-the-beaten-restaurant-path, those who've discovered this "charming hole-in-the-wall" exhort others to "be adventurous" and try it.

Hot Lips Pizza 🅂 20 11 15 $11
1909 SW Sixth Ave. (bet. College & Hall Sts.), 503-224-0311
Raleigh Hills Fred Meyer Shopping Ctr., 4825 SW 76th Ave. (bet. Beaverton-Hillsdale Hwy. & Scholls Ferry Rd.), Beaverton, 503-297-8424
■ The deep dish on these "thin-crust" and pan pizza shops is all about "fresh", "seasonal ingredients"; boosters blow kisses at their "gourmet inventions" (including an "apple, blue cheese and walnut" Waldorf version), "zesty sauce" and use of "farmers' market" "organic veggies"; N.B. there's beer and wine at the Sixth Avenue location only.

Huber's　　　　20　23　20　$24
411 SW Third Ave. (bet. Stark & Washington Sts.), 503-228-5686
■ Portland's Downtown oldie (since 1879) but goodie, this American "institution" talks turkey by serving Thanksgiving dinner "any time of the year", as well as a popular Spanish coffee that "flames before your eyes"; history lovers "take visitors" here for the "turn-of-the-century elegance", but some snipe about the "smoke drifting from the bar" where a new generation is "having a good time."

Hudson's Bar & Grill S　　　21　24　20　$30
Heathman Lodge, 7801 NE Greenwood Dr. (bet. 41st St. & Parkway Dr.), Vancouver, WA, 360-816-6100
■ "Leave the mall and head for the forest" to this NW–New American bistro, serving "excellent" local fare including "yummy seafood cakes" in an "inviting" room with a chill-fighting fireplace; "great Sunday jazz" and guest chefs keep travelers coming back to this Heathman property in Vancouver's otherwise "lackluster" dining scene.

Hunan S　　　19　16　17　$19
Morgan's Alley, 515 SW Broadway (Washington St.), 503-224-8063
■ Those who like it "hot hot hot" head to this Downtown Chinese where the "consistent" fare is "always good", particularly the potstickers; others blast the "red vinyl" decor, but it remains an "institution", especially for lunch.

Hungry Dog Burrito S　　　17　11　13　$10
2310 NW Everett St. (23rd Ave.), 503-226-1978
■ For "fast, cheap Mission-style burritos", they travel in packs to this counter-service taqueria in Northwest, a doggone "pretty part of town"; though the signature dishes weigh in at one barkin' pound, the "preparations are healthful", including "excellent grilled chicken" fillings.

Il Fornaio S　　　20　22　19　$29
115 NW 22nd Ave. (Burnside St.), 503-248-9400
◪ "Load up on the bread" for olive-oil dipping at this "light, airy" affiliate of a California-based Italian chain in Northwest where "regional menus" impress, particularly "divine squash ravioli"; the wine selection also elicits bravos, though naysayers sniff that service is "uninformed" and food "formulaic."

Il Piatto S　　　23　22　20　$28
2348 SE Ankeny St. (24th Ave.), 503-236-4997
■ *Amici* of this "romantic retreat in Southeast" endorse wholeheartedly its "imaginative" Italian cuisine, starring "outrageous polenta with portobellos" and "excellent gnocchi"; the "softly lit" "warm and luscious" interior makes "hip" hearts beat faster", but regulars recommend reservations at this "bustling" – some say "cramped" – trattoria (check out the "tiny" bathroom).

India House [S] 21 | 15 | 18 | $19
1038 SW Morrison St. (11th Ave.), 503-274-1017
◪ If you sikh a naan-starter that's "as good as it gets" for very little bread, go to this Downtown Indian where "great okra and lamb tandoori" also stand out among the "not fancy" but "dependable" fare; a few home-wreckers holler that while the "owners are nice", service can be "sloppy."

JAKE'S FAMOUS CRAWFISH [S] 24 | 23 | 23 | $35
401 SW 12th Ave. (Stark St.), 503-226-1419
■ A Portland "grande dame" that's been "earning its reputation every day" since 1892, this NW seafooder in Downtown serves a "wide variety" of "incredibly fresh" and "well-prepared fish" and shellfish, especially "can't-be-beat oysters"; with "professional service" and "historic art" on the walls, it's "a must for out-of-towners", though a few crabs claim the "salads and vegetables need work."

Jake's Grill [S] 22 | 22 | 21 | $32
Governor Hotel, 611 SW 10th Ave. (Alder St.), 503-220-1850
■ Everything's jake at this "classic" American surf 'n' turf, an "upscale" "brass rail" Downtown grill in the Governor Hotel that lures "crab-cake connoisseurs" as well as those who ride herd over "lunchtime blue plate specials" and bar bargains ("happy-hour hamburgers are the best in town"); warning to cigarophobes: this "good-old-boys' place" has a "tolerant smoking policy" in the bar area.

J & M Cafe [S]🚫 21 | 19 | 19 | $13
537 SE Ash St. (6th Ave.), 503-230-0463
■ This "cute" American cafe in an Eastside ex-warehouse dishes up "consistently good" breakfast, from basted eggs to burritos accompanied by "bottomless coffee" in assorted funky mugs; go for "people-watching" lunch and "best-ambiance brunch" too, but alas, no dinner.

Jarra's Ethiopian Restaurant 18 | 10 | 16 | $19
1435 SE Hawthorne Blvd. (14th Ave.), 503-230-8990
◪ "A little goes a long way with the bread" (spongy injera) at this "friendly" family-run African on Hawthorne where you can mop up "some of the best and spiciest Ethiopian food on the planet" with your hands instead of a fork; those who find it jarring jibe "the decor leaves much to be desired", as does the "glacial" (as in slow) service.

Jo Bar & Rotisserie [S] 21 | 22 | 20 | $27
715 NW 23rd Ave. (bet. Irving & Johnson Sts.), 503-222-0048
■ Hipsters and people-watchers call this "sleek" but "very comfortable" NW bistro a "welcome respite from the frenzied crowds of 23rd Avenue" with "delectable salmon salad" and "great desserts from Papa Haydn" (its next-door parent); brunch- and lunch-goers acclaim it as "an all-time favorite", and later on, barflies swarm for "great drinks."

JOEL PALMER HOUSE 27 | 25 | 24 | $42

600 Ferry St. (6th St.), Dayton, 503-864-2995

■ It's "worth the drive to Dayton" in wine country to dine at this "remodeled historic house" that's known for "classic, chef-run gourmet" NW cuisine; "mushroom mavens" pop in for "fabulous" fungi appearing in everything from salad to cheesecake, but the "zingy grilled meats" and "rich coq au vin" are also good picks; the "lovely setting", a "happy" staff and "caring proprietors" cap the experience, though it costs a little morel than some would like.

John Street Cafe [S] 24 | 18 | 24 | $15

8338 N. Lombard St. (John Ave.), 503-247-1066

■ "A bright spot in a once-bustling part of town," this North Portland American-Eclectic offers "outstanding omelets and corned beef hash" for breakfast and lunch specials that seem fresh-picked out of "mom's garden"; the owners, formerly of the Tabor Hill Cafe, "have a great formula" that makes "lucky" loyalists feel "like family."

Kells Irish Restaurant & Pub ◐ [S] – | – | – | M

112 SW Second Ave. (bet. Ash & Pine Sts.), 503-227-4057

This upmarket Irish in Downtown is known for its St. Pat's Day festival and single-malt whiskey list that's no blarney – it's the largest in the Pacific Northwest; the pub fare includes "great corned beef and cabbage", shepherd's pie and a Guinness chocolate cake served in a "lively atmosphere" that features Gaelic entertainment.

Ken's Home Plate 22 | 13 | 19 | $15

1208 NW Glisan St. (12th Ave.), 503-517-8935
1852 SE Hawthorne Blvd. (19th Ave.), 503-236-9520

■ "Why cook?" when chef "Ken [Gordon] knows what mashed potatoes are all about" at this Hawthorne and Pearl twin set of Eclectic comfort-food "gourmet takeouts" with limited on-site dining; it's "like going into mom's kitchen" and coming out with "Southern-fried chicken and anything chocolate", such as "yummy homemade Oreos."

Khun Pic's Bahn Thai ⇏ ▽ 23 | 23 | 13 | $21

3429 SE Belmont St. (bet. 34th & 35th Aves.), 503-235-1610

■ Picture this: the "best Thai" served in a "beautifully decorated" Victorian in Belmont; the "wonderful" curries made-to-order by the chef-owner are "great every time", but the customized cuisine can result in "slow service."

Koji Osakaya [S] 20 | 15 | 16 | $22

1502 NE Weidler St. (15th Ave.), 503-280-0992
7007 SW Macadam Ave. (Texas St.), 503-293-1066
606 SW Broadway (bet. Alder & Morrison Sts.), 503-294-1169

(continued)

Koji Osakaya
*11995 SW Beaverton-Hillsdale Hwy. (Lombard Ave.),
Beaverton, 503-646-5697*
☑ Sushi and soba seekers say this "solid" Japanese chain
serves "consistently great", "luscious melt-in-your-mouth"
raw fish and "fresh" Asian "comfort food" matched up
with "sumo wrestling on TV"; some carp that "table
service is slow" and wish they'd "turn down the lights."

Kornblatt's Delicatessen 🆂   19 | 12 | 15 | $15 |
628 NW 23rd Ave. (bet. Hoyt & Irving Sts.), 503-242-0055
☑ Kvellers call this Northwest Jewish deli "the best in
town", with "matzo ball soup that will cure any cold",
"darn good bagels" and "great" sandwiches; kvetchers
counter "New York it ain't", with "overpriced" fare and
Manhattan-style service – "pity."

La Buca 🆂   19 | 13 | 15 | $14 |
*40 NE 28th Ave. (Couch St.), 503-238-1058
2309 NW Kearney St. (23rd Ave.), 503-279-8040*
■ For "fast" "no-frills quality pasta", this "cheap but savory
self-service" Italian duo in Northeast and Northwest offers
a "convenient" alternative; big mouths mention "pesto
mashed potatoes – the ultimate comfort food" and consider
the "take-and-go concept" "perfect for singles" or those
in a "hurry for a movie."

La Calaca Comelona   20 | 16 | 11 | $14 |
*1408 SE 12th Ave. (bet. Hawthorne Blvd. & Madison St.),
503-239-9675*
■ Amigos attest this "charming" Central Mexican on
Hawthorne offers "authentic country cooking", featuring
"the best pork carnitas" and "fresh juices"; the "amazing
Day-of-the-Dead decor" (the name translates as 'hungry
skeleton') and pictures of Frida Kahlo and Diego Rivera add
to the ambiance, but some knock the "nil service."

La Catalana 🆂⌀   22 | 18 | 20 | $29 |
2821 SE Stark St. (28th Ave.), 503-232-0948
■ It's "Barcelona revisited" at this "romantic" Southeast
Spanish, a "cozy" "find" for couples or groups who seek
"superb tapas" such as "those aioli potatoes", as well as
"excellent paella" and "affordable wines"; a few, however,
feel "the service falls short."

La Cruda 🆂   17 | 14 | 11 | $12 |
2500 SE Clinton St. (25th Ave.), 503-233-0745
■ "Serve yourself" at this "casual" cantina where locals
feast on "huge burritos" topped by a trip to the "creative
salsa bar"; the bar menu and a "funky" "yard-sale
ambiance" at this "hot spot" attract the area's Gen Xers.

La Prima Trattoria S
20 | 19 | 21 | $23
4775 SW 77th Ave. (Scholls Ferry Rd.), Beaverton, 503-297-0360
◪ Admirers sing arias about this Beaverton "storefront" Italian, praising the "great pizzas, pastas and salads", "warm, inviting" interior, "reasonable prices" and "wonderful service"; atonalists argue it's "inconsistent", "suburban mediocre" and "no place for a quiet dinner."

LASLOW'S NORTHWEST S
25 | 21 | 24 | $40
2327 NW Kearney St. (bet. 23rd & 24th Aves.), 503-241-8092
■ The "spot-on", "sophisticated" NW–Contemporary French fare served in this "heart-of-Northwest" restored house is "like eating in your best friend's dining room"; "inventive" chef Eric Laslow has moved from his digs on Broadway to turn out "incredible seafood stew" and award- winning pumpkin-custard crab cakes, while "friendly" hostess/ wine whiz Connie Laslow provides "lots of personal attention."

L'Auberge S
23 | 22 | 23 | $38
2601 NW Vaughn St. (bet. 26th & 27th Aves.), 503-223-3302
■ This French bistro in Northwest is a "cozy" "classic you can always go back to" with a "fancy farmhouse" air, fireplace included; a new chef means a once-"stuffy" menu has been retooled to include "simple fare", particularly at the bar, where "fantastic mushroom soup", burgers and "excellent poached lemon cheesecake" compose a meal of "unassuming goodness."

LE BOUCHON
23 | 18 | 21 | $31
517 NW 14th Ave. (bet. Glisan & Hoyt Sts.), 503-248-2193
■ "*Vive la France*!" cry a legion of *amis* of this "adorable" French-owned bistro in the Pearl that serves *classiques* such as "better-than-Parisian" onion soup and "outstanding sweetbreads and duck confit" at "moderate prices" in a "small, hip setting" that a few find "too noisy"; the "bubbly hostess" (and chef's wife) adds "a touch of class", though some defectors decry the staff as "snippy."

Legin ●S
20 | 12 | 15 | $20
8001 SE Division St. (82nd Ave.), 503-777-2828
◪ "Yum-yum dim sum" is just one part of this sprawling Southeast Chinese, which also features "fresh shellfish"; although a few foes find the 1,300-seat space "noisy" and the service "surly", fans feel it's a "Hong Kong fantasyland"; P.S. go on "weekends for the best variety."

LEMONGRASS THAI ⊉
25 | 19 | 17 | $24
1705 NE Couch St. (17th Ave.), 503-231-5780
■ Chef-owner Shelley Siripatrapa creates "standout" "gourmet" Thai in Northeast in a "beautiful old Victorian" with "fresh flowers galore"; proponents pucker up for "distinctly flavored" basics like chicken-coconut soup and "heavenly garden rolls", but "with a no-reservations policy except for large groups, you can "expect to wait."

Little Wing Cafe 20 | 13 | 16 | $15

529 NW 13th Ave. (bet. Glisan & Hoyt Sts.), 503-228-3101
■ This "casual" New American–Eclectic "jewel" hidden in a Pearl District alley shines with "great sandwiches", "super soups" and "delectable desserts" including "the best coconut cake in the world"; those who wing it for dinner say it offers "an affordable eatery in the increasingly pricey" nabe and appreciate the "phenomenal service."

London Grill S 23 | 24 | 24 | $41

Benson Hotel, 309 SW Broadway (bet. Oak & Stark Sts.), 503-295-4110
■ A "refined, romantic and rewarding" experience is the standard at this Downtown "institution" in the Benson Hotel, where the Continental-NW cuisine continues to epitomize "timeless fine dining"; for 30 years, chef Xavier Bauser has delivered "outstanding and original food presentation" supported by "smooth" "formal service" and an award-winning wine selection; P.S. the $25 prix fixe Sunday brunch is "a favorite."

Lucy's Table 23 | 22 | 22 | $36

706 NW 21st Ave. (Irving St.), 503-226-6126
■ Lucy has no 'splainin' to do at this "creative" New American–Mediterranean in Northwest serving "artfully prepared", "palate-pleasing" suppers that might include "always-perfect risotto", "earthy scallops" and cannelloni that "brings tears to your eyes" from a kitchen that will also "accommodate special dietary needs"; "lovely service" and a "pretty, quiet setting" make this place "perfect for two."

Macheezmo Mouse S 14 | 11 | 13 | $10

Portland Int'l Airport, 7000 NE Airport Way, 2nd fl. (I-205), 503-280-2208
1200 NE Broadway (12th Ave.), 503-249-0002
Pioneer Pl., 700 SW Fifth Ave. (Morisson St.), 503-248-0917
6141 SW Macadam Ave. (California St.), 503-245-1617
10719 SW Beaverton-Hillsdale Hwy. (107th Ave.), Beaverton, 503-646-6000
8870 SE Sunnyside Rd. (bet. 84th & 93rd Aves.), Clackamas, 503-659-4400
1435 NW 185th Ave. (Walker Rd.), Hillsboro, 503-629-5049
Washington Sq. Mall, 9585 SW Washington Sq. Rd. (Hwy. 217), Tigard, 503-639-2379
◪ Known for "fast, healthy Mexican food", this local chain offers as bait "alternative cuisine" that makes vegetarians squeak with delight, especially the "nice salsa bar", "burritos with black beans and brown rice" and the 'Power Salad'; others who feel like lab animals say "they're still experimenting" and "Mex wasn't meant to be medicine", but at least no one feels trapped by the "great-value" prices.

Marco's Cafe & Espresso Bar S　21 | 15 | 19 | $18
3449 NE 24th Ave. (Fremont St.), 503-287-8011
7910 SW 35th Ave. (Multnomah Blvd.), 503-245-0199
■ "Feels like mom cooked for you" at this duet of Eclectic "neighborhood" cafes where a "big menu" with nightly specials offers up "honest" dishes like "imaginative salads," "super omelets" and "beloved red spuds"; families say "it's a great place for kids" with "breakfast all day", though the claustrophobic complain "it's too crowded on weekends."

Marrakesh S　21 | 24 | 22 | $26
1201 NW 21st Ave. (Northrup St.), 503-248-9442
◪ "Sit on the floor, eat with your hands and dance with the belly dancers" at this "exotic" Northwest Moroccan where "authentic" but "messy" food, cushioned with pillow seating, low tables and even lower lights, creates a "cultural learning experience" that's "best for a big group"; a few express that the Marrakesh "show" outshines the fare.

Maya's Taqueria S　18 | 12 | 14 | $11
1000 SW Morrison St. (10th Ave.), 503-226-1946
■ It's a "taco fiesta" at this Downtown Mexican that aficionados acclaim as "authentic, fast and funky"; the "fun decor" compensates for the "cafeteria-style service", and the multi-flavored margaritas and regional beers make the signature 'super burritos' even easier to swallow.

McCormick & Schmick's S　23 | 21 | 22 | $32
235 SW First Ave. (Oak St.), 503-224-7522
■ "Portland through and through", this "solid", "elegant" Downtown seafooder (with a NW accent) is on the upswing again with young chef Paulino Miranda; expect to "feast on appetizers" like the "best calamari", but save room for "always-fresh daily sheet selections" and keep in mind the "inexpensive bar menu" during happy hour.

McCormick's Fish House & Bar S　23 | 20 | 22 | $32
9945 SW Beaverton-Hillsdale Hwy. (99th Ave.), Beaverton, 503-643-1322
◪ Trawl for the "best seafood in the suburbs" at this Beaverton M&S chain link , serving a "wide selection" of "never-fail fish and shellfish" and "the best Cobb salad"; though a few mutineers mumble about "mundane side dishes" and a "formula ambiance", more are hooked by the "wide selection and wine list" and the "cozy bistro feel."

McMenamins Black Rabbit S　19 | 21 | 19 | $27
McMenamins Edgefield, 2126 SW Halsey St. (238th Dr.), Troutdale, 503-669-8610
■ A refurbished poor farm in Troutdale, this Northwesterner is the most upscale of the McMenamin brothers' litter, reaping praise for its "fantastic location" (near a "beautiful vineyard" and garden) and "relaxing" vibe; the fare's "always good", the wine "excellent" and the staff "super."

McMenamins Courtyard Restaurant ⬤🅂
15 | 22 | 15 | $17

McMenamins Kennedy School, 5736 NE 33rd Ave. (Killingsworth St.), 503-249-3983

◪ Senior delinquents can "drink and smoke in 'Detention'" at this "inspired" elementary school transformed into a brewpub/movie theater in Northeast, where the "basic" fare – pizza, pastas and "fabulous burgers" – is secondary to the "innovative location" and entertainment; disciplinarians declare the menu's "uninspired" and service "uneven" but admit that the art-filled hallways and community garden provide "a delightful change of pace."

McMenamins on the Columbia ⬤🅂
15 | 19 | 15 | $18

1801 SE Columbia River Dr. (State Rte. 14), Vancouver, WA, 503-255-9879

◪ For a "sunny-day beer on the water", raft to this "casual" New American Vancouver brewpub in a growing riverfront area and dine on "consistently good light fare", such as burgers, sandwiches and salads; malcontents moan that airplane noise eclipses the view, and "so-so" service gets 'em hopping mad.

Metronome 🅂
21 | 17 | 19 | $21

1426 NE Broadway (bet. 14th & 15th Aves.), 503-288-4300

◪ This NW-Eclectic in Northeast puts a song in the hearts of some with "consistently good food" such as "fabulous curry coconut soup" in concert with the music memorabilia of the married owners (who both play French horn with Oregon orchestras); discordant voices find the ambiance flat and wish the service were sharper; N.B. a new chef may outdate the above food rating.

Milo's City Cafe 🅂
19 | 16 | 18 | $15

1325 NE Broadway (bet. 13th & 14th Aves.), 503-288-6456

■ Eggheads scramble Northeast to this "happy" American-NW "non-diner diner" that dishes up "the best traditional eggs Benedict" and "scrumptious smoked salmon hash" (with "excellent variations") on a daytime-only menu of "basics prepared with love and finesse"; eggspect to put in nesting time for weekend breakfasts because "dang it, they've been discovered."

Misohapi 🅂
20 | 15 | 19 | $15

1123 NW 23rd Ave. (bet. Marshall & Northrup Sts.), 503-796-2012

■ Find "fresh, hot, bountiful, well-spiced and balanced" dishes at this "simple", recently expanded Thai-Vietnamese on a Northwest corner; the bento-box lunch is "so inexpensive, it's almost robbery", and "frugal, hungry and in-a-hurry" noodle nuts are bowled over at dinner as well.

Montage ◐ [S] 🚫 | 17 | 18 | 15 | $18
(fka Le Bistro Montage)
301 SE Morrison St. (3rd Ave.), 503-234-1324
◪ This "spicy" Southeast Cajun-Eclectic attracts scenesters with its late-night "funky" atmosphere, "communal seating" and gimmicks like 'oyster shooters'; while revelers rejoice in "mac 'n' cheese done different ways", jambalaya and leftovers "taken home in foil swans", party-poopers proclaim "it's too cute for its own good" and sniff that the service "needs a serious attitude adjustment."

Morton's of Chicago [S] | 24 | 23 | 23 | $53
213 SW Clay St. (bet. 2nd & 3rd Aves.), 503-248-2100
■ It's an "elite eating experience" at this Downtown steakhouse newcomer that's an instant "classic" for fans of "corn-fed, succulent" steak, the "highly recommended Godiva chocolate cake" and "comfortable, upscale decor"; while a few beef about the chain's "intrusive" custom of presenting raw items from the menu before your meal and are cowed by the "oh-so-expensive" tariff, the majority feel that the "fabulous" food and "pampering service" are "worth their daughters' college tuition."

Mother's Bistro & Bar [S] | 23 | 22 | 22 | $25
409 SW Second Ave. (bet. Stark & Washington Sts.), 503-464-1122
■ "Thanks, mom" say boys and girls for the "stylish" take on American "down-home comfort food" at this new Downtown "treasure" where chef-owner Lisa Schroeder "makes you feel welcome", as do the "outstanding staff" and "sunny living-room" setting that's not "fancy-schmancy"; "tasty matzo ball soup" and "great chicken 'n' dumplings" are "faves"; N.B. don't miss the 'Mother of the Month' specials.

Nicholas' Restaurant [S] 🚫 | 24 | 10 | 17 | $12
381 SE Grand Ave. (bet. Oak & Pine Sts.), 503-235-5123
■ Both "college students and executives" fall into this Southeast "hole-in-the-wall with some of the best Middle Eastern food ever", including "huge" homemade pitas and "an incredible meze plate" at "ridiculously low prices"; while some Bette Davis types cry "what a dump", others rejoin "that's part of the appeal"; N.B. Nicholas' daughters have opened their own joints in Southeast: Hoda's and Ya Hala.

Nick's Italian Cafe [S] | 24 | 18 | 23 | $38
521 NE Third St. (bet. Evans & Ford Sts.), McMinnville, 503-434-4471
◪ You may "share this nondescript dining room with at least one local" vintner at this 25-year-old Italian "wine-country legend" in McMinnville where "every course is a dream", including "fragrant minestrone" and "sublime pasta" partnered with "great Oregon pinots" at "excellent prices"; the not-so-keen nudge "the quality needs picking up" and it's "over the hill", but most maintain "it's worth the drive."

Noho's Hawaiian Cafe [S] 19 | 13 | 18 | $17
2525 SE Clinton St. (bet. 25th & 26th Aves.), 503-233-5301
515 SW Carolina St. (Macadam Ave.), 503-977-2771
Islander Hawaiian Cafe
11820 NE Fourth Plain (117th Ave.), Vancouver, WA, 360-883-3137
■ Big Kahunas "would do the hula" for this "wonderful" Hawaiian trio where "huge portions" of "good sticky rice", "dreamy garlic chicken" and other island specialties provide "cheap eats" for lunch or dinner (though a few pupu their authenticity); each outpost varies in decor, but all are child-friendly and make you "feel like family"; N.B. the Vancouver location is now separately owned.

¡OBA! RESTAURANTE [S] 23 | 25 | 21 | $34
555 NW 12th Ave. (Hoyt St.), 503-228-6161
■ "Pretend you're on vacation" at this "always-jamming" Nuevo Latino in the "trendy Pearl", where the "gorgeous" decor is the perfect backdrop for the "beautiful people" at the "hot bar scene"; holidayers "go for the margaritas and stay for the creative food", including a "to-die-for Caesar", "the best coconut shrimp" and "fabulous tuna", but the worldly-weary warn it's "deafeningly loud."

Obi Japanese Sushi Bar 23 | 16 | 18 | $25
101 NW Second Ave. (Couch St.), 503-226-3826
■ It may be "low on the local radar screen", but this "funky little" Old Town Japanese scores high marks for "well-prepared fresh sushi" and "good mochi ice cream"; regulars recommend a seat "near the TV so you can watch the master work while you drink a cold Kirin."

Old Spaghetti Factory, The [S] 14 | 19 | 17 | $16
715 SW Bancroft St. (Macadam Ave.), 503-222-5375
12725 SE 93rd Ave. (Sunnyside Rd.), Clackamas, 503-653-7949
18925 NW Tanasbourne Dr. (185th Ave.), Hillsboro, 503-617-7614
◪ For "good-value family dining", this "bustling" Italian chain is "always a favorite", serving "hearty" full-meal deals that include spumoni for dessert; industrial types tout the "rustic decor", but some organize against the "mass-produced" fare: "everything looks different but tastes the same."

Old Wives' Tales [S] 18 | 13 | 17 | $16
1300 E. Burnside St. (13th Ave.), 503-238-0470
◪ "Budget-minded" "crunchy-granola" types and "veggie parents" hightail it to this storied Eclectic-Vegetarian in Southeast offering much-loved Hungarian mushroom soup, a "great salad bar" and a kids' "playroom that promotes imagination"; a few modernists mutter the "service and food are still in the '70s."

Original Pancake House [S] ⊄ 24 | 17 | 19 | $14

8601 SW 24th Ave. (Barbur Blvd.), 503-246-9007

■ "Unchanged for almost 50 years", this "gracious" breakfast "landmark" in Southwest (Portland's "the mother church" of a nationwide 82-franchise network) continues to stack up accolades; "adult children" adore the "textbook consistency" of Dino-size 'Dutch Babies' and eat up the "world's best German pancakes"; although a few flap about the "long waits", the "splendid" fare and "comforting retro feel" make it all "worth it."

ORITALIA [S] 22 | 26 | 21 | $39

Westin Portland, 750 SW Alder St. (Park Ave.), 503-295-0680

◪ "Italy meets Asia" at this "stylish" Downtown Fusion newcomer in the Westin Hotel, part of a West Coast chain that offers an "imaginative lunch menu" of 'Zen Tapas' and "intriguing combos" (try ravioli in soy broth) at dinner; the "'in' crowd" comes out for the "hip bar", attracted by the "striking interior" featuring "deep colors, dramatic lights" and velvet-curtained booths, but some say *sayonarderci* to the concept, calling it "pretentious" and "pricey."

PALEY'S PLACE BISTRO & BAR [S] 28 | 23 | 26 | $43

1204 NW 21st Ave. (Northrup St.), 503-243-2403

■ For a "perfect experience", most places pale next to this "touch-of-class" NW-French bistro in a "charming" "converted house" in Northwest, where the "superior" cuisine "never misses"; "gracious" owners and a "knowledgeable staff" serve "sweetbreads to die for" and other "exceptional entrees" with "well-chosen wines"; while treasure hunters dig the "superb complimentary goodies" before and after your meal, wallet-watchers wail "you need to be William Paley to afford it."

Pambiche 22 | 17 | 18 | $19

2811 NE Glisan St. (28th Ave.), 503-233-0511

■ This Northeast Cuban yearling with an "intimate feel" provides "the best reason to establish diplomatic relations with Castro", serving "wonderful" dishes that dance with "intense flavors that match the decor colors", as well as 30 South American wines; the onsite "knockout bakery" means you won't want to skip the "killer desserts."

Papa Haydn East [S] 22 | 17 | 20 | $23

5829 SE Milwaukie Ave. (bet. Knight & Ramona Sts.), 503-232-9440

■ A longtime destination for "colossal", "museum-quality" desserts, this "casual" NW cafe in Sellwood also serves "large beautiful salads", sandwiches and pastas as well as "yummy brunches"; favorite sons and daughters say the eastside Papa is "way cozier" than its sleeker westside sib.

Papa Haydn West 🅂 | 22 | 19 | 20 | $25 |
701 NW 23rd Ave. (Irving St.), 503-228-7317
■ "Start with dessert and work your way backward" at this NW–New American bistro in Northwest that's a "favorite after a show", offering a "quietly buzzing, candlelit atmosphere" with a "nice street view"; the "appealing and tasty" fare plays second fiddle to the "sinfully delicious" sweets, so "eat light and indulge."

Paparazzi Pastaficio 🅂 | 23 | 18 | 20 | $25 |
4439 SW Beaverton-Hillsdale Hwy. (45th Ave.),
503-892-6686
2015 NE Broadway (21st Ave.), 503-281-7701
■ "Share, because everything's good" at this "informal" Italian duo now on both sides of the river, offering "ultra-crispy pizza appetizers", "pastas with delicious sauces", "authentic gnocchi" and the "best risotto" with picture-perfect "pleasant service"; the "charming atmosphere" at the Broadway spot features film-star stills, and the newer location (in Melting Pot's former digs) spotlights owner Sara Medici's artwork.

Paragon Restaurant & Bar ◗🅂 | 19 | 20 | 18 | $29 |
1309 NW Hoyt St. (13th Ave.), 503-833-5060
■ This "honest" New American in the Pearl offering such standbys as "always-reliable calamari and Caesar" is a "neighborhood eatery" and "perfect business-lunch spot" that moonlights as a "boisterous bar" that's "great for people-watching"; its "warm environment" is enhanced by "cozy" booths and amplified by outdoor seating.

Pasta Veloce | 20 | 14 | 16 | $13 |
1022 SW Morrison St. (bet. 10th & 11th Aves.),
503-916-4388
933 SW Third Ave. (Salmon St.), 503-223-8200
246 N. Main Ave. (3rd St.), Gresham, 503-492-9534
12700 SW N. Dakota St. (Scholls Ferry Rd.), Tigard,
503-521-1099 🅂
■ When you want "cheap, upscale pasta served lightening fast", this "dependable" "cafeteria-style" Italian chain is a port in a storm; fans find it "fun to watch food prepared" and propose penne *alla zucca* and tortellini *rustica* along with "unexpected combinations"; P.S. the Downtown branch is a "favorite before events."

Pazzoria 🅂 | 21 | 17 | 17 | $12 |
625 SW Washington St. (6th Ave.), 503-228-1695
■ For "a quick bite at lunch" or a "simple morning" meal, you can't beat this "delightful" Downtown Italian bakery/cafe adjoining its elegant sibling, Pazzo Ristorante; coffee drinks, muffins and cakes, a "good salad sampler" and pizza by the slice slung by an "excellent staff" make this one of Portland's most appealing values.

Pazzo Ristorante S   23 | 23 | 22 | $33
Hotel Vintage Plaza, 627 SW Washington St. (Broadway),
503-228-1515
■ The "classic" yet "imaginative" Italian fare at this
Downtown "perennial pleaser" in the Hotel Vintage Plaza
takes an upswing with newcomer chef Nathan Logan in
the *cucina* cooking "yummy Piedmont beef", "orgasmic"
filled pastas and "excellent desserts"; stylish touches like
the "lively bar", open kitchen and "special-occasion wine
room" make it "a good place to entertain" as well.

PEARL BAKERY   27 | 18 | 19 | $11
102 NW Ninth Ave. (Couch St.), 503-827-0910
■ Doughboys "could live on bread" alone, provided its
provenance is this Pearl District artisanal bakery that's "as
close to a Parisian pâtisserie" as you get in Portland; the
staff of life comes in many styles ("Italian, Swiss, German")
and formats ("perfect pastries", "to-die-for cookies and
cakes" and "super sandwiches"), all shaped by top talents;
while it's cheap, this pearl has a price: "limited seating."

Perry's On Fremont   19 | 18 | 19 | $22
2401 NE Fremont St. (24th Ave.), 503-287-3655
■ A "warm, inviting" ambiance and "eclectic decor" are
the starters at this Northeast old "reliable" serving a "vast
menu" of faves such as chicken pot pie and "outrageous
desserts" and cookies; regulars like to "kick back and
relax" over "great big drinks" on the "sunny dinner patio."

Pho Van Vietnamese S   24 | 18 | 19 | $15
1919 SE 82nd Ave. (bet. Division & Stark Sts.), 503-788-5244
■ Pho phreaks fancy this decade-old Vietnamese that
recently moved into "beautifully decorated", "pleasant
surroundings" in Southeast; noodle-heads slip in for
"hearty", "great-flavored" soups, but a few feel the "grilled
pork is even better" and advocate "avocado smoothies" –
all abetted by "great service."

Piazza Italia S   – | – | – | M
1129 NW Johnson St. (11th Ave.), 503-478-0619
This breezy newcomer in the Pearl transports you to Italy's
sidewalks as co-owner Gino Schettini fills your juice
glass with pinot grigio and delivers al dente pastas in
bright yellow ceramic dishes in a tile-floored storefront
'gastronomia' where you can also buy imported delicacies
such as cheeses and sausages; N.B. no menus here, just
a changing board listing a half-dozen items.

Pizzicato S   22 | 13 | 17 | $14
1630 SE Bybee Blvd. (Milwaukie Ave.), 503-736-0174
705 SW Alder St. (bet. Broadway & Park Ave.), 503-226-1007
505 NW 23rd Ave. (Glisan St.), 503-242-0023
2811 E. Burnside St. (28th Ave.), 503-236-6045

(continued)
Pizzicato
*Hillsdale Shopping Ctr., 6358 SW Capitol Hwy. (bet. Berta &
Sunset Blvds.), 503-452-7166*
1749 SW Skyline Blvd. (Hwy. 26, Sylvan exit), 503-221-8784
4217 NE Fremont St. (42nd Ave.), 503-493-2808
1708 SW Sixth Ave. (Mill St.), 503-227-5800
*Oak Hills Shopping Ctr., 14740 NW Cornell Rd. (Hwy. 26),
503-531-8989*
1900 NE 162nd Ave. (18th St.), Vancouver, WA, 360-891-2081
■ This citywide upmarket chain bakes "the best in New Age
pizza" – "innovative", "hearty" and "gourmet" ("who would
have thought potatoes would work on a pie?") – though
they're almost topped by "an excellent spinach salad" and
"delicious Caesar"; each location's decor varies enough
for some to adjudge the atmosphere "inconsistent."

Plainfields' Mayur S   24   23   22 $34
852 SW 21st Ave. (Burnside St.), 503-223-2995
■ "Gourmet" Indian cuisine enthusiasts endorse the
"exquisitely spiced food" at this longtimer residing in a
Southwest Victorian, citing in particular the "wonderful
dahi wada" and "creamy curries", complemented by an
"extraordinary wine cellar"; the "fancy surroundings",
"elegant table settings" and "remarkable" service provide a
"unique and wonderful treat in every way."

Portland Steak & Chophouse S   22   21   21 $34
*Embassy Suites Downtown, 121 SW Third Ave. (bet. Ash &
Pine Sts.), 503-223-6200*
■ "Clicking smoothly on every count", this Downtown
hotel turf 'n' (some) surfer steers you right with "superb
steaks", "the best fish 'n' chips on land" and a "killer"
happy-hour menu (try the "to-die-for chicken livers"); leather
booths and "pampering" service create an "I-want-to-
live-there" experience that's "worth every cent."

Portofino S   19   16   19 $27
8075 SE 13th Ave. (Tacoma St.), 503-234-8259
☑ Romantic regulars feel like "rolling their last meatball with
their nose" to their spouses (à la *Lady and the Tramp*) at this
"relaxed" Sellwood Italian known for "hearty, comforting
pastas", especially with "terrific vodka tomato sauce" at
"reasonable" prices; however, some see "slippage" since
the departure of the former owner.

Produce Row Cafe S ⌷   15   13   14 $13
204 SE Oak St. (2nd Ave.), 503-232-8355
■ Hopheads insist this Eastside beer garden has the "best
taps in town", with 27 brews flowing and 200 others in
bottles; despite its name, the "menu is carnivore-centric",
serving "filling" sandwiches, burgers and chili; live music
and "great happy-hour prices" produce a favorite setting
in which "to while away the afternoon."

Raccoon Lodge & Brew Pub S | 15 | 17 | 15 | $18

7424 SW Beaverton-Hillsdale Hwy. (Scholls Ferry Rd.), 503-296-0110

☑ A "brewpub on steroids" in Southwest suburbia, this amply-sized beer hall offers equally ample portions of American "meat-and-potatoes fare", including five types of "excellent" fries with nine sauces; while happy campers find the grub "tasty", foes fire back "forget the food – just drink."

Red Electric Cafe S | 21 | 17 | 19 | $17

6440 SW Capitol Hwy. (Bertha Blvd.), 503-293-1266

■ "Don't blink or you'll miss" this three-squares-a-day American in Hillsdale where the "solid breakfast" features make-your-own omelets; at later meals, a "mean meat loaf" and "good blue plate specials" will give you a rosy glow, and the electricity bill is always "reasonable."

RED HILLS PROVINCIAL DINING S | 26 | 22 | 23 | $37

276 Hwy. 99 W. (3rd St.), Dundee, 503-538-8224

■ About 800 wines, with 20-plus by the glass, attract oenophiles to this Northwesterner in Dundee, where chef-owners Nancy and Richard Gehrts create a changing menu of "intense dishes one could never prepare at home" served in a "wonderful old" house with a patio for outdoor dining; though most find the service "friendly", a few feel the staff's "a little too down-home for such a classy place."

Red Star Tavern & Roast House ◑S | 21 | 22 | 20 | $31

Fifth Avenue Suites Hotel, 503 SW Alder St. (5th Ave.), 503-222-0005

☑ Wood-grilled and rotisserie "meat reigns supreme" at this "comfortably fancy" Downtown "power spot", which also offers a "nice dessert menu" to accompany the American "home cookin' with flair"; "business-type" hombres giddy-up for the "warm" cowpoke decor and "great bar", but service reviews range from "very good" to "not acceptable."

RESTAURANT MURATA | 26 | 17 | 21 | $33

200 SW Market St. (bet. 2nd & 3rd Aves.), 503-227-0080

■ "Mothers from Tokyo" are impressed by the sushi at this upmarket Downtown Japanese across from Keller Auditorium, and favorite sons and daughters declare that "with diligence and planning, you can have an authentic" multi-course meal (call two days ahead); "udon and soba lunchtime favorites" and tatami rooms also attract adherents.

Restaurant Russia S | ▽ | 19 | 15 | 18 | $18

6433 SE Foster Rd. (bet. 64th & 65th Aves.), 503-771-8873

☑ "Ironically, the only place in town for Russian food in a city with a large Slavic population", this Southeast yearling entices glasnosters with live entertainment, "authentic" borscht, dumplings and stroganoffs and native wines and vodka; a few cold warriors warn of indifferent service.

Rheinlander S
− − − M
5035 NE Sandy Blvd. (50th Ave.), 503-288-5503
"Come hear the strolling accordion player" and singing
waiters, who set the tone at this family-friendly German
stalwart (since 1963) in Northeast offering a traditional
hearty menu of schnitzel cordon bleu, *hasenpfeffer* (rabbit)
and apple strudel, served with Rhine wines.

Riccardo's Ristorante
22 18 20 $35
16035 SW Boones Ferry Rd. (Bryant Rd.), Lake Oswego,
503-636-4104
■ This longtime "favorite" Lake Oswego Italian has a high
romance quotient with its "fabulous garden patio"; foodies
find *amore* as well, with "imaginative polentas" and a
wide selection of veal; the owners are "wonderful" and
the wine service "knowledgeable", but some are not
enamored of the interior, which they say "needs updating."

Ringside Steakhouse S
21 18 21 $35
2165 W. Burnside St. (22nd Ave.), 503-223-1513 ◗
14021 NE Glisan St. (140th Ave.), 503-255-0750
◪ "Red meat, red booths and red lights" prevail at this
"old-fashioned" duo; ringers maintain it "puts chains to
shame" and "five generations have enjoyed wonderful
steaks and onion rings" served by "professional waiters";
the wrung-out say the "nothing-special" steaker "needs
updating"; N.B. the more youthful Eastside branch serves
lunch, while the Northwesterner is dinner only.

Rustica S
18 18 18 $22
1700 NE Broadway (17th Ave.), 503-288-0990
◪ Rustic types amble to this Northeast Italian, where "good
soup-and-half-sandwich combos" at lunch and dinnertime
"scrumptious lasagna" with a side of toys create a family-
friendly "casual dining experience"; city slickers sniff that
the "menu reads better than it tastes."

Ruth's Chris Steak House S
24 22 23 $48
309 SW Third Ave. (Oak St.), 503-221-4518
■ "They have it down" at this "classy" chain link Downtown
whose offerings "picky steak enthusiasts" call "fantastic",
with sides like "to-die-for garlic mashed potatoes" and
amenities like a cigar bar, "great cocktails" and "wonderful
service"; even those who find it "the most expensive beef
in town" can't stop themselves from "going back for more."

SABURO'S SUSHI HOUSE S
26 11 14 $22
1667 SE Bybee Blvd. (bet. 16th & 17th Aves.), 503-236-4237
■ This Westmoreland "Tokyo-style telephone booth of a
restaurant" calls converts with "unbelievably fresh sushi"
in "huge portions" as well as "good green-tea ice cream
and plum wine"; be warned the decor is "humble" and
seating limited; still, connoisseurs continue to redial,
saying it's "worth it all."

Saigon Kitchen

19 | 10 | 15 | $16

835 NE Broadway (9th Ave.), 503-281-3669 Ⓢ
3829 SE Division St. (39th Ave.), 503-236-2312

◩ "Great spring rolls" and "especially good pad Thai" make this old faithful Vietnamese-Siamese duo in Northeast and Southeast a "great value" for a "quick lunch" and takeout; although there's "no ambiance" and staff "tries to get you out ASAP", supporters won't miss Saigon, saying it's worth "a drive through a blinding snowstorm."

Salvador Molly's

21 | 19 | 17 | $18

1523 SW Sunset Blvd. (Capitol Hwy.), 503-293-1790

◼ "Wild, spicy and fun", this Hillsdale Caribbean–Nuevo Latino serves "edible sunshine" including "amazing smoothies", "the best roast pork in town" and "superb jerk chicken" accompanied by "loud, bright music" best classified as "Elvis goes to Jamaica."

Sammy's Restaurant & Bar Ⓢ

18 | 18 | 19 | $26

333 NW 23rd Ave. (bet. Everett & Flanders Sts.), 503-222-3123

◩ In a Northwest hot spot, this "solid" NW-American stirs up a "spicy Bloody Mary" and puts on a "super weekend breakfast" and a lunch that includes "the best roasted turkey sandwiches in town"; with sidewalk tables in fair weather, "great people-watching" is guaranteed, though some critics carp the food is "consistently mediocre."

Santa Fe Taqueria Ⓢ

16 | 12 | 12 | $14

831 NW 23rd Ave. (Kearney St.), 503-220-0406

◼ "Big yummy burritos" and "can't-go-wrong tacos" entice Gens X, Y and Z to this "fast and funky" Northwest Mexican where food is "assembled to order" cafeteria-style for enjoying inside or outside at the crowded sidewalk tables with "a decent margarita on sunny days."

Saucebox

23 | 21 | 19 | $28

214 SW Broadway (Burnside St.), 503-241-3393

◼ Though it's a "scene, scene, scene", this "hip" Bruce Carey–owned Downtown Pan-Asian serves totally "rockin' food" including "edamame [soybeans] instead of a bread basket" and the "best sauced salmon"; the "swank", "smoky" ambiance, late-night DJs and "fantastic cocktails" drive a few to "drink, drink, drink."

Sayler's Old Country Kitchen Ⓢ

18 | 14 | 19 | $25

10519 SE Stark St. (105th Ave.), 503-252-4171
4655 SW Griffith Dr. (Beaverton-Hillsdale Hwy.), Beaverton, 503-644-1492

◪ The "steak-shaped menu" speaks volumes for this pair of "old-fashioned" family-owned "institutions" in Beaverton and Southeast where you'll also sail in for "killer fried chicken" and other "affordable", trend-free options, served by a longtime staff that "treats you like family"; the fashion-forward fuss that the fare "needs updating."

Serratto ●S
18 23 20 $33

2112 NW Kearney St. (21st Ave.), 503-221-1195

☑ Co-owner Michael Cronan catches the overflow of his next-door Caffe Mingo with this expansive two-year-old Northwest Italian where there's "no wait"; "authentic" pastas are partnered with a broad selection of native vino, and admirers anticipate the new chef's skill will bring the kitchen up to par with the "gorgeous decor."

Siam S
▽ 24 15 21 $20

3800 SW Cedar Hills Blvd. (Hall Blvd.), Beaverton, 503-626-6535

■ Supported by an "outstanding" menu, "interesting specials" rule at this Beaverton Thai, where a "pleasant room" and "friendly, unpretentious service" help keep Intel and Nike workers running back for more.

SOUTHPARK SEAFOOD GRILL & WINE BAR S
21 22 20 $33

901 SW Salmon St. (Park Ave.), 503-326-1300

☑ A Heathman Group "stylish" remake, this Downtown Mediterranean boasts an "imaginative wine list" perfect for the menu's "wide choice of seafood", including "great oysters" and "yummy crab cakes"; although the "modern, open decor" attracts culture-vultures headed for the nearby Center for the Performing Arts, critics carp the fare's "inconsistent" and "way overpriced."

Springwater Grill S
▽ 20 19 21 $26

6716 SE Milwaukie Ave. (Bybee Blvd.), 503-232-2442

■ Hope springs eternal that this "pleasant" Westmoreland newcomer will continue to satisfy supporters of its "evolving menu focused on NW fare" as well as Eclectic items and happy-hour bargains in the "comfortable bar"; the "great ambiance" and "good value" make the loss of the popular Fiddleheads in this space easier to bear.

Stanich's ⊅
21 11 16 $12

5627 SW Kelly Ave. (Flower St.), 503-246-5040
4915 NE Fremont St. (49th Ave.), 503-281-2322

■ "If you liked it 30 years ago, you'll still like" this 51-year-old tavern-cum-"burger place supreme" in Northeast whose self-proclaimed 'World's Greatest Hamburger' provides what some armchair physicians call "a great hangover" cure; "neat sports memorabilia" in a "smoky bar atmosphere" only enhances this "Portland institution"; N.B. the Southwest sib is just a kid, having opened in 1987.

Stickers Asian Cafe S
20 17 17 $15

6808 SE Milwaukie Ave. (Bybee Blvd.), 503-239-8739

■ "Not your father's Chinese restaurant", this Sellwood Pan-Asian is praised for its "good-snacking" versions of Eastern street food and, of course, potstickers, all "well priced and delicious"; the "cute, tiny" space is decorated with artwork and photos collected by the owner.

Sungari Restaurant   25 | 21 | 22 | $25
735 SW First Ave. (Yamhill St.), 503-224-0800

■ "At last, outstanding Chinese" cheer champions of this "upscale" Downtown recent arrival; "everyone raves" about the "subtly seasoned" Szechuan fare, including "the best moo shu pork" and other "high-style" dishes, served in an "elegant atmosphere"; N.B. check out adventurous choices from the wine list: Alsatian, German and Californian.

Sushi Takahashi   18 | 18 | 16 | $19
24 NW Broadway (Burnside St.), 503-224-3417
Takahashi S
10324 SE Holgate Blvd. (103rd Ave.), 503-760-8135

■ You'll find "fast, affordable fun" at both these kitschy tastes of Japan" where you "gotta love discount night", the "generous portions" and the "nice sake selection"; despite fishy "silliness" (patrons "pull a piece of $1.25 sushi" from a countertop train at the Old Town location), the "food keeps 'em coming back" there and to the Southeast station.

Swagat Indian Cuisine S   20 | 13 | 16 | $19
2074 NW Lovejoy St. (21st Ave.), 503-227-4300
4325 SW 109th Ave. (bet. Beaverton-Hillside Hwy. & Canyon Rd.), Beaverton, 503-626-3000

■ This "jewel-in-the-crown" Indian duet puts on an "oft-craved", "fantastic, cheap lunch buffet" and serves "solidly reliable authentic" dinner dishes; reviewers remark that both the Beaverton and Northwestern branches "could use some help with the decor."

Sweet Basil S   – | – | – | M
3135 NE Broadway (32nd Ave.), 503-281-8337

Herbalists are heading to this new Thai in a Northeast home (ex Laslow's on Broadway) whose Siamese chef-owner prepares favorites such as curries and noodle dishes; lunch and dinner guests dine in one of several elegant rooms or on a sweet patio in the summer.

Sweetwater's Jam House ◑S   19 | 19 | 15 | $21
3350 SE Morrison St. (34th Ave.), 503-233-0333

■ It's always jamming at this "hipster hot spot" in Belmont spinning Caribbean-Cajun "clean-your-sinuses" cuisine, including "great cod fritters", "excellent ribs" and "authentic goat curry" with "strong rum drinks" in an "offbeat setting" that makes you "feel like you're on vacation"; N.B. the next-door sib Voudou Cafe does lunch with a Creole slant.

Syun Izakaya S   ▽ 28 | 23 | 22 | $27
209 NE Lincoln St. (2nd Ave.), Hillsboro, 503-640-3131

■ "Fresh, delicious sushi", an "authentic" sake bar and "unusually generous portions" earn ovations at this Hillsboro haven where you can also satisfy a yen for "out-of-this-world tempura"; though the "unlikely setting is an ex library", some won't shush about the "sporadic service."

Tabor Hill Cafe 🗒   15 | 13 | 16 | $19
3766 SE Hawthorne Blvd. (38th Ave.), 503-230-1231
☒ This snug American cafe in busy Hawthorne exudes a
"neighborhood ambiance" with "friendly service" and
"inexpensive" traditional fare at breakfast, lunch and
dinner; those who miss the former owners (now at John
Street Cafe) sigh "it's not what it used to be."

Tao of Tea, The 🗒   20 | 24 | 19 | $12
3430 SE Belmont St. (bet. 34th & 35th Aves.), 503-736-0119
Portland Classical Chinese Garden, 239 NW Everett St.
(bet. 2nd & 3rd Aves.), 503-224-8455
■ They sympathize with "hard-core tea lovers" at this
Southeast teahouse-cum-"sanctuary from the city's
madness"; the "'60s hippie atmosphere" may make you
"meditative" as you "turn off your cell phone and order up"
from a menu of 120 exotic brews and "great flatbreads" with
a variety of toppings, Japanese mochi ice cream and other
goodies; N.B. the new Everett Street branch is unrated and
serves only Chinese teas and snacks.

Tapeo   25 | 20 | 21 | $30
2764 NW Thurman St. (bet. 27th & 28th Aves.), 503-226-0409
■ "Tantalizing tapas" "transport you to the Mediterranean
coast" at this Spanish "gem" in Northwest that's "fun and
crowded"; the "grazing" menu features "authentic" dishes
that, expense-wise, can "add up but are still a good value",
and the all-Iberian wine list also constitutes "a lesson
on sherry" taught by chef-owner Ricardo Segura, whose
personality gives this place a "great buzz."

Taqueria La Sirenita 🗒 ⌿   – | – | – | I
2817 NE Alberta St. (28th Ave.), 503-335-8283
This "always-great" Mexican in the up-and-coming Alberta
corridor in Northeast serves "cheap, authentic" soup,
shrimp cocktail, tacos and burritos in a bright, tight space;
though "off the beaten path", it's "worth the trip every
time" according to its growing fanship.

Taqueria Nueve 🗒   – | – | – | M
28 NE 28th Ave. (Burnside St.), 503-236-6195
This Northeast Mexican newcomer goes beyond rice and
beans, offering Oaxacan-inspired dishes using some NW
ingredients including free-range chicken, wild boar tacos
and wild mushroom enchiladas; warm colors and festive
tableware make this an appealing dinner destination.

Tara Thai House 🗒   19 | 15 | 18 | $20
1310 NW 23rd Ave. (Overton St.), 503-222-7840
■ This "serene" Northwest Laotian-Thai in a remodeled
house serves "exceptional soups, spring rolls and pad
Thai" and the "house noodles are pure comfort food", but
what really leaves an impression is the "dreamy deck" that's
"under a huge oak tree."

Tennessee Red's Barbecue Co. S   20 | 10 | 13 | $15
2133 SE 11th Ave. (Grant St.), 503-231-1710
☑ Take the family for brawny BBQ at this Southeast joint serving "outstanding ribs" with "a variety of unique sauces" and sentimental Southern dishes like mustard greens and sweet potato pie; nevertheless, nostalgists note that new ownership means it's "not as good as in the past."

Thai Kitchen S   ▽ 23 | 16 | 20 | $20
Walker Ctr., 2840 SW Cedar Hills Blvd. (Walker Rd.), Beaverton, 503-626-7150
■ Even those who "avoid strip malls make an exception" to shop at this Beaverton Thai where the "hot and fresh", "finely prepared" fare is "always excellent"; the ravenous reveal that the "friendly service is sometimes slow."

Thai Orchid S   22 | 16 | 18 | $19
2231 W. Burnside St. (bet. 22nd & 23rd Aves.), 503-226-4542
10075 SW Barbur Blvd. (Capitol Hwy.), 503-452-2544
Tanasbourne Town Ctr., 18070 NW Evergreen Pkwy. (185th Ave.), Beaverton, 503-439-6683
120 N. Main Ave. (Powell Blvd.), Gresham, 503-491-0737
18740 Willamette Dr. (Fairview Way), West Linn, 503-699-4195
1004 Washington St. (Evergreen Blvd.), Vancouver, WA, 360-695-7786
■ A "solid performer among the Thais", this ever-blooming chain loops through the city and beyond, offering a "nicely spicy" "standard menu" of "fabulous soups", "flavorful" curries and "extraordinary specials"; although the decor differs according to location, the food is "consistent."

Thai Touch S   19 | 9 | 18 | $14
4806 SE Stark St. (48th Ave.), 503-230-2875
☑ Undaunted by the "deplorable decor", devotees want to reach out and touch the "lovely green curry", "spicy green beans" and other "excellent" dishes at this small Siamese in Southeast; those untouched deem it simply "decent", claiming "the competition's better."

Thai Villa S   19 | 10 | 16 | $19
670 N. State St. (D Ave.), Lake Oswego, 503-635-6164
☑ "Spicy" defines the fare at this Lake Oswego Thai where the "spectacular beef soup" and red and green curries attract admirers, though some villify the "dry" dishes.

Thanh Thao S   22 | 10 | 17 | $15
4005 SE Hawthorne Blvd. (40th Ave.), 503-238-6232
Thanh Thao II S
8355 SE Powell Blvd. (82nd Ave.), 503-775-0306
■ Those in the know "go early on weekend nights" to these Hawthorne and Southeast "down-home" Siamese-Vietnamese twins, where the "reasonable", "terrific" fare features "excellent eggplant" as well as an array of vegetarian dishes that make this duo a "great place to share."

Thien Hong ◐S
22 ┃ 13 ┃ 18 ┃ $15

6749 NE Sandy Blvd. (bet. 67th & 68th Aves.), 503-281-1247
■ With this "newly decorated" Chinese convert (from Vietnamese) in Northeast, regulars rave about the large menu's "great salt-and-pepper squid" ("the best I've had anywhere"); takeout is popular with all ages, and late-night hours make this a favorite among the nocturnal.

3 DOORS DOWN CAFE
25 ┃ 20 ┃ 23 ┃ $30

1429 SE 37th Ave. (Hawthorne Blvd.), 503-236-6886
■ "Style and substance without pretension" is openly proclaimed by proponents of this Mediterranean-NW in Hawthorne, where the "giant portions" of "mamma-mia penne with vodka sauce" and other "imaginative pastas" are "easy to split" (which ensures you'll "save room for banana cream pie"); no one can slam the "romantic" atmosphere and "bend-over-backward service", but its many regulars "wish it were bigger."

Three Square Grill S
21 ┃ 15 ┃ 20 ┃ $20

Hillsdale Shopping Ctr., 6320 SW Capitol Hwy. (bet. Bertha & Sunset Blvds.), 503-244-4467
■ This Hillsdale "family place in a strip mall exceeds expectations" with its "imaginative" American "comfort" food with a strong Southern accent; squareheads scramble for hoppin' John and "to-die-for strawberry shortcake" as well as "great hash" for brunch; added attractions include "revolving art shows" and "fun music on weekends."

TINA'S S
28 ┃ 22 ┃ 25 ┃ $40

760 Hwy. 99 W. (opp. fire station), Dundee, 503-538-8880
■ "Perennial wine country star" that sparkles with NW-French fare in Dundee; the "sophisticated" "ingredients shine through" in "super sautéed oysters" and "fab beef tenderloin", all "well matched" by "superb" *vins d*'Oregon and warmed by "friendly" service; though some whine about the "city prices", most "find excuses to make the trip."

Trianon S
18 ┃ 17 ┃ 19 ┃ $31

9225 SW Allen Blvd. (Scholls Ferry Rd.), Beaverton, 503-245-2775
◪ Latter-day Madame de Pompadours clamor for "classic Continental, heavy on the béarnaise" at this Beaverton institution whose specialties include "underrated" dill pickle soup; it offers "great ambiance" in a sprawling setting that's "good for a meeting", but *les critiques* carp about the "stuffy", "vintage '70s" decor and "salty" fare.

Tully's Coffee
19 ┃ 13 ┃ 14 ┃ $10

(fka Marsee Baking)
Portland Int'l Airport, 7000 NE Airport Way, 503-281-7000 S
519 SW Sixth Ave. (Alder St.), 503-973-5000 S
1220 SW Fourth Ave. (bet. Jefferson & Madison Sts.), 503-294-6000

(continued)

(continued)
Tully's Coffee
City Hall, 845 SW Fourth Ave. (bet. Taylor & Yamhill Sts.),
503-226-9000
210 SW Fourth Ave. (Pine St.), 503-952-5000 **S**
1625 SE Bybee Blvd. (16th Ave.), 503-952-5000
935 NE Broadway (10th Ave.), 503-280-8800 **S**
1323 NW 23rd Ave. (Overton St.), 503-295-5900 **S**
Tanasbourne Town Ctr., 2711 NW Town Center Dr.
(185th Ave.), Beaverton, 503-533-9400 **S**
406 A Ave. (4th St.), Lake Oswego, 503-697-5600 **S**
☑ This bakery chain allows you to sit inside or out as you
sample its homemade soups, sandwiches and pastries;
converts call it a "carbohydrate paradise" for its "amazing"
bagels and "fabulous" desserts, but a recent buyout prompts
protests over "snail-slow" service and "inconsistent" food.

Tuscany Grill **S**　　　　**23** **22** **21** **$30**
811 NW 21st Ave. (bet. Johnson & Kearney Sts.), 503-243-2757
■ "Everything's just right" at this "cozy, authentic and
romantic" Italian in Northwest, from "the smile at the door"
to the "scrumptious food", especially the spinach ravioli
that "makes you want to lick your plate", the "wonderful
lamb" and "unbeatable halibut"; the rustic room provides
a "friendly" drop-in on a trattoria-thick corner, and the
"summertime streetside dining is a treat."

TYPHOON! **S**　　　　**25** **18** **19** **$23**
2310 NW Everett St. (23rd Ave.), 503-243-7557
TYPHOON! ON BROADWAY **S**
Imperial Hotel, 400 SW Broadway (Stark St.), 503-224-8285
■ Bangkok-born chef-owner Bo Kline has stormed Portland
and beyond with her "world-class", "always packed"
Downtown and Northwest Siamese twins, serving the
"most imaginative Thai in town"; reviewers rain praise
on her "mind-boggling menu" including "great curries",
"heavenly 'pine cone fish'" and a "legendary tea selection";
"exotic surroundings" add to the "upscale feel", as do the
tariffs, but while "prices are high", it's "worth it."

Umenoki　　　　　　　**18** **16** **20** **$21**
2330 NW Thurman St. (bet. 23rd & 24th Aves.), 503-242-6404
☑ Admirers say *arigato* for 50 kinds of sushi and bento
specials at this Northwest Japanese and find the fare
"excellent", the bamboo-screened decor "authentic"
and the service "personable"; detractors dis the dishes,
saying they're "so-so" while the service is "slow"-slow.

Uogashi　　　　　　　**20** **18** **16** **$22**
107 NW Couch St. (1st Ave.), 503-242-1848
■ Serving the usual suspects ("great sushi" and tempura),
this "wonderful" Old Town Japanese uses "organic produce"
and hosts cooking classes; although the ambiance is
"authentic", a few feel the service needs improvement.

Utopia Cafe S　　▽ 19 17 22 $12
3308 SE Belmont St. (33rd Ave.), 503-235-7606
■ Folks find a bit of nirvana at this "small" New American–Eclectic "breakfast oasis" on Belmont serving "make-me-swoon blue corn pancakes" and "great baked goods", as well as lunch specials "loved by vegans"; chef-owner Joanne Perkins is "warm and welcoming", and outdoorsy types regain paradise on the patio.

Veritable Quandary S　　21 20 20 $28
1220 SW First Ave. (bet. Jefferson & Madison Sts.), 503-227-7342
■ Though it's now over 30, folks still trust this "tried-and-true" Downtown NW bistro with an Italian slant whose proximity to Keller Auditorium makes it "great for a pre-event dinner"; the "delicious" menu includes "gourmet" dishes like osso buco and "fabulous pastas", but some are in a veritable quandary over smoke from the "happening bar"; P.S. the patio is the "best place for a summer cocktail."

Vista Spring Cafe S　　18 18 18 $20
2440 SW Vista Ave. (Spring St.), 503-222-2811
■ "A local hangout you'd drive across town for", this "cozy", kid-friendly American-Eclectic "fixture" "tucked away in quiet" Portland Heights serves a "gourmet pizza" that elicits encores, while others spring for "delicious soups", mac 'n' cheese and homemade marionberry pie; N.B. grab a wooden window booth for the best vistas.

Vita Cafe S⌿　　– – – I
3024 NE Alberta St. (30th Ave.), 503-335-8233
Vegetarians plant themselves in this Eclectic Northeast cafe where the "funky, fresh and flavorful" dishes include "creative country-fried tempeh steak" (and a hormone-free hamburger for holdouts); art-covered walls and wooden booths create a setting regulars call "good for families."

Widmer Gasthaus S　　19 19 18 $19
955 N. Russell St. (Interstate Ave.), 503-281-3333
■ This "fun place to meet the gang and have a burger" under the Fremont Bridge in North Portland also pours homemade "well-crafted brews" to accompany "just-like-Germany schnitzels, spaetzles" and "rainy-day goulashes" with a NW spin; the roomy space is "great for parties" and *kinder*-friendly as well.

Wild Abandon S　　22 19 22 $25
2411 SE Belmont St. (25th Ave.), 503-232-4458
■ No need to abandon hope when you enter this "sassy" (both cuisine- and decor-wise) Belmont "so-busy-it's-crazy" cafe "with a social conscience", where you feast on "inventive" Eclectic fare featuring "clever combos" like polenta lasagna; it's also a "favorite for breakfast", and while at dinner you and your neighbors sit "elbow-to-elbow", you won't mind bending yours for "fresh lime margaritas."

WILDWOOD RESTAURANT & BAR 🅂

| 27 | 23 | 24 | $39 |

1221 NW 21st Ave. (Overton St.), 503-248-9663

■ Homegrown chef and best-selling author "Cory Schreiber gave Portland a gift when he opened" this "wildly popular" "NW cuisine icon" in Northwest that "does justice to local provender" and pays "attention to sustainable farming" and "boutique wines"; loyalists "love watching the open kitchen" turn out "incredible duck", "excellent Washington mussels" and "fresh desserts" served in an "intriguing milieu" (where "cheek-to-jowl" dining can produce "thunderous noise").

Wilfs

| – | – | – | E |

Union Station, 800 NW Sixth Ave. (Irving St.), 503-223-0070

In a restored century-old train station in the Pearl, this 25-year-old does "classic" Continental and NW cuisine in a clubby setting featuring wingback chairs, while waiters perform "solid" tableside service on the Caesar salad, steak Diane and crêpes suzette; celestial types find "piano bar heaven" Wednesday–Saturday.

William's on 12th 🅂

| 24 | 22 | 23 | $38 |

207 SE 12th Ave. (bet. Burnside & Stark Sts.), 503-963-9226

■ "Wunderkind" chef-owner William Henry takes a "bold approach" to French bistro fare in the "unscenic" Southeast in an "upper-class Bohemian", "comfortable dining room"; supporters swoon for "vibrant seared scallops" and other "superlative" entrees at "below-market prices", and though some say this yearling "still makes a few mistakes", most folks are decidedly Friends of Bill.

WINTERBORNE

| 26 | 21 | 24 | $36 |

3520 NE 42nd Ave. (Fremont St.), 503-249-8486

■ Turning "meat-and-potatoes girls" into born-again fish freaks, this seafood-only old-timer speaks with both NW and French accents in a "small, cozy" Northeast setting; "whatever they suggest, order it" is one school of thought, but consider the "unique crab juniper" and "terrific sautéed oysters", remembering that "every entree is special" and so are you with "personal attention from the staff" (that strikes a few as "interfering").

Ya Hala

| – | – | – | I |

8005 SE Stark St. (80th Ave.), 503-256-4484

Opened by a member of a local restaurant family (begat by Nicholas) in Southeast, this "undiscovered" Lebanese yearling shares space with a small Middle Eastern grocery store; it features an open kitchen baking fresh pita bread, grilling lamb kebabs, stuffing grape leaves and mashing hummus in a unhurried, eager-to-please ambiance.

Yen Ha 🌙 [S] 21 | 11 | 16 | $18

6820 NE Sandy Blvd. (68th Ave.), 503-287-3698

◩ If you have a yen for "quality Vietnamese eats", head to this Northeast longtimer featuring 150 items ranging from familiar (BBQ beef) to exotic (frogs' legs), all at "bargain prices"; however, a few find the food no laughing matter, saying "there's better in the neighborhood"; N.B. an adjoining karaoke bar supplies late-night entertainment.

Yoko's [S] ▽ 23 | 17 | 20 | $21

2878 SE Gladstone St. (bet. 28th & 29th Aves.), 503-736-9228

■ This "small, quaint" sushi "standby" in Southeast is a "favorite", as skillful with "all the standards" as it is with "original", "innovative selections" – don't miss a duo of dynamic dishes, the "fun Batman and Dynamite rolls"; a rockin' "lively atmosphere" makes it "worth the wait", allowing "plenty of time for sake."

Zell's: An American Cafe [S] 22 | 16 | 19 | $16

1300 SE Morrison St. (13th Ave.), 503-239-0196

■ Reviving the "lost art of breakfast", this American-Eclectic cafe in Southeast serves that important meal all day; Zell-lots savor "scones served when you sit down", followed by "carbo-fruity entrees" like German pancakes and other "fresh, fresh, fresh" fare; the "kitschy decor" and "unhurried" ambiance make this "a happy place to dine."

Portland
Indexes

CUISINES
LOCATIONS
SPECIAL FEATURES

CUISINES

African
Baobab
Horn of Africa
Jarra's Ethiopian

American (New)
Alameda Cafe
Besaw's Cafe
Chez What?
Clarke's
Hudson's B&G
J & M Cafe
Little Wing Cafe
Lucy's Table
McMenamins/Columbia
Papa Haydn West
Paragon
Utopia Cafe

American (Traditional)
Alameda Brewhse.
Anne Hughes
Beaches
Beaterville Cafe
Bijou Cafe
Billy Reed's
BridgePort Ale
Byways Cafe
Cadillac Cafe
Caswell
Cup & Saucer Cafe
Foothill Broiler
Fuller's Coffee Shop
Goose Hollow Inn
Hall St. Grill
Huber's
Jake's Grill
John St. Cafe
Milo's City Cafe
Mother's Bistro
Original Pancake House
Perry's On Fremont
Raccoon Lodge
Red Electric Cafe
Red Star Tavern
Sammy's
Sayler's
Tabor Hill Cafe
Three Sq. Grill
Vista Spring Cafe
Zell's

Asian
Oritalia
Tao of Tea

Bakery
Berlin Inn
Grand Central Bakery

Il Fornaio
Pazzoria
Pearl Bakery
Tully's Coffee

Barbecue
Buster's Texas-Style BBQ
Campbell's BBQ
Doris' Cafe
Tennessee Red's BBQ

Brazilian
Brasilia

Cajun/Creole
Montage
Sweetwater's Jam Hse.

Caribbean
Salvador Molly's
Sweetwater's Jam Hse.

Chinese
Bamboos
Dragonfly
Fong Chong
FuJin
Good Day
Hunan
Legin
Sungari
Tao of Tea
Thien Hong

Coffeehouse/Dessert
Papa Haydn East
Papa Haydn West
Tully's Coffee

Coffee Shop/Diner
Byways Cafe
Cadillac Cafe
Fat City Cafe
Fuller's Coffee Shop
Milo's City Cafe

Continental
London Grill
Trianon
Wilfs

Cuban
Pambiche

Deli/Sandwich Shop
Daily Cafe/Rejuvenation
Grand Central Bakery
Kornblatt's Deli
Little Wing Cafe
Produce Row Cafe

Dim Sum
Fong Chong
Legin

Eclectic/International
Alameda Cafe
Brazen Bean
Bread & Ink Cafe
Caswell
Chameleon
Compass World Bistro
Counter Culture
Daily Cafe/Rejuvenation
Dot's Cafe
Fusion
Grant House
Hands on Café
Henry's Cafe
John St. Cafe
Ken's Home Plate
Little Wing Cafe
Marco's Cafe
Old Wives' Tales
Oritalia
Springwater Grill
Utopia Cafe
Vista Spring Cafe
Vita Cafe
Wild Abandon
Zell's

Ethiopian
Jarra's Ethiopian

French
Bluehour
Cafe des Amis
Castagna
Clarke's
Couvron
Heathman
Tina's
Winterborne

French (Bistro)
Brasserie Montmartre
Cafe Castagna
Cafe des Amis
Esplanade
L'Auberge
Le Bouchon
Paley's Place
William's on 12th

French (New)
Couvron
Laslow's Northwest

German
Berlin Inn
Gustav's Bier Stube
Rheinlander
Widmer Gasthaus

Greek
Alexis
Berbati
Eleni's Estiatorio

Hamburgers
Beaterville Cafe
BridgePort Ale
Bugatti's Caffe
Burgerville USA
Byways Cafe
Cadillac Cafe
Chez What?
Foothill Broiler
Jo Bar & Rotisserie
McMenamins/Columbia
McMenamins Courtyard
Produce Row Cafe
Stanich's
Widmer Gasthaus

Hawaiian
Noho's

Health Food
Counter Culture
Macheezmo Mouse
Old Wives' Tales

Hot Dogs
Dog House
Good Dog/Bad Dog

Indian
Bombay Cricket Club
India House
Plainfields' Mayur
Swagat

Irish
Kells Irish Restaurant & Pub

Italian
(N=Northern; S=Southern;
N&S=Includes both)
Alessandro's (N&S)
Assaggio (N&S)
Bastas Trattoria (N&S)
Bluehour (N)
Bugatti's Caffe (N&S)
Bugatti's Rist. (S)
Cafe Castagna (N)
Caffe Mingo (N)
Clarke's (N)
Cozze (N&S)
Fratelli (N&S)
Genoa (N&S)
Gino's (N&S)
Giorgio's (N)
Il Fornaio (N&S)
Il Piatto (N)
La Buca (N&S)
La Prima Trattoria (N&S)

Nick's Italian Cafe (N)
Old Spaghetti Factory (N&S)
Oritalia (N&S)
Paparazzi Pastaficio (N&S)
Pasta Veloce (N&S)
Pazzo (N)
Pazzoria (N&S)
Piazza Italia (N&S)
Portofino (N&S)
Riccardo's (N&S)
Rustica (N&S)
Serratto (N&S)
3 Doors Down (N&S)
Tuscany Grill (N)
Veritable Quandary (N&S)

Japanese
Big Dan's
Bush Garden
Celadon
Koji Osakaya
Obi Japanese
Restaurant Murata
Saburo's Sushi
Sushi Takahashi
Syun Izakaya
Umenoki
Uogashi
Yoko's

Jewish
Kornblatt's Deli

Korean
Celadon

Kosher
Counter Culture

Laotian
Tara Thai

Lebanese
Abou Karim
Al-Amir
Cedar's
Hoda's
Nicholas'
Ya Hala

Mediterranean
Bluehour
Lucy's Table
Southpark Seafood
Tapeo
3 Doors Down

Mexican/Tex-Mex
Cafe Azul
Chevys
Chez Jose East
El Burrito Loco
Esparza's Tex Mex
Hungry Dog Burrito

La Calaca Comelona
La Cruda
Macheezmo Mouse
Maya's Taqueria
Santa Fe Taqueria
Taqueria La Sirenita
Taqueria Nueve

Middle Eastern
Abou Karim
Al-Amir
Bombay Cricket Club
Garbonzos
Hoda's
Nicholas'
Ya Hala

Moroccan
Casablanca
Marrakesh

Nuevo Latino
¡Oba!
Salvador Molly's

Pacific Northwest
Alexander's
Besaw's Cafe
Bistro 921
Caprial's Bistro
Cassidy's
Columbia River Ct.
Dundee Bistro
Esplanade
Hall St. Grill
Harborside
Heathman
Higgins
Hudson's B&G
Jake's Famous Crawfish
Jo Bar & Rotisserie
Joel Palmer Hse.
Laslow's Northwest
London Grill
McCormick & Schmick's
McMenamins Black Rabbit
Metronome
Milo's City Cafe
Paley's Place
Papa Haydn East
Papa Haydn West
Red Hills
Red Star Tavern
Sammy's
Springwater Grill
Taqueria Nueve
3 Doors Down
Tina's
Veritable Quandary
Widmer Gasthaus
Wildwood

Wilfs
Winterborne

Pan-Asian
Celadon
Dragonfish
Dragonfly
Saucebox
Stickers Asian Cafe

Pizza
Accuardi's
Beaches
BridgePort Ale
BridgePort Brew Pub
Bugatti's Caffe
Cafe Castagna
Caswell
Escape From N.Y.
Goose Hollow Inn
Hot Lips Pizza
La Prima Trattoria
McMenamins Courtyard
Paparazzi Pastaficio
Pazzoria
Pizzicato
Vista Spring Cafe

Pub Food
Alameda Brewhse.
BridgePort Ale
BridgePort Brew Pub
McMenamins/Columbia
McMenamins Courtyard
Produce Row Cafe
Stanich's

Russian
Restaurant Russia

Seafood
Dan & Louis' Oyster Bar
Harborside
Jake's Famous Crawfish
Jake's Grill
Legin
McCormick & Schmick's
McCormick's Fish House
Portland Steak
Southpark Seafood
Winterborne

Senegalese
Baobab

Southern/Soul
Bernie's
Delta Cafe
Doris' Cafe
Tennessee Red's BBQ
Three Sq. Grill

Southwestern
Chez Grill

Spanish
Colosso
Fernando's Hideaway
La Catalana
Tapeo

Steakhouse
El Gaucho
Hall St. Grill
Hayden Island Steak
Jake's Grill
Morton's of Chicago
Portland Steak
Ringside Steakhse.
Ruth's Chris
Sayler's

Tapas
Colosso
Fernando's Hideaway
La Catalana
Tapeo

Tearoom
Tao of Tea

Thai
Dragonfly
Khun Pic's Bahn Thai
Lemongrass Thai
Misohapi
Saigon Kitchen
Siam
Sweet Basil
Tara Thai
Thai Kitchen
Thai Orchid
Thai Touch
Thai Villa
Thanh Thao
Typhoon!

Vegetarian
(Most Chinese, Indian and
Thai restaurants usually offer
vegetarian dishes; *vegan)
Counter Culture*
Cup & Saucer Cafe*
Macheezmo Mouse
Old Wives' Tales
Utopia Cafe*
Vita Cafe

Vietnamese
Misohapi
Pho Van Vietnamese
Saigon Kitchen
Thanh Thao
Yen Ha

LOCATIONS

Beaumont
Alameda Brewhse.
Alameda Cafe
Marco's Cafe
Perry's On Fremont
Pizzicato
Stanich's

Beaverton/Tigard
Beaches
Bush Garden/Soba
Buster's Texas-Style BBQ
Chevys
Hall St. Grill
Hot Lips Pizza
Koji Osakaya
La Prima Trattoria
Macheezmo Mouse
McCormick's Fish House
Paparazzi Pastaficio
Pasta Veloce
Raccoon Lodge
Sayler's
Siam
Swagat
Thai Kitchen
Thai Orchid
Trianon
Tully's Coffee

Chinatown/Old Town
Accuardi's
Alexis
Fong Chong
Good Day
Obi Japanese
Sushi Takahashi
Tao of Tea
Uogashi

Clackamas
Chevys
Gustav's
Macheezmo Mouse
Old Spaghetti Factory

Clinton Street
Dot's Cafe
Henry's Cafe
La Cruda
Noho's

Downtown
Abou Karim
Al-Amir
Alessandro's
Alexander's
Berbati
Bijou Cafe
Bistro 921

Brasserie Montmartre
Bush Garden
Cassidy's
Dan & Louis' Oyster Bar
Dragonfish
El Gaucho
Esplanade
Fernando's Hideaway
Good Dog/Bad Dog
Harborside
Heathman
Higgins
Hot Lips Pizza
Huber's
Hunan
India House
Jake's Famous Crawfish
Jake's Grill
Kells Irish Restaurant & Pub
Koji Osakaya
London Grill
Macheezmo Mouse
Maya's Taqueria
McCormick & Schmick's
Morton's of Chicago
Mother's Bistro
Oritalia
Pasta Veloce
Pazzo
Pazzoria
Pizzicato
Portland Steak
Red Star Tavern
Restaurant Murata
Ruth's Chris
Saucebox
Southpark Seafood
Sungari
Tully's Coffee
Typhoon! on B'way
Veritable Quandary

Hawthorne
Bombay Cricket Club
Bread & Ink Cafe
BridgePort Ale
Burgerville USA
Cafe Castagna
Casablanca
Castagna
Chez Grill
Compass World Bistro
Cup & Saucer Cafe
FuJin
Garbonzos
Jarra's Ethiopian
Ken's Home Plate
La Calaca Comelona

Tabor Hill Cafe
Thanh Thao
3 Doors Down

Hillsboro
Chevys
Macheezmo Mouse
Old Spaghetti Factory
Syun Izakaya

Hillsdale
Garbonzos
Pizzicato
Red Electric Cafe
Salvador Molly's
Three Sq. Grill

Johns Landing
Brasilia
Cedar's

Lake Oswego
Chevys
Clarke's
Riccardo's
Thai Villa
Tully's Coffee

Lloyd Center/NE Broadway
Cadillac Cafe
Chez Jose East
Colosso
Dragonfly
Grand Central Bakery
Macheezmo Mouse
Metronome
Milo's City Cafe
Paparazzi Pastaficio
Rustica
Saigon Kitchen
Sweet Basil
Tully's Coffee

Metro Area
Bugatti's Caffe
Bugatti's Rist.
Bush Garden
Buster's Texas-Style BBQ
Macheezmo Mouse
Pizzicato
Thai Orchid
Tully's Coffee

Multnomah Village
Fat City Cafe
Marco's Cafe

Northeast Portland
Bernie's
Billy Reed's
Burgerville USA
Chameleon
Chez What?
Counter Culture

Dog House
Doris' Cafe
El Burrito Loco
Gustav's
Horn of Africa
Koji Osakaya
La Buca
Lemongrass Thai
McMenamins Courtyard
Pambiche
Pizzicato
Rheinlander
Ringside Steakhse.
Taqueria La Sirenita
Taqueria Nueve
Thien Hong
Vita Cafe
Winterborne
Yen Ha

North Portland
Beaterville Cafe
Hayden Island Steak
John St. Cafe
Widmer Gasthaus

Northwest Portland
Bamboos
Bastas Trattoria
Besaw's Cafe
Big Dan's
Brazen Bean
Cafe des Amis
Caffe Mingo
Celadon
Escape From N.Y.
Foothill Broiler
Garbonzos
Hungry Dog Burrito
Il Fornaio
Jo Bar & Rotisserie
Kornblatt's Deli
La Buca
Laslow's Northwest
L'Auberge
Lucy's Table
Marrakesh
Misohapi
Paley's Place
Papa Haydn West
Pizzicato
Ringside Steakhse.
Sammy's
Santa Fe Taqueria
Serratto
Swagat
Tapeo
Tara Thai
Thai Orchid
Tuscany Grill

Typhoon!
Umenoki
Wildwood

Out of Metro Area
Columbia River Ct.

Pearl District
Baobab
Bluehour
BridgePort Brew Pub
Byways Cafe
Cafe Azul
Daily Cafe/Pearl
Fratelli
Fuller's Coffee Shop
Giorgio's
Ken's Home Plate
Le Bouchon
Little Wing Cafe
¡Oba!
Paragon
Pearl Bakery
Piazza Italia
Wilfs

Southeast Portland
Anne Hughes
Berlin Inn
Burgerville USA
Campbell's BBQ
Caswell
Cozze
Daily Cafe/Rejuvenation
Delta Cafe
Esparza's Tex Mex
Fusion
Genoa
Hoda's
Il Piatto
J & M Cafe
Khun Pic's Bahn Thai
La Catalana
Legin
Montage
Nicholas'
Old Wives' Tales
Pho Van Vietnamese
Produce Row Cafe
Restaurant Russia
Saigon Kitchen
Sayler's
Sushi/Takahashi
Sweetwater's Jam Hse.
Tao of Tea
Tennessee Red's BBQ
Thai Touch
Thanh Thao II
Utopia Cafe
Wild Abandon

William's on 12th
Ya Hala
Yoko's
Zell's

Southwest Portland
Chez Jose West
Couvron
Goose Hollow Inn
Hands on Café
Koji Osakaya
Macheezmo Mouse
Noho's
Old Spaghetti Factory
Original Pancake House
Pizzicato
Plainfields' Mayur
Stanich's
Thai Orchid
Tully's Coffee
Vista Spring Cafe

Troutdale/Gresham
Buster's Texas-Style BBQ
El Burrito Loco
McMenamins Black Rabbit
Pasta Veloce
Thai Orchid

Vancouver, WA
Beaches
Burgerville USA
Buster's Texas-Style BBQ
Chevys
Grant House
Hudson's B&G
McMenamins/Columbia
Noho's/Islander
Pizzicato
Thai Orchid

Westmoreland/Sellwood
Assaggio
Caprial's Bistro
Eleni's Estiatorio
Gino's
Papa Haydn East
Pizzicato
Portofino
Saburo's Sushi
Springwater Grill
Stickers Asian Cafe
Tully's Coffee

Wine Country
Dundee Bistro
Joel Palmer Hse.
Nick's Italian Cafe
Red Hills
Tina's

SPECIAL FEATURES

Brunch
(Best of many)
Berlin Inn
Besaw's Cafe
Bijou Cafe
Billy Reed's
Brasserie Montmartre
Bread & Ink Cafe
Chez What?
Columbia River Ct.
Compass World Bistro
Grant House
Hands on Café
Harborside
Hayden Island Steak
Heathman
Hudson's B&G
Il Fornaio
Jo Bar & Rotisserie
London Grill
Old Wives' Tales
Papa Haydn East
Papa Haydn West
Red Electric Cafe
Red Star Tavern
Southpark Seafood
Springwater Grill
Sweetwater's Jam Hse.
Three Sq. Grill
Trianon
Veritable Quandary
Wildwood
Zell's

Buffet
(Check prices, days
and times)
Brasilia
Counter Culture
Horn of Africa
India House
London Grill
Swagat

Business Dining
Alessandro's
Alexander's
Bluehour
Bush Garden
Caprial's Bistro
Castagna
Dragonfish
Dundee Bistro
El Gaucho
Esplanade
Fratelli

Genoa
Grant House
Hall St. Grill
Hayden Island Steak
Heathman
Higgins
Hudson's B&G
Hunan
Il Fornaio
Jake's Famous Crawfish
Jake's Grill
Jo Bar & Rotisserie
Laslow's Northwest
L'Auberge
London Grill
McCormick & Schmick's
McCormick's Fish House
Morton's of Chicago
Nick's Italian Cafe
¡Oba!
Oritalia
Paley's Place
Pazzo
Plainfields' Mayur
Portland Steak
Red Star Tavern
Restaurant Murata
Ringside Steakhse.
Ruth's Chris
Serratto
Southpark Seafood
Thai Orchid
Tina's
Typhoon!
Veritable Quandary
Wildwood
Wilfs

Caters
(Best of many)
Abou Karim
Al-Amir
Berlin Inn
Bush Garden
Buster's Texas-Style BBQ
Cadillac Cafe
Campbell's BBQ
Caprial's Bistro
Chameleon
Compass World Bistro
Cozze
Daily Cafe/Rejuvenation
Doris' Cafe
Dragonfly
Fratelli

Hands on Café
Hoda's
Hudson's B&G
Hunan
Il Piatto
India House
Jake's Grill
Jo Bar & Rotisserie
Ken's Home Plate
Kornblatt's Deli
La Buca
Laslow's Northwest
McMenamins Black Rabbit
McMenamins/Columbia
McMenamins Courtyard
Mother's Bistro
Noho's
Pambiche
Papa Haydn East
Papa Haydn West
Pazzo
Pizzicato
Red Hills
Salvador Molly's
Springwater Grill
Sungari
Swagat
Sweetwater's Jam Hse.
Syun Izakaya
Taqueria Nueve
Tully's Coffee
Tuscany Grill
Typhoon!
Wild Abandon

Cigar Friendly

Brazen Bean
Bush Garden
Dragonfish
El Gaucho
Hall St. Grill
Harborside
Jake's Grill
McMenamins Black Rabbit
McMenamins Courtyard
Morton's of Chicago
Mother's Bistro
Ringside Steakhse.
Ruth's Chris
Sammy's
Sayler's
Veritable Quandary

Delivers*/Takeout

(Nearly all Asians, coffee
shops, delis, diners and
pasta/pizzerias deliver or do
takeout; here are some
interesting possibilities;
D=delivery, T=takeout; *call
to check range and charges,
if any)
Abou Karim (T)
Alameda Brewhse. (T)
Alameda Cafe (T)
Al-Amir (T)
Alexis (T)
Anne Hughes (T)
Baobab (T)
Bastas Trattoria (T)
Berbati (T)
Berlin Inn (T)
Bernie's (T)
Besaw's Cafe (T)
Bijou Cafe (T)
Bombay Cricket Club (T)
Bread & Ink Cafe (T)
BridgePort Ale (T)
Bugatti's Rist. (T)
Burgerville USA (T)
Caffe Mingo (T)
Campbell's BBQ (T)
Cassidy's (T)
Caswell (T)
Chevys (T)
Chez Grill (T)
Chez Jose East (T)
Colosso (T)
Counter Culture (T)
Cozze (T)
Dan & Louis' Oyster Bar (T)
Delta Cafe (T)
Dog House (T)
Doris' Cafe (T)
El Burrito Loco (T)
Esparza's Tex Mex (T)
Foothill Broiler (T)
Fusion (T)
Garbonzos (T)
Gino's (T)
Good Dog/Bad Dog (T)
Gustav's Bier Stube (T)
Hungry Dog Burrito (T)
Il Fornaio (T)
Jo Bar & Rotisserie (T)
John St. Cafe (T)
Kells Irish Restaurant & Pub (T)

La Buca (T)
La Calaca Comelona (T)
La Cruda (T)
Marco's Cafe (T)
Maya's Taqueria (T)
McMenamins/Columbia (T)
Metronome (T)
Montage (T)
Mother's Bistro (D,T)
Nicholas' (T)
Noho's (D,T)
Old Spaghetti Factory (T)
Old Wives' Tales (T)
Pambiche (T)
Papa Haydn East (T)
Papa Haydn West (T)
Paparazzi Pastaficio (T)
Pazzoria (T)
Pearl Bakery (T)
Perry's On Fremont (T)
Red Star Tavern (T)
Rustica (T)
Salvador Molly's (T)
Santa Fe Taqueria (T)
Sayler's (D,T)
Springwater Grill (T)
Stanich's (T)
Swagat (T)
Sweetwater's Jam Hse. (T)
Tabor Hill Cafe (T)
Three Sq. Grill (T)
Trianon (T)
Tully's Coffee (D,T)
Tuscany Grill (T)
Widmer Gasthaus (T)
Ya Hala (T)
Zell's (T)

Dessert/Ice Cream

Bijou Cafe
Bluehour
Bread & Ink Cafe
Burgerville USA
Castagna
Compass World Bistro
Dundee Bistro
Grant House
Heathman
Hudson's B&G
Laslow's Northwest
Marco's Cafe
Mother's Bistro
Paley's Place
Papa Haydn East
Papa Haydn West
Pazzo

Dining Alone

(Other than hotels, coffee
shops, sushi bars and places
with counter service)
Abou Karim
Alameda Cafe
Bijou Cafe
Bluehour
Bread & Ink Cafe
Counter Culture
Foothill Broiler
Garbonzos
Grant House
Henry's Cafe
Higgins
Il Fornaio
Jo Bar & Rotisserie
Marco's Cafe
McCormick & Schmick's
McCormick's Fish House
Mother's Bistro
Old Wives' Tales
Papa Haydn East
Papa Haydn West
Pizzicato
Red Electric Cafe
Saucebox
Thai Orchid
Tully's Coffee
Veritable Quandary
Zell's

Entertainment

(Check days, times and
performers for entertainment;
D=dancing; best of many)
Al-Amir (D/belly dancer/guitar)
Alexander's (D/piano)
Alexis (belly dancer)
Berbati (band/belly dancer)
Billy Reed's (blues/reggae)
Brasilia (D/Latin)
Brasserie Mont. (jazz/magician)
Bush Garden (karaoke)
El Gaucho (flamenco guitar)
Esplanade (jazz)
Fernando's Hideaway (D/DJ)
Gustav's Bier Stube (D)
Heathman (jazz)
Hudson's B&G (jazz/piano)
Kells Irish (Celtic)
Legin (D/karaoke)
Marrakesh (D/belly dancer)
McCormick & Schmick's (piano)
McMenamins Courtyard (bands)
Paragon (blues/jazz)
Restaurant Russia (D/Russian)
Rheinlander (German)
Saucebox (DJ)

Typhoon! on B'way (jazz)
Wilfs (piano bar)
Yen Ha (karaoke)

Fireplace

Bamboos
Beaches
Columbia River Ct.
Dundee Bistro
El Gaucho
Heathman
Hudson's B&G
Il Fornaio
Jake's Famous Crawfish
L'Auberge
McCormick's Fish House
Papa Haydn West
Paragon
Plainfields' Mayur
Raccoon Lodge
Red Hills
Ringside Steakhse.
Sayler's
Tina's
Trianon

Game in Season

Bastas Trattoria
Beaches
Billy Reed's
Bluehour
Castagna
Dan & Louis' Oyster Bar
Dundee Bistro
Grant House
Heathman
Higgins
Hudson's B&G
Il Fornaio
Joel Palmer Hse.
La Catalana
Le Bouchon
London Grill
McMenamins Black Rabbit
Paley's Place
Rheinlander
Serratto
Tuscany Grill
Wildwood

Historic Interest

(Year opened; *building)
1849 Grant House*
1857 Joel Palmer Hse.*
1879 Huber's
1886 McCormick & Schmick's*
1892 Jake's Famous Crawfish
1898 Wilfs*
1903 Besaw's Cafe
1907 Dan & Louis' Oyster Bar
1909 Jake's Grill*

1911 McMenamins/Rabbit*
1912 London Grill*
1915 McMenamins Courtyard*
1921 Columbia River Ct.
1927 Billy Reed's*
1941 Fuller's Coffee Shop
1944 Ringside Steakhse.
1946 Sayler's
1949 Stanich's

Hotel Dining

Benson Hotel
　El Gaucho
　London Grill
Columbia Gorge Hotel
　Columbia River Ct.
DoubleTree Hotel
　Hayden Island Steak
Embassy Suites Downtown
　Portland Steak
Fifth Avenue Suites Hotel
　Red Star Tavern
Governor Hotel
　Jake's Grill
Heathman Hotel
　Heathman
Heathman Lodge
　Hudson's B&G
Hilton Portland
　Alexander's
　Bistro 921
Hotel Vintage Plaza
　Pazzo
Imperial Hotel
　Typhoon! on B'way
McMenamins Edgefield
　McMenamins Black Rabbit
McMenamins Kennedy School
　McMenamins Courtyard
Paramount Hotel
　Dragonfish
RiverPlace Hotel
　Esplanade
Westin Portland
　Oritalia

"In" Places

Assaggio
Beaches
Bluehour
BridgePort Brew Pub
Cafe Castagna
Caprial's Bistro
Castagna
Fratelli
Higgins
Hudson's B&G
Jake's Famous Crawfish
Jake's Grill
Laslow's Northwest

¡Oba!
Oritalia
Paley's Place
Paragon
Pazzo
Serratto
Southpark Seafood
Veritable Quandary
Wildwood

Late Late – After 12:30
(All hours are AM)
Brasserie Montmartre (1)
Cassidy's (2)
Caswell (2)
Chez Grill (1)
Colosso (2)
Dot's Cafe (2)
El Gaucho (1)
Kells Irish Restaurant & Pub (2)
McMenamins/Columbia (1)
McMenamins Courtyard (1)
Montage (2)

Meet for a Drink
(Most top hotels and the
following standouts)
Alameda Brewhse.
Assaggio
Beaches
Billy Reed's
Bluehour
Brasserie Montmartre
Brazen Bean
BridgePort Ale
BridgePort Brew Pub
Cafe Castagna
Caswell
Chevys
Chez Grill
Colosso
Dundee Bistro
Fernando's Hideaway
Gino's
Giorgio's
Goose Hollow Inn
Hall St. Grill
Harborside
Higgins
Huber's
Jake's Famous Crawfish
Kells Irish Restaurant & Pub
L'Auberge
McCormick & Schmick's
McCormick's Fish House
McMenamins Black Rabbit
McMenamins/Columbia
McMenamins Courtyard
Morton's of Chicago
Mother's Bistro

¡Oba!
Oritalia
Paley's Place
Paragon
Raccoon Lodge
Ringside Steakhse.
Ruth's Chris
Saucebox
Serratto
Southpark Seafood
Springwater Grill
Sweetwater's Jam Hse.
Tapeo
Veritable Quandary
Widmer Gasthaus
Wildwood
Wilfs

Noteworthy Newcomers (17)
Baobab
Bluehour
Cafe Castagna
Clarke's
Dundee Bistro
Eleni's Estiatorio
El Gaucho
Fratelli
Giorgio's
Grant House
Hoda's
Laslow's Northwest
Pambiche
Sungari
Sweet Basil
Ya Hala

Offbeat
Beaterville Cafe
Brazen Bean
Caswell
Chez What?
Counter Culture
Delta Cafe
Dog House
Dot's Cafe
Esparza's Tex Mex
Fusion
Good Dog/Bad Dog
Jarra's Ethiopian
La Calaca Comelona
Marrakesh
McMenamins Courtyard
Montage
Noho's
Pambiche
Salvador Molly's
Stickers Asian Cafe
Sweetwater's Jam Hse.

Tao of Tea
Vita Cafe
Wild Abandon
Ya Hala

Outdoor Dining

(G=garden; P=patio;
S=sidewalk; T=terrace;
W=waterside; best of many)
Accuardi's (P,S)
Alameda Brewhse. (S)
Alameda Cafe (S)
Bastas Trattoria (P)
Beaches (P,W)
Berlin Inn (G)
Bernie's (G)
Besaw's Cafe (P)
Billy Reed's (P)
Bluehour (P,S)
Bombay Cricket Club (P)
Brazen Bean (P)
BridgePort Brew Pub (P)
Bugatti's Rist. (P)
Bush Garden (P)
Cadillac Cafe (P)
Campbell's BBQ (P)
Castagna (S)
Celadon (P)
Chameleon (P)
Chevys (P)
Chez Jose East (P)
Chez What? (P)
Clarke's (T)
Columbia River Ct. (P,W)
Compass World Bistro (G)
Cozze (P)
Cup & Saucer Cafe (P)
Dragonfish (S)
Dragonfly (P,S)
Dundee Bistro (P)
Esplanade (P,S,T,W)
Fernando's Hideaway (T)
Gino's (S)
Giorgio's (P,S)
Grand Central Bakery (S)
Grant House (G,P)
Hall St. Grill (P)
Hands on Café (P)
Harborside (P,W)
Huber's (P,S)
Hudson's B&G (P)
Il Fornaio (P)
Jake's Grill (S)
Joel Palmer Hse. (P)
John St. Cafe (P)
Khun Pic's Bahn Thai (P)
Koji Osakaya (P)
Kornblatt's Deli (P)
La Buca (P,S)

L'Auberge (P)
Little Wing Cafe (T)
Lucy's Table (P,S)
McMenamins/Columbia (P,W)
McMenamins Courtyard (P)
Metronome (S)
Noho's (P)
Noho's/Islander (S)
Paley's Place (P)
Pambiche (S)
Papa Haydn East (S)
Papa Haydn West (P)
Paragon (G,P,S,T)
Pasta Veloce (P,S)
Pazzo (T)
Perry's On Fremont (G,P)
Pizzicato (S,T)
Plainfields' Mayur (G,P)
Portland Steak (S)
Produce Row Cafe (P)
Raccoon Lodge (P)
Red Electric Cafe (P)
Red Hills (P)
Riccardo's (P,T)
Ringside Steakhse. (P)
Saigon Kitchen (P)
Salvador Molly's (T)
Sammy's (P,S)
Sayler's (P)
Serratto (P)
Siam (P)
Stickers Asian Cafe (S)
Sweet Basil (P)
Sweetwater's Jam Hse. (S)
Syun Izakaya (P)
Tapeo (P)
Taqueria La Sirenita (P)
Tara Thai (P)
Trianon (P)
Tully's Coffee (S)
Utopia Cafe (P)
Veritable Quandary (P)
Widmer Gasthaus (P)
Wild Abandon (P)
Wildwood (P)

Parking/Valet

(L=parking lot;
V=valet parking;
*=validated parking)
Abou Karim (V)
Accuardi's*
Alexander's (L,V)*
Bamboos (L)
Bastas Trattoria (L)
Beaches (L)
Beaterville Cafe (L)
Big Dan's (L)
Bistro 921 (L)

Bluehour (V)
Bombay Cricket Club (L)
Bugatti's Rist. (L)
Bush Garden (L,V)*
Buster's Texas-Style BBQ (L)
Cadillac Cafe (L)
Cafe des Amis (L)
Caffe Mingo (L,V)*
Campbell's BBQ (L)
Chameleon (L)
Chevys (L)
Chez Grill (L)
Chez Jose East (L)
Clarke's (L)
Columbia River Ct. (L)
Couvron (L)
Cozze (L)
Daily Cafe/Rejuvenation (L)
Delta Cafe (L)
Dog House (L)
Doris' Cafe (L)
Dundee Bistro (L)
El Gaucho (V)*
Esplanade (V)
Foothill Broiler (L)
Fusion (L)
Garbonzos (L)
Giorgio's (L)
Hall St. Grill (L)
Hands on Café (L)
Harborside*
Heathman (V)
Hudson's B&G (L)
Il Fornaio (L,V)
Jake's Grill (V)
Jarra's Ethiopian (L)
Jo Bar & Rotisserie (L)*
Joel Palmer Hse. (L)
Koji Osakaya (L)
La Buca (L)
La Calaca Comelona (L)
La Prima Trattoria (L)
Legin (L)
London Grill (V)*
Lucy's Table (V)
Marco's Cafe (L)
McCormick & Schmick's (L)
McCormick's Fish House (L)
McMenamins/Columbia (L)
McMenamins Courtyard (L)
Morton's of Chicago (V)
Obi Japanese*
Old Spaghetti Factory (L)
Old Wives' Tales (L)
Original Pancake House (L)
Oritalia (V)
Paley's Place (L)
Papa Haydn East (L)
Papa Haydn West (L)*

Paparazzi Pastaficio (L)
Pasta Veloce (L)
Pazzo (V)
Pearl Bakery (L)
Perry's On Fremont (L)
Pho Van Vietnamese (L)
Pizzicato (L)*
Plainfields' Mayur (L)
Portland Steak*
Portofino (L)
Raccoon Lodge (L)
Red Electric Cafe (L)
Red Hills (L)
Red Star Tavern (V)*
Ringside Steakhse. (L,V)
Ruth's Chris (V)
Saburo's Sushi (L)
Salvador Molly's (L)
Sammy's (L)
Sayler's (L)
Serratto (L,V)*
Siam (L)
Southpark Seafood (L)*
Springwater Grill (L)
Stanich's (L)
Stickers Asian Cafe (L)
Swagat (L)
Thai Orchid (L)
Thai Touch (L)
Thai Villa (L)
Thien Hong (L)
Tina's (L)
Trianon (L)
Tully's Coffee (L)
Tuscany Grill (V)
Umenoki (L)
Uogashi (L)
Widmer Gasthaus (L)
Wildwood (L)
William's on 12th (L)
Winterborne (L)

Parties & Private Rooms
(Any nightclub or restaurant
charges less at off-times;
* indicates private rooms
available; best of many)
Alameda Brewhse.
Al-Amir
Alexander's*
Alexis
Berlin Inn*
Billy Reed's*
Bistro 921
Brasserie Montmartre
Brazen Bean
Bread & Ink Cafe
BridgePort Brew Pub*
Bush Garden*

Cadillac Cafe
Cafe Azul
Caprial's Bistro*
Casablanca*
Cassidy's*
Chameleon*
Chevys*
Chez Grill*
Clarke's*
Columbia River Ct.*
Compass World Bistro
Counter Culture
Dan & Louis' Oyster Bar*
Doris' Cafe
Dundee Bistro*
El Gaucho*
Esparza's Tex Mex*
Esplanade*
Fernando's Hideaway*
Fratelli
Genoa*
Giorgio's
Good Day
Hall St. Grill*
Harborside
Hayden Island Steak
Heathman*
Horn of Africa
Hudson's B&G*
Hunan
Il Fornaio*
Jake's Grill*
Joel Palmer Hse.*
Kells Irish Restaurant & Pub*
La Catalana*
La Prima Trattoria
Legin*
London Grill*
Marrakesh
McCormick & Schmick's
McCormick's Fish House
McMenamins Black Rabbit*
McMenamins Courtyard*
Misohapi*
Morton's of Chicago*
Mother's Bistro*
Nick's Italian Cafe*
Noho's*
¡Oba!
Old Spaghetti Factory*
Old Wives' Tales
Oritalia*
Paley's Place*
Papa Haydn East
Paragon*
Pasta Veloce
Pazzo*
Perry's On Fremont
Plainfields' Mayur*

Portofino
Raccoon Lodge*
Red Electric Cafe*
Red Hills*
Red Star Tavern*
Restaurant Murata
Rheinlander*
Ringside Steakhse.*
Rustica
Ruth's Chris*
Saigon Kitchen
Sammy's*
Saucebox
Sayler's*
Serratto*
Southpark Seafood
Stanich's*
Sungari
Swagat
Sweetwater's Jam Hse.
Thai Orchid*
Thai Touch*
Thai Villa
3 Doors Down
Tina's*
Trianon*
Tuscany Grill
Typhoon!*
Umenoki
Uogashi
Vista Spring Cafe
Widmer Gasthaus*
Wild Abandon
Wilfs
William's on 12th
Winterborne

People-Watching
Assaggio
Bijou Cafe
Bluehour
Brazen Bean
Cafe Castagna
Delta Cafe
El Gaucho
Esparza's Tex Mex
Goose Hollow Inn
Heathman
Higgins
Il Fornaio
Jake's Famous Crawfish
Jake's Grill
Jo Bar & Rotisserie
McCormick & Schmick's
Montage
¡Oba!
Oritalia
Paragon
Pazzo

Red Star Tavern
Ruth's Chris
Saucebox
Serratto
Southpark Seafood
Veritable Quandary
Wildwood

Power Scene
Bluehour
El Gaucho
Heathman
Jake's Famous Crawfish
Jake's Grill
McCormick & Schmick's
McCormick's Fish House
Morton's of Chicago
¡Oba!
Oritalia
Pazzo
Portland Steak
Red Star Tavern
Ruth's Chris
Southpark Seafood
Veritable Quandary
Wildwood

Pub/Bar/Microbrewery
Alameda Brewhse.
BridgePort Ale
BridgePort Brew Pub
Gustav's Bier Stube
Harborside
Kells Irish Restaurant & Pub
McMenamins Black Rabbit
McMenamins/Columbia
McMenamins Courtyard
Produce Row Cafe
Stanich's
Widmer Gasthaus

Quiet Conversation
Cafe des Amis
Castagna
Celadon
Couvron
Dundee Bistro
Fratelli
Genoa
Grant House
Joel Palmer Hse.
Lemongrass Thai
London Grill
Marrakesh
Oritalia
Plainfields' Mayur
Red Hills
Riccardo's
Ringside Steakhse.
Tao of Tea
Tina's

Wilfs
Winterborne

Romantic
Assaggio
Bluehour
Brazen Bean
Cafe des Amis
Casablanca
Castagna
Columbia River Ct.
Couvron
Dundee Bistro
El Gaucho
Esplanade
Fratelli
Genoa
Giorgio's
Heathman
Higgins
Hudson's B&G
Il Piatto
Joel Palmer Hse.
La Catalana
Laslow's Northwest
L'Auberge
Lemongrass Thai
London Grill
Lucy's Table
Marrakesh
Morton's of Chicago
Nick's Italian Cafe
¡Oba!
Oritalia
Paley's Place
Pazzo
Plainfields' Mayur
Red Hills
Riccardo's
Ringside Steakhse.
Serratto
3 Doors Down
Tina's
Tuscany Grill
Veritable Quandary
William's on 12th
Winterborne

Senior Appeal
Alessandro's
Alexander's
Bistro 921
Bugatti's Caffe
Dan & Louis' Oyster Bar
Esplanade
Giorgio's
Goose Hollow Inn
Grant House
Gustav's Bier Stube

Hall St. Grill
Hayden Island Steak
Jake's Famous Crawfish
Kornblatt's Deli
La Prima Trattoria
Marco's Cafe
McCormick & Schmick's
McCormick's Fish House
McMenamins Black Rabbit
McMenamins Courtyard
Morton's of Chicago
Mother's Bistro
Nick's Italian Cafe
Old Wives' Tales
Perry's On Fremont
Red Hills
Red Star Tavern
Rheinlander
Riccardo's
Ruth's Chris
Sayler's
Southpark Seafood
Springwater Grill
Syun Izakaya
Thai Orchid
Three Sq. Grill
Tina's
Vista Spring Cafe
Widmer Gasthaus
Wilfs
Zell's

Singles Scene

Beaches
Bluehour
Brasserie Montmartre
Brazen Bean
BridgePort Ale
Cafe Castagna
Caswell
Chevys
Chez Grill
Colosso
Escape From N.Y.
Esparza's Tex Mex
Harborside
Hot Lips Pizza
Jake's Famous Crawfish
Jake's Grill
Kells Irish Restaurant & Pub
McMenamins Black Rabbit
McMenamins/Columbia
McMenamins Courtyard
Montage
¡Oba!
Oritalia
Paragon
Raccoon Lodge
Saucebox

Serratto
Springwater Grill
Veritable Quandary
Wildwood

Sleepers
(Good to excellent food,
but little known)
Big Dan's
Casablanca
Cedar's
Chameleon
Counter Culture
Daily Cafe/Rejuvenation
Dog House
Good Day
Henry's Cafe
Horn of Africa
J & M Cafe
John St. Cafe
Khun Pic's Bahn Thai
Obi Japanese
Pazzoria
Siam
Springwater Grill
Stickers Asian Cafe
Syun Izakaya
Thai Kitchen
Thien Hong
Uogashi
Yoko's

Teenagers & Other Youthful Spirits

Accuardi's
Big Dan's
Bugatti's Caffe
Burgerville USA
Chez What?
Delta Cafe
Escape From N.Y.
Macheezmo Mouse
Maya's Taqueria
Misohapi
Montage
Noho's
Old Spaghetti Factory
Original Pancake House
Pambiche
Pizzicato
Raccoon Lodge
Rheinlander
Stickers Asian Cafe
Tao of Tea
Taqueria La Sirenita
Tully's Coffee

Teflons

(Get lots of business, despite so-so food, i.e. they have other attractions that prevent criticism from sticking)
Billy Reed's
Chevys
Macheezmo Mouse
McMenamins Courtyard
Old Spaghetti Factory
Produce Row Cafe
Raccoon Lodge

Theme Restaurant

Burgerville USA
Casablanca
Chevys
Dog House
Good Dog/Bad Dog
Joel Palmer Hse.
Kells Irish Restaurant & Pub
Marrakesh
McMenamins Courtyard
Old Spaghetti Factory
Original Pancake House
Pasta Veloce
Rheinlander
Tao of Tea
Tapeo

Visitors on Expense Account

Bluehour
Cafe Azul
Cafe des Amis
Couvron
El Gaucho
Grant House
Heathman
Higgins
Jake's Famous Crawfish
Jake's Grill
Joel Palmer Hse.
London Grill
McCormick & Schmick's
Morton's of Chicago
Oritalia
Paley's Place
Portland Steak
Red Star Tavern
Ringside Steakhse.
Ruth's Chris
Southpark Seafood
Wildwood

Wine/Beer Only

Accuardi's
Alameda Cafe
Anne Hughes
Assaggio

Bamboos
Baobab
Berlin Inn
Bijou Cafe
Bread & Ink Cafe
BridgePort Ale
BridgePort Brew Pub
Bugatti's Caffe
Bugatti's Rist.
Bush Garden
Cadillac Cafe
Caffe Mingo
Casablanca
Cedar's
Compass World Bistro
Counter Culture
Cozze
Cup & Saucer Cafe
Daily Cafe/Rejuvenation
Dan & Louis' Oyster Bar
Escape From N.Y.
FuJin
Fusion
Garbonzos
Good Day
Good Dog/Bad Dog
Goose Hollow Inn
Grand Central Bakery
Henry's Cafe
Hoda's
Hungry Dog Burrito
Il Piatto
India House
J & M Cafe
Ken's Home Plate
Khun Pic's Bahn Thai
La Buca
La Prima Trattoria
Lemongrass Thai
Little Wing Cafe
Macheezmo Mouse
Marco's Cafe
Marrakesh
Maya's Taqueria
Milo's City Cafe
Misohapi
Nick's Italian Cafe
Noho's/Islander
Old Wives' Tales
Pambiche
Papa Haydn East
Paparazzi Pastaficio
Pasta Veloce
Pazzoria
Piazza Italia
Pizzicato
Produce Row Cafe
Restaurant Murata

Restaurant Russia
Saburo's Sushi
Saigon Kitchen
Siam
Stanich's
Sushi Takahashi
Swagat
Sweet Basil
Syun Izakaya
Tabor Hill Cafe
Tapeo
Tara Thai
Thai Kitchen
Thai Orchid
Thai Villa
Thanh Thao
Thien Hong
3 Doors Down
Three Sq. Grill
Typhoon!
Umenoki
Vista Spring Cafe
Vita Cafe
Widmer Gasthaus
William's on 12th
Winterborne
Yoko's

Winning Wine List

Assaggio
Bastas Trattoria
Bluehour
Cafe Castagna
Caprial's Bistro
Castagna
Columbia River Ct.
Couvron
Dundee Bistro
Fratelli
Genoa
Gino's
Heathman
Higgins
Jake's Famous Crawfish
Joel Palmer Hse.
Laslow's Northwest
Morton's of Chicago
Nick's Italian Cafe
¡Oba!
Oritalia
Paley's Place
Pazzo
Red Hills
Ringside Steakhse.
Southpark Seafood
Tina's
Tuscany Grill
Veritable Quandary
Wildwood

Worth a Trip

Dayton
    Joel Palmer Hse.
Dundee
    Dundee Bistro
    Red Hills
    Tina's
Hillsboro
    Syun Izakaya
Hood River
    Columbia River Ct.
McMinnville
    Nick's Italian Cafe
Troutdale
    McMenamins Black Rabbit
Vancouver, WA
    Grant House
West Linn
    Bugatti's Rist.

Young Children

(Besides the normal fast-food
places; * indicates children's
menu available)
Accuardi's
Alameda Brewhse.*
Besaw's Cafe
Bijou Cafe
Bistro 921
BridgePort Ale
Bugatti's Caffe
Burgerville USA
Byways Cafe
Campbell's BBQ
Chevys*
Chez Grill
Chez Jose East*
Cup & Saucer Cafe
Dan & Louis' Oyster Bar*
Dog House
Doris' Cafe*
El Burrito Loco
Escape From N.Y.
Esplanade*
Foothill Broiler
Fuller's Coffee Shop
Gino's*
Good Dog/Bad Dog
Grant House
Gustav's Bier Stube*
Hall St. Grill*
Hands on Café
Hayden Island Steak
Hoda's*
Hungry Dog Burrito
Il Fornaio
Il Piatto*
Kornblatt's Deli*
Legin

Little Wing Cafe*
Macheezmo Mouse
Marco's Cafe*
Marrakesh*
Maya's Taqueria
McMenamins Black Rabbit
McMenamins Courtyard
Misohapi
Mother's Bistro
Noho's*
Old Spaghetti Factory
Old Wives' Tales*
Original Pancake House
Paparazzi Pastaficio
Pasta Veloce*
Perry's On Fremont*
Pizzicato*

Red Electric Cafe
Rheinlander
Rustica
Salvador Molly's*
Santa Fe Taqueria
Sayler's
Springwater Grill*
Stickers Asian Cafe
Sushi Takahashi
Taqueria La Sirenita
Tennessee Red's BBQ
Three Sq. Grill
Tully's Coffee
Vista Spring Cafe
Widmer Gasthaus
Zell's

Wine Vintage Chart
1985-1999

This chart is designed to help you select wine to go with your meal. It is based on the same 0 to 30 scale used throughout this *Survey*. The ratings (prepared by our friend **Howard Stravitz**, a law professor at the University of South Carolina) reflect both the quality of the vintage and the wine's readiness for present consumption. Thus, if a wine is not fully mature or is over the hill, its rating has been reduced. We do not include 1987, 1991 or 1993 vintages because they are not especially recommended for most areas.

	'85	'86	'88	'89	'90	'92	'94	'95	'96	'97	'98	'99
WHITES												
French:												
Alsace	24	19	22	28	28	23	27	25	22	23	25	22
Burgundy	23	24	19	25	21	23	22	26	28	25	24	25
Loire Valley	–	–	–	26	25	–	22	24	26	23	22	23
Champagne	28	25	24	26	29	–	–	24	27	24	24	–
Sauternes	22	28	29	25	27	–	–	22	23	24	23	–
California:												
Chardonnay	–	–	–	–	–	–	22	26	22	26	23	26
REDS												
French:												
Bordeaux	26	27	25	28	29	18	24	25	24	23	24	22
Burgundy	24	–	23	26	29	22	21	26	27	25	24	25
Rhône	25	19	25	28	27	15	23	25	22	24	27	25
Beaujolais	–	–	–	–	–	–	–	23	21	24	23	24
California:												
Cab./Merlot	26	26	–	21	28	25	27	26	25	26	23	25
Zinfandel	–	–	–	–	–	–	26	25	24	23	22	23
Italian:												
Tuscany	26	–	23	–	26	–	23	25	19	28	25	24
Piedmont	25	–	25	28	28	–	–	23	26	28	26	25